Ski Style

CultureAmerica

Karal Ann Marling
Erika Doss

SERIES EDITORS

Ski Style

SPORT AND CULTURE IN THE ROCKIES

Annie Gilbert Coleman

 University Press of Kansas

© 2004 by the University Press of Kansas
All rights reserved

Published by the University Press of Kansas (Lawrence, Kansas 66049), which was
organized by the Kansas Board of Regents and is operated and funded by Emporia
State University, Fort Hays State University, Kansas State University, Pittsburg State
University, the University of Kansas, and Wichita State University

Library of Congress Cataloging-in-Publication Data
Coleman, Annie Gilbert.
  Ski style : sport and culture in the Rockies / Annie Gilbert Coleman.
    p. cm. — (CultureAmerica)
  Includes bibliographical references and index.
  ISBN 0-7006-1341-2 (alk. paper)
    1. Skis and skiing—Social aspects—Colorado.   2. Skis and skiing—Economic
aspects—Colorado.   3. Skis and skiing—Colorado—History.   I. Title.
II. Culture America.
  GV854.9.S63C65   2004
  796.93'09788—dc22   2004008739

British Library Cataloguing in Publication Data is available.

Printed in the United States of America

10 9 8 7 6 5 4 3 2 1

The paper used in this publication meets the minimum requirements of the American
National Standard for Permanence of Paper for Printed Library Materials z39.48-1984.

For Jon

CONTENTS

ACKNOWLEDGMENTS

I have gotten a lot of funny looks over the years when I told people I was working on a history of Colorado skiing. Serious historians, they implied, must have heftier things to think about. And I may not always be too serious. Quite a number of people and institutions, however, shared my enthusiasm for the project and helped me along the way. This book originated as a dissertation at the University of Colorado. I could not have asked for a better pair of mentors than Patty Limerick and Phil Deloria, who taught me to be a historian and a colleague by treating me like one. Lee Chambers provided invaluable comments, Bill Travis gave his enthusiasm and geographical perspective, and Julie Greene jumped thoughtfully into the history of the ski industry when I needed her. Clark Whitehorn, Cathy Lavender, and Ken Orona were a great source of energy, cheer, and support.

Financial assistance for the dissertation came from the University of Colorado History Department's Douglas A. Bean Memorial Faculty Research Stipend and Pile Fellowship, the Roaring Fork Research Scholarship funded by Ruth Whyte, Dr. Giles D. Toll, and the American Historical Association. Individuals who helped me research include Charlie Langdon at the *Durango Herald;* Mary Walker and Ingrid Schierling Burnett at the Tread of Pioneers Museum; Sue Spearing at the Grand County Historical Society; Jeff Leich at the New England Ski Museum; the kind folks at the University of Colorado Archives, Denver Public Library, and Colorado Historical Society; and Lisa Hancock, Georges Odier, Ann Hodges, and Jody Phillips at the Aspen Historical Society. Thanks go, especially, to all the men and women who so generously shared their experiences and perspectives with me on tape. Interviewing them was my favorite part of the research, and I feel honored to have met them all.

Another set of scholars and friends helped me revise the dissertation into what you have before you. Johnny Faragher, Virginia Scharff, and Elliott West helped me sharpen my ideas with generous gifts of attention over the years; Morten Lund and Margaret Supplee Smith offered expertise and insight on ski history; Hal

Rothman helped me think about tourism; and John Allen, Frieda Knobloch, and Benjamin Rader gave thoughtful and thorough comments on the manuscript. Thanks go especially to Nancy Scott Jackson and Peggy Shaffer, whose clear eyes, sharp wits, and encouraging spirits helped me realize my goals for this book. At Indiana University–Purdue University, Indianapolis, the School of Liberal Arts supported my writing with timely and much appreciated summer research grants. There, colleagues David Craig, Kevin Cramer, Wietse deBoer, Owen Dwyer, Margie Ferguson, Stephen Heathorn, Miriam Langsam, Monroe Little, Jack McKivigan, Nancy Robertson, Bill Schneider, Scott Seregny, Michael Snodgrass, and Catherine Souch all contributed to this project in some important way, be it reading parts of the manuscript, bouncing ideas around, enforcing deadlines, or generally helping me deal with the life of an assistant professor. Jennifer Johnson made beautiful maps. Among them all, these smart people greatly improved this book, and I claim any lurking mistakes as my own.

I am happy to thank my father, John J. Gilbert, whose love of learning encouraged me to become a historian, and my mother, Cally C. Gilbert, whose optimism and tendency to procrastinate I embrace in myself every day. My brother John taught me to ski with an intensity and boldness that opened a new world to me. Barb, Tom, and Cherie Coleman have become avid supporters of my work, which I appreciate all the time. Thanks also to my soccer teammates in Boulder, Denver, and Indianapolis, whose simultaneous encouragement to run and to write kept me focused, and to my women friends in academia, in my neighborhood, and from Williams, who consistently strive to do it all with humor and grace—or at least without making too big of a mess. Thank you Harry, for keeping my priorities straight (as only a three-year-old can), and Louise, for your excellent timing. And thank you Jon, whose creative spirit animates our home (along with the cat and the basset hounds), skips through my life, and alights on these pages.

I skied Aspen Mountain once and had a great time — 1995, I think it was. The sun was shining. I zoomed down smooth slopes and felt like I was gliding along the skin of the earth. For a different thrill I chose steep moguls, turning quickly on the very edge of control. Riding up the chairlift I chatted with a new acquaintance or looked out at the surrounding peaks. I was happy to be there, but I took care to distinguish myself from those "others" who came to see the celebrities, nightlife, boutiques, and high society for which Aspen had become famous. I wore my old ski boots (secondhand from a friend), good racing skis I had on loan from a shop, and clothes I had skied in twelve years ago. I was a fashion nightmare, but I made my choices consciously. Between my ratty outfit and my impressive skiing, I thought, it would be clear that I belonged in that town and on that mountain. I was there not because I had money or wanted to be part of the "in crowd" but because I was a good skier, at home in the Rockies, and deserved some respect. This is all rather embarrassing to admit, but it illustrates how the physical act of skiing is not just about descending a mountain. It never was. This book explains how skiing is about style, spectacle, and status as much as it is about nature, physical experience, and sport.

Of course, the physical allure of the sport is important. One nineteenth-century outdoorsman wrote that "the ski has an unpleasant way of running in opposite directions, of getting crossed, and finally of piling the pupil in a snow-bank." "But," he continued, "to one who is persistent the joys of jumping and running with the ski are finally opened." Skiing "may appear to be dangerous," he said, "but it is exhilarating."[1] An author in 1905 similarly wrote, "as the experienced skidor [skier] dashes down the crusted hillsides with the speed of the wind, there comes to the sport an added exhilaration and excitement that positively knows no equal."[2]

Skiing has always produced more than endorphins, however; it also forges a connection between the skier and the physical environment. In 1928, for instance, Marjorie Perry and her friend Elinor

Eppich Kingery reveled in the big curves they made as they skied down from Rollins Pass "with the perfect powdered snow swirling in the air."[3] When I asked a longtime Denver skier what had attracted him to the sport as a nine-year-old in the mid-1930s, he readily answered, "being in the mountains." "The feeling of rhythm," he said, and "to some extent the speed, but mostly the feeling of being able to come into synchrony with the mountains and the snow."[4] When she skied slowly, one woman explained in 1938, "I feel myself a part of the deep silence, lost in the magnificence of something so much bigger and more enduring than anything I am or can do, that the present is gone completely."[5] Expert powder skier Dolores LaChapelle echoed this sensation in the 1990s. "Once this rhythmic relationship to snow and gravity is established on a steep slope," she wrote, "there is no longer an I and snow and the mountain, but a continuous flowing interaction."[6] Through the act of skiing, skiers could enter a landscape that felt wild and natural — they could gain access to something fundamental, pristine, and authentic — and they did it during a century when "nature" grew both increasingly appealing and elusive.

Beyond connecting people to an idealized landscape, skiing also acquired powerful cultural meaning. Many women and men interpreted the experience as liberating. Beth Sinclair learned to ski in the late 1930s and said that what attracted her to the sport was "the freedom and the speed." Fellow Aspen resident Cherie Oates, who took up the sport in the 1940s, also liked to ski downhill fast. "I'd be picking up pieces [of equipment and clothes] out of the trees [after a fall], I'd always be losing something," she told me, "but there was just a real thrill about that, a real challenge . . . [and] a freedom that you're on your own power."[7] One author in 1947 waxed poetic about his experiences skiing above Aspen in the Montezuma Basin. "There's no sensation like it," he wrote. "You just soar."[8]

Descriptions of skiing in terms of thrill, exhilaration, freedom, and personal connection to the mountain landscape are so pervasive that they have reached the point of cliché. The sensation of flying down a mountain on skis has attracted people to the sport since its very beginning, and it still does, but that sensation is not all that people get from it. They connect with nature, and they also act out an identity — a sense of belonging to a club, a town, a class, or some group that makes them feel grounded. My ties to the sport grew largely from the fact that I grew up in Hanover, New Hampshire, a town with a long ski history and a strong local youth program. That I took a semester off from Williams College to compete as a freestyle skier in Europe said much about my race and my class identity, although at the time I saw it as a chance to express my independence and try on the role of World Cup competitor. It didn't quite fit, and I gave up that life for academia, where I grew curious about the millions of people who ski for reasons quite different from my own. On the day that I skied Aspen Mountain I tried to emphasize those differences, but like everyone else on the slope, I used the sport to define who I was and how I fit in. We were all accomplishing this, self-consciously or not, through a landscape and a consumer culture that located us firmly in the late twentieth century.

Why people ski has much to do with historical context — the relationships of labor and gender, region, consumption, and class that surround each skier and give meaning to the world around him or her. This book is more than a history of skiing and the ski industry.[9] It traces how the meaning of skiing has changed and grown throughout the twentieth century, but it also seeks to explain how skiing is tied up with questions of place and identity. It connects the history of a physical act (skiing down a mountain) with stories of economic development (the rise of the ski industry) and cultural change (the identity formation of skiers and ski towns). Examining the connections among skiing, its practitioners, its promoters, and Colorado's very real mountains offers a view into the larger issues of how cultural meanings become inscribed on the landscape and how landscapes in turn influence culture. In selling the experience of skiing and combining recreation with a powerful consumer culture, Colorado's ski industry had a big impact on individual skiers, destination resorts, and the American West. In the end, it redefined the social, physical, economic, and imaginary landscape of the Colorado Rockies at the same time it made them the focus of a national leisure industry, ethic, and style. Places like Vail and Aspen have become powerful cultural icons as well as economic models.

Skiing began in the Rocky Mountains during the late nineteenth century, as an activity that was either free or considered work. Some experts skied for a living; others won local acclaim and occasionally prize money for their skill. Mining towns supported local skiing through special clubs that staged competitions and integrated the sport into the fabric of their communities. European resorts and instructors introduced the idea that skiing could be a leisure commodity in the early twentieth century, a concept Coloradans slowly incorporated into their own regional identity. After World War II, Americans began to sell the sport through nascent destination resorts and develop a ski industry that thrived in the American West. New management techniques and corporate mergers gradually turned this industry into one that was more concerned with the business of consumption than with skiing. This process of commodification has resulted more recently in vacation packages that can feature deluxe accommodations and dining, spa treatments, the Wild West, European cosmopolitanism and romance, and local celebrities, as well as powder snow, athletic adventure, and rugged scenery. It has become unclear, in other words, exactly what is for sale.

The reason for this muddle is that, although the physical act of sliding down a mountain remains at the heart of the skiing experience, skiers came to want much more than that when they visited destination ski resorts. They bought a set of associations that mediated their relationship to "wild" mountain landscapes, enveloped them in mythical western and alpine communities, and enhanced their personal identities. All this was possible because, through the twentieth century, the sport of skiing became associated with increasingly different and conflicting images — of work and leisure, community and celebrity, wilderness and development, European Alps and the American West, masculinity and femininity, and physical liberation and dictatorial consumer culture. These images emerged as a product of skiers' consumer demands, local boosters' efforts to attract visitors, and strategies from within the ski industry to promote skiing, its destination resorts, and related products.

Resolving the tensions between these disparate images was not necessary; in fact, skier-tourists have come to expect a range of contradictory experiences from their vacations, and it pays to offer consumers a wide variety of choices. Wild yet accessible landscapes, exhilarating but safe skiing, images of the past separated from local history, and highly developed service industries with no visible workers are part of what has made skiing so popular. Maintaining images and landscapes that are at such odds with each other has come to characterize the most successful destination ski resorts. Places such as Aspen, Vail, and Steamboat Springs seem to be glitzy, self-referential shells of their natural, western, and European pasts. They can still feel real, however, largely due to the grace with which they maintain the tensions surrounding their mountain landscapes, local community identities, and the race, class, and gender of their skiing customers. These tensions have a history, and they are what made Colorado's ski industry at once so successful and so problematic. How those tensions grew up together to create the resorts we know today is also the story of how sport, landscape, community identity, and skier identity formed one another in the twentieth century.

Scholars have discussed cultural landscapes as "our unwitting autobiography, reflecting our tastes, our values, our aspirations, and even our fears, in tangible, visible form." People create these landscapes; they bear a system of signs we can use to think about our culture.[10] But people also move through, consume, and internalize the world around them, so landscapes pass messages back to society. Ski resort landscapes play an important role in this book because they are at once reflections of the society and economy that built them and material actors that influenced skier behavior, identity, and consumer culture.[11] Designers shaped resorts to remind visitors of European alpine villages, Victorian mining towns, or scenes from the Wild West. These places offer countless, almost constant, opportunities to consume food, fashion, and social life as well as skiing itself; and they provide visitors with different stages on which they can advertise themselves and their purchases. (Or, in my case, high-quality gear that was either old or on loan.) More than a visual landscape, ski resorts not only shape skiers' kinetic experience as they first ride up and then ski down the mountain; they also offer new roles for skiers to try on, and they help create mythic pasts for the towns below. The transformation of mountain landscapes goes hand in hand with the formation of skier and ski town identities, as well as the history of the ski industry.

Skiers' relationship to the mountains changed significantly during the twentieth century. Unlike many other sports, the practice of skiing revolves around a relatively undeveloped landscape. The scenery, the weather, the physical experience of gliding (and sometimes falling) down a mountain, and a personal connection to the wilderness all contribute to skiers' enjoyment of their sport in fundamental ways. Early skiers had little difficulty finding mountain landscapes they could hike up and descend on their own. As ski resorts grew and the ski industry sold the experience to as many skiers as possible, the mountains changed along with skiers' expectations. By the late twentieth century, skiers wanted both the "natural" experience of skiing and a comfortable vacation. They wanted, in other words, high-speed chairlifts, well-groomed slopes, ski-in restaurants, and a guarantee of safety at the same time that they demanded scenic views, isolated trails, a connection to nature, and the thrill of speed.

Fulfilling these contradictory expectations required some pretty fancy footwork on the part of ski area managers and the ski industry as a whole. They developed their resorts to accommodate more trails, lifts, lodges, and people — hiring more workers and altering the mountains in the process. Similarly, the demand for more service workers both on and off the slopes eventually threatened the wild experience skiing had come to represent. So while built landscapes and an expanded labor force grew more necessary, so did the need to hide all evidence of their existence. Captains of the ski industry negotiated such tensions by effectively erasing labor from the landscape and defining their mountains as "natural" whenever and however possible.[12]

The growth of skiing in Colorado produced and depended on a second set of tensions focused on the notion of community identity. Situated firmly in mountain towns during the late nineteenth century, skiing developed as a local sport, continually influenced by people moving to the Rockies from other places. European immigrants from Scandinavia and the Alps fundamentally shaped the way people skied in Colorado and the West at the same time that local mountain communities integrated the sport — and those immigrants — into their own social, economic, and cultural fabric. Skiing thus grew as both an imported and a homegrown phenomenon; immigrant skiers became local experts and community members. Mountain towns that had once been developed for mining and ranching took on new identities, as leisure and sport inscribed a different set of economic relationships on their landscapes. The growth of recreational tourism and the ski industry after World War II melded skiing into mountain economies further by encouraging outsiders to visit these towns. Images of the Wild West, Victorian culture, or the European Alps — or some mix of all three — drew new visitors by emphasizing aspects of the town and the sport's past. Destination skiers hoped to experience skiing in an authentic Rocky Mountain community and sought out "locals" to verify that experience. At the same time, these skiers — as typical tourists — wanted to see behind the town's facade and participate in the community themselves.[13] Most skiing tourists stayed for a week or two, but others moved in every winter or even permanently, and by the late twentieth century, some vacationers had become foundations of the local community. This wide variety and constant migration of people created places where everyone, to some degree, was at once local and tourist, insider and outsider.

It was out of this confusing mix that the ski industry crafted its product, and part of that product was the community itself. Local businesses, resort marketers, and other members of the ski industry tried to attract skiers on vacation by re-creating the local landscape and its history. They played up the colorful, exotic, and mythic aspects of the town's past at the expense of the less glamorous reality of working-class immigration and extractive economies.[14] They tried to turn late-twentieth-century mountain towns into European alpine villages, Victorian mining towns, the Wild West, or some mixture of each. They defined resort towns as solid western communities inhabited by authentic locals rather than the transient muddle of working people, migrant skiers, transplanted tourists, and second-home owners who actually lived there. Although these images bore some connection to the ethnic or economic orientation of the town's past, they created a kind of never-never land for skier-tourists that existed in tension with the real history of the town's people, culture, and economy. The popularity of these mythic places only increased the discord surrounding them, because the working people who actually supported resort town economies could no longer afford to inhabit them.

The rise of Colorado's ski industry produced a final set of tensions centered on skiing's resort culture and the social identity of its participants. A collection of working-class immigrants brought skiing to Colorado from Scandinavia and the European Alps, and ski resorts advertised their own authenticity by flaunting European ski instructors, restaurants, and architecture. This move created a white, European, alpine identity that blurred national boundaries and sold ski vacations to an elite crowd. Skiing and its landscapes thus came to be associated with a manufactured image of wealth and celebrity well after the sport had spread beyond fancy European resorts and into the American middle class. Skiing's whiteness, too, existed in uneasy tension with the ethnically diverse people who lived near resorts, worked in their kitchens, or liked to ski.

The culture that helped define skiing as white and elite developed similar problems surrounding gender. Women and men had both enjoyed skiing since the sport's introduction in the late nineteenth century. Ski culture historically focused on heroic male skiers and masculine instructors, however, as the sport highlighted the potentially unfeminine act of flying down a mountain.[15] Male and female skiers alike found this physical experience to be empowering, but ski industry marketers defined the act of skiing in much more limiting and gendered ways. Skiing sold as a social activity, as a family vacation, and as an opportunity to display fashionable bodies highlighted women's traditional roles as girlfriends, mothers, and sexual objects. Even ski equipment and teaching workshops designed specifically for women emerged within a larger consumer culture that defined female skiers primarily as consumers and only secondarily as athletes. This liberating physical experience thus came enmeshed in a ski culture that called that very experience into question.

This series of tensions and contradictions surrounding the "natural" condition of the sport's landscape, local community identity, and a wealthy, white, and gendered ski culture arose as the meaning of skiing in Colorado changed throughout the twentieth century. That history forms the central narrative of this book, and it explains how destination resort skiing and its landscapes grew to be so compelling, so problematic, and so popular. It also situates the growth of the ski industry and the development of its landscapes firmly in a series of larger historical contexts.

During its early years, Colorado skiing grew as a direct result of Scandinavian immigration and the Rocky Mountain mining economy. Wealthy tourists and European instructors soon brought Alpine skiing and its accompanying resort culture to American cities in the East and West. By the 1930s, Coloradans were incorporating various visions of the sport into their local communities and struggling to create nascent ski areas. This period of skiing development came to an end after World War II. With the close of the war, a number of important changes helped establish a ski industry in America. Veterans of the U.S. Army's 10th Mountain Division won international respect as skiers and returned to build ski businesses and resorts of their own. National economic growth, technological advances, and energetic consumption helped ski area managers develop appealing mountain landscapes and supported the expansion of other ski-related businesses. By 1960, the modern ski industry had taken shape in Colorado and attached a specific and powerful consumer culture to skiing and its resorts.

After this period of formation, the ski industry matured. As its economic momentum grew, the industry manufactured destination resort landscapes in concert with its own consumer culture. The relationships among skiing, the local economy, Europe, and the Rocky Mountains became confused as industry leaders wedded images of whiteness, class, and wilderness to mythic communities disconnected from their historic roots, their multiethnic labor force, and their built landscapes. Creating such places encouraged skiers to expect both wild and developed mountains, a culture in which they could live out particular ethnic and gender identities, and an authentic community that would transport them to the Wild West, an alpine village, or both.

Colorado's mountain landscapes and its style of destination resorts have made its ski areas the most famous and the most popular in the nation. The growth of the ski industry changed the economy, environment, and identity of the Rockies at the same time it developed its product. Places such as Vail, Aspen, and Steamboat Springs have become the standards by which other destination resorts are measured and the center of a national leisure industry, largely because of the way they juggle their social, economic, and environmental realities with the experience, landscape, and images they sell. Their product has changed as the meaning of skiing has become more varied since the nineteenth century and less directly attached to notions of work and local community. The industry created places where Texas church groups, grandmothers who had skied in the 1950s, and young male snowboarders could all have a good time by consuming mountain landscapes, quaint towns, ski fashion, and even other skiers. When I skied Aspen Mountain, I loved the physical thrill of it and the chance to be outside, but I also have to admit that I liked seeing the famous town, acting like I belonged on the mountain, being able to tell people I had skied there, and spotting a celebrity or two.

Spectacle and opportunities for consumption now compete with the kinetic attraction of the sport in ways that make the history of skiing relevant to larger developments in American cultural history. First, it resonates with historical trends in popular culture and celebrity. In the 1920s, radio and popular journalism helped usher in America's "golden age of sport" by allowing the whole country to follow and cheer the likes of Red Grange, Bobby Smith, and Babe Ruth. The growth of advertising, public relations, and Hollywood's film industry converged with this to support the rise of national heroes and celebrities, offering up famous personalities for consumption through the press, popular films, or products they endorsed.[16] Films shot in Sun Valley and Aspen promos featuring resident Gary Cooper made the stars and the resorts look good. This phenomenon accelerated in the decades after World War II with the increased visibility and new marketing opportunities presented by television. By the late twentieth century, a number of western ski towns had earned national reputations, because where celebrities lived and played had become a matter of popular consumption.

The growth of the ski industry also illuminates developments in sports history. Like its recreational cousins golf and tennis, skiing originated partly as a pastime for members of the elite. Participating in these sports required access to country clubs or winter resorts and so reinforced social bonds among members of the upper class. Many Americans felt flush during the 1920s and after World War II, however, and all three recreational sports enjoyed much higher and broader levels of participation during those periods than before. After the 1970s, these sports became accessible in new ways as real estate developers used golf courses, tennis courts, and ski areas to draw investors, and large destination resorts incorporated sports into the package of leisure experiences they marketed to visitors.[17]

Broad cultural changes also influenced who played sports and why. Popular images of the "new woman" in the 1920s advertised athletic femininity, and the women's movement in the 1970s encouraged women to take control of their bodies and use them as athletes. It did not hurt that American female skiers bettered the men to national acclaim at the 1948 and 1952 Olympics.[18] The ski industry benefited from national shifts in gender norms and leisure spending, and it helped create those trends, too. It also has an important relationship to American youth culture. In hiring "ski bums" from the 1950s through the 1970s and providing spaces for "freestyle" skiing and snowboarding after that, ski resorts incorporated potentially subversive groups of young people, accepted them as customers, and gave them a forum to express themselves.

All of this happened in highly developed landscapes that the industry defined as natural. The distance between resorts' advertised wilderness and actual ski area terrain has reached oceanic proportions by now, but it makes sense, given other national trends during the later twentieth century. Skiing came of age when industrial, technological, urban, and suburban development threatened the wilderness that Americans held increasingly dear.[19] At the same time the fledgling environmental movement mobilized to safeguard that wilderness, ski industry marketers packaged remnants of it and sold it to skiers across the country. They were not alone in this enterprise — nature tourism and stores such as the Nature Company have also thrived under these conditions, and they each allow Americans to consume natural resources in the name of protecting them.[20]

Region as well as wilderness gave western ski resorts their cachet, and this phenomenon, too, resonates with larger historical trends. Products of popular culture have mythologized the landscape of the American West (from *The Virginian* to John Ford's films and *Dances with Wolves*) and made it available to readers and moviegoers. Dude ranches gave tourists authentically western experiences in safe, vacation-sized bites beginning in the 1920s. More recently, Ralph Lauren and Robert Redford's *Sundance* catalog translated the West into material goods that promised to enhance consumers' identities by conjuring up powerful mythic images.[21] Ski resorts have been selling this association for decades and fit snugly into a long tradition of western mythologizing and western tourism, but they push it further by promoting consumption of the West through the physical act of skiing. Being able to list the resorts you have skied mirrors the serious tourist's practice of visiting every national park or seeing a set of famous attractions — it gives you a kind of status, and it also associates you with particular landscapes.[22] In their economic success as well, Colorado ski resorts introduced a western style of development to the nation. Vail and Aspen rank with Disneyland, Las Vegas, gangsta rap music, and California skateboarding as powerful cultural influences and economic models.[23]

The history of Colorado's ski industry sits comfortably among larger narratives of the twentieth century, including the histories of mass media and celebrity, sports, gender, youth culture, wilderness, the West, and consumer culture. These companions help explain the ski history of Colorado, and it, in turn, helps explain them. By the late twentieth century, consumption had become the vehicle through which Americans could get closer to nature, the West, and the type of person they would like to be, without leaving the reality of their sedentary and suburban lifestyles. Colorado's ski industry made this possible for all sorts of people, no matter what their skiing ability, by offering myriad experiences, landscapes, images, and identities for sale. Skiing itself became optional. Buying a vacation or a ski jacket, or even watching MTV's Extreme Games, opened a world of possibilities to the consumer, and Americans have reached the point where they take this ability for granted.

Witness the boom in surfer girl fashion. I admire much about women surfers: their grace and strength, their intimacy with the ocean, and their success in a male-dominated sport. Not too many women and girls surf, but a lot (like me) wish they did. We want this because, after some professional women surfers gained media attention and films like *Blue Crush* hit the box office, we realized exactly how great the sport was and how cool young women surfers were.[24] Though access to the beach and time for developing skills remain tough to find, we can all express our would-be identities as surfer babes through vicarious consumption. Clothes once made specifically for surfers are now marketed nationwide. Pottery Barn Kids sells surf-themed linens, rugs, and lamps. Movies, magazines, and reality TV shows let us into the surfing world as hopeful spectators. These goods call forth exciting images of riding waves off beautiful beaches with youthful independence. We consume surfing as a style, a spectacle, and an attitude more than a sport, though it is fundamentally rooted in a physical experience. All this illustrates just how tenuous the connections between outdoor sports and the images we devour really are. What a history of the ski industry can do is show us how they got that way.

1

Snowshoe Itinerants and Flying Norsemen
Early Skiing in Colorado

John Dyer rose from bed early one February morning, strapped on a pair of ten-foot-long skis, and headed out into the snowstorm toward Oro City, Colorado. He had reached timberline, traveling slowly over deep snow, when he said, "all of a sudden I felt a jar, and the snow gave way under me, and a noise struck my ear like a death-knell." About 150 feet ahead he found a crack six inches wide where the snow had settled, and a week later an avalanche filled the entire gorge below. "I felt better on the upper side of the break," Dyer later wrote mildly, noting that he reached the top of the Continental Divide at daybreak.[1] Dyer made regular ski trips through the Rocky Mountains, crisscrossing the Continental Divide in every kind of weather with a heavy pack on his back and only himself to rely on. Subzero weather, avalanches, and disorienting storms constantly threatened his life, and he was known throughout Summit County and South Park for his strength, endurance, and daring.

Although Dyer might bring to mind images of extreme athleticism, he represents a distinctly nineteenth-century version of the Colorado skier. He got out of bed and entered the storm that day in 1864 because he had to deliver the mail. He had made his skis himself and carried his bag from mining camp to mining camp for $18 a week, since his primary vocation as a Methodist minister did not pay well.[2] Both occupations required constant travel, enabling him to earn some money on the side by exchanging miners' gold dust for greenbacks. For Dyer, more than fifty other mailmen, and a few other

Colorado

ministers, risking their lives on skis was a necessary by-product of their jobs. Work, not play, led them into the mountains. And unlike modern-day extreme skiers, they did not have to seek out undeveloped terrain; in nineteenth-century Colorado, it surrounded them at every turn. Injury and death loomed large. Dyer had received the offer to subcontract the winter mail delivery after his predecessor died on Mosquito Pass.[3] Other mail carriers were found wandering deliriously, pinned in the snow by their own mailbags, or frozen to death.

This intimacy with danger, the mountainous winter wilderness, and work made the experience of skiing in nineteenth-century Colorado very different from what it is today. Colorado residents, attracted to the mountains by promising ore deposits, grazing lands, and farming opportunities, faced long, lonely winters. Skiing, or Norwegian snowshoeing, as they called it, helped them move around during the winter to a degree that would have been impossible otherwise. These women and men created a tradition of skiing in Colorado that acknowledged its Scandinavian roots; it centered on the local economy and regularly crossed the boundaries between work and leisure. This skiing took on gendered meanings from the start, since women and men both donned Norwegian snowshoes and incorporated the sport into their daily lives, their work, and their play in different ways. Although men and women defined their skiing differently, it equipped them both to participate in the regional economy that had drawn them to the mountains in the first place.

Neither this economy nor the sport attached to it remained static, however. Economic changes heralded by the railroads and the crash of 1893 redefined skiing as more recreational than work related, though working-class Scandinavian immigrants continued to shape the sport. Now more of an antidote to the declining mining economy than a necessary result of that economy, skiing acquired wealthier enthusiasts and a new set of gendered and class meanings even within small mountain towns. By the 1920s, Coloradans had organized myriad local clubs, competitions, and spectacular events designed to draw skiers to the sport and to their communities. Throughout this transformation, skiing's connections to the local economy, to Scandinavia, and to gendered notions of work and leisure remained strong.

Skiing to Work

Skiing became a part of Rocky Mountain culture as soon as miners, ranchers, and settlers entered the region in the mid-nineteenth century.[4] The Pikes Peak gold rush of 1859 first put Denver on the map and sent hopeful miners into the surrounding mountains. These "poor man's diggings," where supposedly only a pick, a shovel, and a strong back were necessary to get rich, got played out rather quickly, changing hands to wealthier capitalists capable of financing more intensive hard rock mines. From the Jackson Diggings near Idaho Springs, the Gregory Diggings near Black Hawk and Central City, and Gold Hill near Boulder, prospectors sought new discoveries in South Park and rushed in subsequent seasons to California Gulch and Oro City, camps in the San Juan Mountains, and Buckskin Joe. By the mid-1860s, gold mining had fizzled, but silver strikes revived fading camps and created new towns, including Caribou, Georgetown, Breckenridge, Leadville, Silverton, Ouray, Telluride, and Aspen. Coal discoveries supported Gunnison and Crested Butte. Throughout the mid and late nineteenth century, the chance of getting rich quickly lured thousands of people into what would become the state of Colorado.

Colorado mining camps came to life in some of the most isolated areas of the region and flickered out as soon as the ore disappeared. Hopeful prospectors guarded their claims and worked them diligently; others bought town lots, set up shop, and tried to develop permanent communities to support their businesses. Both endeavors were a gamble and help explain why small groups of working people might choose to spend their winters in a harsh mountain landscape. Staying and working through the winter helped them establish a toehold in towns where economic success proved all too elusive. These communities, such as they were, looked equally tenuous from a demographic standpoint. Women and children were few and far between; residents consisted mainly of young, single, transient men.[5] This bleak social and economic framework proved fertile ground for the development of skiing in Colorado.

Most directly, skiing arrived in the Rocky Mountains with Scandinavian immigrants. An integral part of Scandinavian culture and history, skiing helped inhabitants of Norway and Sweden travel and hunt as long as 4,000 years ago, and evidence also supports prehistoric use of skis in Siberia and

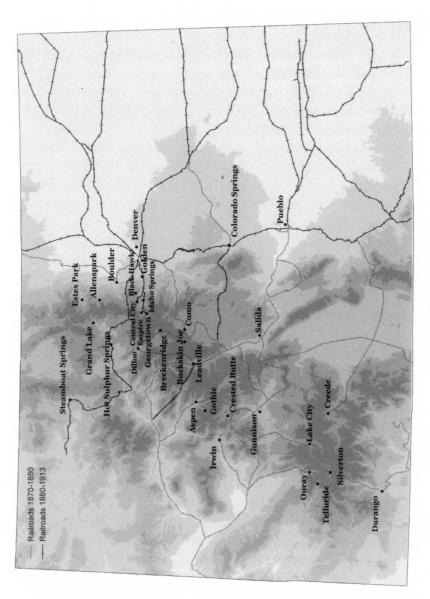

Historic railroads and towns

Steamboat Springs

Grand Lake

Hot Sulphur Springs

Estes Park

Allenspark

Boulder

Dillon Central City Black Hawk

Empire

Georgetown Idaho Springs

Denver

Golden

Breckenridge

Buckskin Joe

Como

Leadville

Salida

Aspen

Gothic

Crested Butte

Colorado Springs

Irwin

Gunnison

Pueblo

Lake City

Creede

Ouray

Silverton

Telluride

Durango

Slovenia. Norse history and mythology celebrated ski god Ull, the goddess Skade, and the legend of young King Sverre, whom two skiers rescued from the jaws of death. By the eighteenth century, the Norwegian government had incorporated the sport into its military, forming ski troops to fight Sweden in 1716.[6] Norwegians also integrated skiing into their culture through the concept of *Idraet,* loosely translated as outdoor "sport" and infused with nationalist sentiment, but also embodying masculine characteristics of strength, manliness, toughness, and the overcoming of fear that would translate easily to late-nineteenth-century Colorado.[7] As such an important aspect of Scandinavian society, skiing became part of the cultural baggage immigrants brought with them across the Atlantic in their search for work and prosperity.

During the nineteenth century, Norway experienced a prolonged economic downturn, and many emigrated to seek their fortunes. Norwegians settled in Minnesota's Red River Valley and elsewhere in the northern Midwest to farm; others took factory jobs. The promise of gold in California, and then the panic of 1857, encouraged Scandinavian midwesterners to join the diverse ethnic mix of people headed farther west. John Tostensen Rue, for instance, arrived in Illinois with his family in 1837. After moving to Wisconsin and changing his name to John Thompson, he joined the rush of miners and settlers headed to California in 1851.[8] In October 1862, the *Sacramento Union* reported that Norwegians had discovered gold at Silver Mountain in 1861 and that "the various districts of the mountain are now to a great extent occupied by that class of citizens." The next summer, the paper reiterated that there were "a great many Norwegians in this portion of the State."[9]

Skiing offered a degree of winter mobility in mining regions that eased the constraints of living in the hinterlands and made Norwegian snowshoeing attractive to all local residents, no matter what their cultural background. Immigrants shared their knowledge of how to make skis with their friends, coworkers, and neighbors. As early as January 1853, one California newspaper noted that "the miners do all their locomotion on snowshoes."[10] The Pikes Peak gold rush in Colorado prompted similar behavior. When the Reverend John Dyer's church assigned him to the Blue River Mission in Summit County and he found himself with a preaching schedule that would take him on regular two-week tours of surrounding mining camps, he said matter-of-factly, "I made me a pair of snow-shoes." A small group of Aspen prospectors acquired similar mobility during the camp's first winter in 1879 when two Swedes among their ranks taught them all how to make and use skis.[11] The Scandinavian immigrants in Colorado's Rockies — and the knowledge they brought with them — proved indispensable to residents when it came to learning how to ski.

And skiing turned out to be important. In this mining world of spent placer claims, disappearing silver veins, and wild prospecting hunches, economic uncertainty ruled the day. A few ranching and farming settlements perched on an equally precarious economic niche in support of the mining industry. These towns and the more established mining camps attracted women and families to the region, but isolating mountain passes and long, cold winters made mining and community building in Colorado extremely difficult. As a means of negotiating this Rocky Mountain terrain, skiing became a necessary part of the local economy and daily life. It connected mountain settlements to distant cities and families, enabled men and women to work during the winter, and provided both with a form of recreation that reinforced their gendered roles within the local economy.

Mail carriers such as John Dyer earned their livelihood on skis. For these men, skiing represented work more than anything else. Their jobs helped sustain local economies by linking them to the outside world. As a minister, Dyer established a communications link of an especially civilizing kind. His regular visits signified a certain degree of town development and the possibility of a permanent church in the future, and they helped define mining camp residents as churchgoing men and women rather than itinerant prospectors and whores. The greenbacks he carried gave miners access to a larger economic system, let them cash in on their digging, and also helped define their bearers as powerful and successful. Perhaps even more important was the mail in his bag. Letters and newspapers connected town residents to national and regional political, commercial, and social events, as well as to distant family members. Alice Denison, a well-educated woman who had moved to Steamboat Springs to look after her ailing nephew in 1885, relied on snowshoeing mail carriers to maintain crucial links with those "outside." In December she wrote to her sister, "We feel as tho' the bottom had fallen out of our very existence at the rumor that we are to have no mail after the 9th of January . . . the mail seemed our only 'holt' on anything earthly."[12] Cramped in small cabins, surrounded by miles of snow and mountains, many nineteenth-century Coloradans depended on skiing mail carriers for their very sanity. More broadly, these mailmen helped sustain local economies by supporting the social and cultural well-being of mountain town communities.

Mountain residents acknowledged the importance of mail carriers' work by granting them legendary status. After John Tostensen Rue emigrated from Norway and followed the gold rush to California, he carried mail ninety miles over the Sierra Mountains, from Carson Valley to Placerville, linking the Great Basin with the Pacific Coast. By doing so, he transformed into "Snowshoe" Thompson, the most famous skiing mail carrier in the West. Likewise, Colorado's own "snow-shoe itinerant," the Reverend John Dyer, became the stuff of legend — at least three mountain peaks bore his name. This kind of heroic skiing took on a specifically masculine meaning in nineteenth-century mountain towns, one characterized by dangerous, demanding, and skilled outside work and one supported by the Norwegian notion of *Idraet*. It was a meaning that resonated with hard rock miners. One man remembered the first mail carrier on Berthoud Pass as "a wonder, the best snow-shoe man ever known in Middle Park. His pack was never less than 70 pounds of mail. . . . He often packed straight through from Empire to Hot Sulphur, going night and day, with no sleep, stopping only for meals."[13] His expertise, work ethic, and physical prowess earned him recognition because that is what miners valued in one another. Mail carriers' reputations also stemmed from the degree to which they overcame the challenges posed by Rocky Mountain weather and natural landscapes. One contemporary called Snowshoe Thompson "a man who laughs at storms and avalanches and safely walks where others fall and perish."[14] This was the kind of masculinity that Rocky Mountain workingmen could appreciate.

Mail carriers sustained local mines and ranches by linking them to the outside world and earned respect through their skiing. The sport supported mountain economies more directly when the vagaries of winter placed whole settlements in danger and residents donned skis to reach safety. The winter of 1898–99, the worst in Colorado history, led to a series of narrow escapes. In the most striking example that year, a persistent storm and dwindling supplies led the people of Hunters Pass (now known as Independence Pass) to abandon their town. They dismantled their homes, built seventy-five pairs of skis with the boards, and slipped, slid, and otherwise made their way down twenty miles to the safety of Aspen.[15] This mass exodus kept the community

Nineteenth-century mail carriers braved extreme winter landscapes on skis and became legends because of it. (Harry A. Christopher Collection, 2–18, Archives, University of Colorado, Boulder Libraries)

of Hunters Pass intact and enabled its residents to return to business as usual once spring came around.

Skiing helped sustain the local economy in more traditional ways as well. Workingmen and -women often relied on skis to accomplish their jobs during the winter. Miners skied their daily commute to and from the mines, which were sometimes located several miles outside of town. Ranchers skied to gather stray animals and accomplish other winter chores. Workingwomen, especially those who tended to people's health and reproduction, also had to ski to do their jobs. Susan Anderson, known to many as "Doc Susie," attended to her patients in and near Fraser no matter what the weather. "I've skied into ditches," she said, "and I've lost my way, now and then, in a blizzard, but nothing to get worried about."[16] The midwife in Steamboat preferred to travel on a toboggan pulled by men on skis rather than under her own propulsion, and she was known to go as far as twenty miles to a patient.[17] Like the mail carriers and workingmen they lived among, these women donned skis and faced winter conditions head-on in order to do their jobs.

Almost every mountain town resident, in fact, became familiar with the winter landscape from atop a pair of Norwegian snowshoes. As one newspaper editor near Irwin and Crested Butte noted, "every man, woman and child had to learn to ski . . . we had to learn if we wanted to go anywhere."[18] Mining, hunting, errands, and social visits required skill on skis, and many newcomers spent their time learning as soon as winter set in. Alice Denison wrote from Steamboat Springs in 1885, "Today the snow is falling fast and I guess is the beginning of winter — that is, when cattle must be driven in from the range . . . and the snow shoeing begins."[19] On a small scale, as a common, local activity, skiing became necessary to conduct business, run the ranch or mine, and keep company during the winter. On one level, this kind of skiing remained purely work related and necessary for each town's basic, economic function. On another level, however, such skiing took on a more social meaning.

Skiing offered, in fact, one of the only forms of winter recreation available in these high mountain towns. The very landscape and weather that cooped people up for long winter months and made it so dangerous to travel long distances also provided local skiers with their own kind of roller-coaster ride. The thrill of moving downhill through the snow was accessible to women as well as men, since both skied around town for work and coordination proved more important in skiing than strength. The sport, in fact, became central to the winter social scene. In Grand Lake, Colorado, an 1883 newspaper article noted that "coasting on snowshoes has taken the place of dancing parties," and "quite a number of our ladies are becoming adept at the art."[20] Socially active women were crucial in nineteenth-century mountain towns, mostly because their activities helped define their town as successful. They sought ways to fill their leisure time that would re-create the social world they had left behind. An amazing number of literary societies and theater groups sprang up in Rocky Mountain mining towns, and skiing served a similar function in the winter. In the 1880s, Norwegian snowshoe parties became popular social events in Aspen, Grand Lake, Tin Cup, White Pine, and Crystal.[21] Such coed skiing enabled residents to get outside and have fun at the same time that it helped fulfill some of the community's basic social and cultural needs.

A clearly masculine activity when applied to mail carriers, miners, and ranchers, skiing took on a differently gendered meaning when women practiced it. Women and men skied as both a kind of work and a form of recreation, but women placed their activity in a more social context. They did errands, visited one another, and toured the area on their snowshoes fairly regularly.[22] They rarely explored distant mountains or challenged the fierce weather associated with heroic skiers. Women's skiing thus acquired a feminine meaning connected to the local landscape, social activities, and women's day-to-day care for the family — a concern that could encompass midwifery and even Doc Susie's work.[23] As historian John Allen observed: "In the [California] gold and silver camps social convention certainly continued to play its perceived role of civilizing society, yet it is clear when 'the beautiful' fell six feet deep that strenuous activity by women on skis was not condemned out-of-hand as un-sexing, non-womanly or simply not permitted. Indeed, skiing was a talent admired in both men and women."[24] This was the case in Colorado towns, as well. Doc Susie, a self-defined novice, limited her skiing to medical emergencies, but Alice Denison enjoyed trekking around

Mountain men and women skied for fun as well as work in the nineteenth century. These early Steamboat Springs residents appear completely at home on their Norwegian snowshoes. (Tread of Pioneers Museum, Steamboat Springs, Colorado)

Steamboat Springs and skiing down hills as a diversion. Both earned respect for their snowy travels. Photos from nineteenth-century mining towns throughout the state show women standing on their snowshoes — dressed in long skirts — with pride and poise.[25]

Efforts to establish their towns as reputable institutions led residents to competitions as well as snowshoe parties. Rather than demonstrating a degree of social sophistication, however, ski races represented a way for mining camps to compete with one another for recognition and prove the toughness of their inhabitants. During the summer months, residents rallied behind their baseball team of local workers, and in the winter they supported their best skiers. Every victory helped assure people that their town — and, by extension, their mines and businesses — had the most strength, integrity, and promise. Men used huge homemade skis, with only a leather toe strap to hold their feet in and one pole for balance and braking. They flew straight down mountainsides at speeds up to seventy miles an hour, mimicking their ritual "race home" from the mines every evening.[26] This kind of skiing emphasized speed, daring, and skill — masculine traits associated with both miners' and mail carriers' work — and onlookers described it in explicitly masculine terms. One Silverton racer skied "like a war-horse thirsting for gore," according to a Denver paper.[27] In February 1881, twenty skiers vied for $25 prize money at Irwin in Gunnison County, and other contests took place over the next few years in Tomichi, Gothic, and Crested Butte.[28] Sixteen of the area's best skiers competed for $37 in prize money at Crested Butte in 1886, racing down the mountain in heats of four abreast. These races illustrated yet another way that skiing emphasized both work and leisure at once. When the race down from the mines became formalized with prize money and spectators, it simultaneously reinforced economic rivalries, celebrated masculine work, and provided an occasion for fun.

As a competitive and spectator sport, moreover, skiing created economic opportunity for local towns through recreation. The Gunnison County Snowshoe Club formed in 1886 after the meet in Crested Butte and immediately proceeded to schedule a series of races for that winter. Gunnison, Irwin, and Gothic all hosted races that season, which offered prize money and attracted a number of competitors and spectators.[29] The club worked especially hard to attract competitors and spectators for the first meet at Gunnison. It placed advertisements in local newspapers, convinced government officials to close schools and courts, and arranged for the Denver and Rio Grande Railroad to run special trains to Gunnison from different mining camps in the region. The club's efforts bore fruit when an estimated 2,000 people showed up to watch the races and contribute to the local economy.[30] Although the Gunnison Club never met again after that first season (ski clubs were more ephemeral and transitory than the mining camps themselves), other mining communities formed snowshoe clubs of their own. Ouray, for instance, formed the Mount Sneffles Snowshoe Club and offered snacks and alcoholic beverages at its ski meetings. The festive air connected with ski clubs and their races encouraged the residents of Hunters Pass to ease tensions by naming their mass exodus to Aspen during the blizzard of 1898–99 "The Annual Race of the Hunters Pass Tenderfoot Snow-Shoe Club."[31] These clubs supported their towns by attracting business, offering community leisure activities, and lightening up a potentially deadly descent.

The races in Colorado and the ski clubs that promoted them reiterated important characteristics of the sport in nineteenth-century Colorado. They focused on the workingmen who skied as part of their jobs as well as for play, although the occasional "Ladies' Race" gave women a chance to compete at a lower level. Scandinavian skiers often carried the day, highlighting the significance of their immigrant culture and earning status for athletic feats akin to those that heroic mail carriers performed for a wage. Mailmen and racing miners blended work and play through sport, and so did mountain town women. Snowshoe clubs and parties served as logical recreational outlets in places where women regularly skied to do their chores. In promoting town rivalries and attracting visitors, ski races also reinforced the ways in which skiing strengthened marginal towns. Skiing linked them to the outside world, helped residents escape physical danger, delivered men and women to their daily jobs, and filled out social and recreational calendars. Initially developed as a necessary form of mobility in harsh winter landscapes, skiing wound up supporting local mountain economies in myriad ways.

During the last quarter of the nineteenth and into the twentieth centuries, however, Colorado's economy — and its skiing — changed. In 1880, Colorado became the number one mining state in the United States, with a total production of $23 million.[32] By 1886, Como (just over Boreas Pass from Breckenridge), Crested Butte, Silverton, and Aspen enjoyed railroad access to the outside world. In 1891, the Rio Grande Southern linked Ridgeway, Telluride, Ophir, and Rico to Durango with a system that crossed four passes and connected Durango to every major San Juan mining district except Creede and Lake City. Railroads reached from Denver to Steamboat Springs in 1909. As mountain towns gained access to the rails, the movement of people, money, mail, ore, and other goods swelled. Railroad tracks altered the map of winter transportation, replacing mail carriers' routes and granting some communities a degree of prosperity and longevity. The culture of snowshoeing mailmen and mountain town skiing persisted in areas that the railroads did not reach, but those towns usually had limited futures.

Many gold camps, including John Dyer's stomping ground of Buckskin Joe and Mosquito, had already boomed and busted by the mid-1860s. The success of silver towns depended largely on access to smelters and outside markets; those unable to attract a railroad faltered quickly. Tumbling silver prices eventually caused more widespread problems, and after the crash of 1893, little remained of Colorado's glory days. The state reported 337 business failures and 435 mines closed within a month. Leadville alone reported 20 business failures, 90 closed mines, and 2,500 men out of work; Aspen, Ouray, Georgetown, Breckenridge, Silverton, and Telluride faced similar devastation.[33] When the government repealed the Sherman Silver Purchase Act in 1893, any hope for recovering silver prices disappeared, and miners fled silver districts en masse. As early as 1900, Colorado's mountains were already dotted with ghost towns. Those communities that survived by farming, ranching, or mining other metals on a small scale quickly developed a more humble, less optimistic tone of life.

This economic shift altered how and why people skied in Colorado. Railroads and busted towns erased the need for skiing mailmen. Mining camp rivalries disappeared with the ore, and so did the ski racing that articulated such competition. Some isolated mountain residents still depended on their snowshoes and passed down their knowledge of the sport to their children, and skiing maintained its intimate connections to mountain towns and their economies, but after 1900, far fewer Coloradans would strap skis on their feet out of necessity. Together, local skiers, Denver residents, and a new cohort of Norwegian immigrants forged a system of ski carnivals and a tradition of recreational skiing that would define the sport in Colorado for years to come.

Refined Tastes

A new wave of Scandinavian immigrants entered the United States in the 1880s and early 1900s, and they brought with them a much more sophisticated version of skiing. Norwegian Sondre Nordheim popularized a binding that attached to the heel and the telemark and christiania style of turns, which enabled skiers to maneuver downhill and even jump with new ease and grace. By the 1860s, jumping competitions had sprouted up throughout Norway and Scandinavia to complement the cross-country races started twenty years earlier, and Nordheim won them handily. He and other skiers from Telemark spread their ideas to those in Christiania (now Oslo), entering contests there and forming the Christiania Ski Club in 1877.[34] The club organized its first national competition two years later, and the Telemark skiers astounded the prince of Denmark and Norway's King Oscar II with their abilities. "From that day on," one Norwegian historian wrote, "the skiing events at Huseby Hill turned into a national occasion for the whole country." Norway's first Nordic Winter Festival would take place at an even better skiing facility in Holmenkollen in 1903. Competitors came from Sweden, and an entire week was dedicated to the celebration of winter sports. National competitions, recreational cross-country skiing and jumping, and community ski clubs entered Scandinavian culture and soon spread across the world.[35]

Norwegian Fritdjof Nansen drew further attention to the sport when he skied across Greenland in 1888. He demonstrated the utility of skiing as a means of transportation, but he also publicized its recreational benefits. In a passage that resonated with meaning for nineteenth-century American outdoors people, Nansen brought the sport of skiing to a new audience. "Where will you find more freedom and excitement," he wrote in 1890, "than in speeding, swift as a bird, down the tree-clad hillside, winter air and spruce branches rushing past your face and eyes, brain and muscles alert, ready to avoid the unknown obstacles which at any moment may be thrown in your path? It is as if all civilization were suddenly washed from your mind and left, with the city atmosphere, far behind. You become one with your skis and with nature."[36]

Nordheim's new technology and technique and Nansen's public infatuation with the sport made recreational skiing accessible and attractive to people in snowy climes all over the world. More than mere physical mobility or community activity, skiing as Nansen described it offered health by liberating skiers from the evils coming to be associated with "civilization" and the city.

These advances in technique and technology came too late to reach the mining camps of California or Colorado, which explains in part why skiing across mountain ranges and racing straight down them represented such heroic feats. When Americans discovered Nordheim's inventions and the resulting ease with which they could ski, more and more of them took up the sport. This new recreational skiing gained appeal outside of isolated mountain towns partly through Americans who headed to Europe. Upper-class Americans accustomed to traveling the world in search of new diversions first came across recreational skiing either in Norway itself or, more probably, in European resorts that offered winter sports. Swiss alpine resorts, for instance, had been popular with other Europeans since the mid-1800s, and by the end of the century, Americans patronized them as well. By 1900, Norwegian ski instructors in St. Moritz were training Swiss ones to complement its winter sports activities. They formed the St. Moritz Ski Club in February 1902, when the 531 guests (55 of whom were Americans) all took part in a "fascinating combination of social climbing, display of wealth, competitiveness, and longing for the simpler life."[37] Other tourists, less concerned with the image of wealth and more with the benefits of outdoor activity, went straight to the source. One magazine author noted in 1901 that "more and more foreigners, and from farther distances, are every year drawn into the fascination of Norway's national sport and they enjoy it as much as do the natives."[38]

European skiing and tourism went hand in hand only for those who could afford travel; this fact would not change over time. Working-class, immigrant Scandinavians, however, also brought this more refined sport to American soil, where it would become part of community life across the northern United States. Economic depression in Norway and other parts of Scandinavia from the 1880s to the 1900s encouraged young men to leave home and try to establish themselves in other countries. Miners, farmers, missionaries, students, mailmen, and other emigrant Norwegians introduced skiing to Australia, New Zealand, Alaska, China, Japan, Chile, Argentina, and even North Africa, as well as Germany, Austria, Switzerland, Italy, France, Russia, and Spain.[39] Quite a number of them wound up in the United States — between 1880 and 1889, almost 680,000 immigrants came from Norway, Sweden, and Denmark to America, making up the fourth largest immigrant group of the decade and

12.7 percent of the period's total immigration.[40] Among the Norwegians who emigrated were forty skiers from Telemark, including Sondre Nordheim and three other King's Cup winners. Most settled in the Midwest, where they formed ski clubs and held competitions. Local clubs sprang up in northern rural areas where pockets of Scandinavians settled and promoted skiing as healthy, outdoor recreation for the community. Initially ethnically exclusive and distinctly working class, these clubs eventually opened up to anyone interested in the sport and exhibited some degree of diversity.[41] In 1891, Scandinavian immigrants formed America's first ski association — the Ski Association for the Northwest — headquartered in St. Paul, Minnesota. The American Ski Association, based in Ishpeming, Michigan, followed in 1905. By 1919, the National Ski Association had united thirty clubs from all over the country, many with names that displayed their Norwegian heritage.[42]

National organizations that promoted skiing as an ideal, healthy outdoor sport attracted the attention and interest of the upper-class outdoor enthusiasts of the 1890s and 1900s, who sought spiritual, physical, and moral refuge in the mountains. The early twentieth century saw increasingly industrialized cities, the seeming decline of American civilization, and the end of the "frontier." For those caught in the city, the primitive and the wild offered sources of spiritual beauty and truth. Echoing Fritdjof Nansen, John Muir wrote that "thousands of tired, nerve-shaken, over-civilized people are beginning to find out that going to the mountains is going home. . . . Mountain parks and reservations are useful not only as fountains of timber and irrigating rivers," he said, "but as fountains of life." Appreciation of the wilderness had spread from a relatively small group of upper-class tourists to become a more middle-class, national cult.[43]

The growth of this movement coincided with the increasing popularity of outdoor recreation that had spread after the Civil War from Europe to the East, and — by the 1890s — to the West as well. Historian Earl Pomeroy noted the conspicuous presence of easterners camping in the Rockies as early as the 1870s, by which time Boston residents had formed the Appalachian Mountain Club. By the 1880s, "westerners were camping on an impressive scale."[44] John Muir's Sierra Club, established in 1892, represented the small but growing population of westerners interested in "exploring, enjoying, and rendering accessible the mountain regions of the Pacific Coast."[45] Reports of new roads and hotels growing up around the Estes Park region of Colorado and the growing popularity of outdoor recreation documented the spread of this wilderness enthusiasm in the Rocky Mountains at the turn of the century. Naturalist Enos Mills embarked on frequent hikes and even winter ski camping trips with his dog, Scotch, in the area that would become Rocky Mountain National Park.[46]

He was not alone in his enthusiasm for Colorado's outdoors. Denver resident Mary Sabin had already climbed seven peaks in the state by 1912, many with her sister, Florence. On April 3, she and James Grafton Rogers invited some friends over to create the Colorado Mountain Club (CMC), which brought interests in the preservation of scenery and wilderness, exercise and outdoor recreation, and tourism together in one group.[47] That first year, the twenty-five charter members took ten trips; in three years, the CMC would be skiing. Urban outdoor clubs like Denver's CMC based their missions on assumptions about the mountain landscape that stemmed directly from their upper-class status and urban location. They understood the mountains as places to visit, play, and preserve rather than as home or a place of work. Like Nansen and Muir, they skied for health and recreation, not out of necessity.

Some Americans developed this perspective at school. Northeastern colleges — home of elite young men — grew interested in cultivating healthy student bodies as well as minds and began to establish outing clubs and amateur ski teams. Dartmouth formed both in 1909, and other New England liberal arts colleges followed. Williams, Middlebury, Harvard, Yale, and the state universities of Vermont and New Hampshire formed their own clubs and began a tradition of intercollegiate ski competitions and winter carnivals.[48] Recreational skiing grew through these channels to become popular among the young well-to-do who had the time, money, and leisure to develop their interest in the outdoors.

The same national club presence that prompted skiing's entrance into northeastern liberal arts colleges also paved the way for the sport in upper-class urban outdoor clubs. College students and mountain club members shared perspectives based on class, urban residence, education, and leisure; their recreational habits reinforced each other, and college students often formed or joined outdoor clubs after they graduated. The Colorado Mountain Club, like its eastern ancestors and the Sierra Club in California, adopted skiing as part of its winter agenda when it held its first annual ski outing to Fern Lake near Estes Park in 1915.[49] Scandinavian ski clubs originating in the

Midwest, European resort skiing, and college outing clubs all encouraged the rise of recreational skiing in Colorado, but the most direct influence came, as it had before, from working-class Scandinavian immigrants who wound up in the Rocky Mountains.

Although fewer Norwegians moved to Colorado than to Minnesota or Michigan in the late nineteenth and early twentieth centuries, those who did had an indelible influence on skiing in the state. One rather typical Norwegian immigrant, with exceptional skill and enthusiasm for the sport, introduced skiing to Denver residents personally. He helped establish a tradition of local ski clubs in Denver and in rural mountain towns where the sport barely remained as a form of transportation. Like John Dyer and the mail carriers, Carl Howelsen became a regional hero, known for his skill and daring. Too, he promoted a kind of skiing that supported local economies, though this skiing served as the beginning of tourism and the antidote to slow times rather than a means to mine or ranch more effectively. Finally, like the Scandinavian immigrants that preceded him to Colorado, he gained status and authenticity because he embodied the roots and history of the sport. He became, in short, the "Flying Norseman."

Carnival Skiing

Son of a shoemaker, Karl Hovelsen was born in Christiania in 1877 and grew up skiing along with his ten brothers and sisters.[50] By 1902, he was winning almost every cross-country and jumping contest he entered, including ones at Holmenkollen and other national competitions. At the Nordic Winter Sports Week in 1903 in Christiania, Hovelsen took home the Prince Regent's Cup for the fifty-kilometer race, King Oscar's Cup for the combined races, and the Holmenkollen Gold Medal, the highest award of the Holmenkollen races. He had won every ski event.

During that time, however, Norway was undergoing an industrial depression that made it difficult for Hovelsen, a stonemason and bricklayer by trade, to find work. In 1905, he immigrated to America, got a job in Chicago, and, as Carl Howelsen(or sometimes Howelson), joined other countrymen in the recently established Norge Ski Club. On a trip to Riverview Amusement Park, he noticed a ride in which cars slid down a ninety-foot tower into a pool and decided to try it on skis. He came back one morning and altered the chute, jumped about sixty feet in the air before landing, and entranced the guards so completely that they let him keep doing it on weekends for the crowds. When the director of the Barnum and Bailey Circus came along and offered him a job, Howelsen convinced two of his Norwegian friends to join him in his adventure. For almost a season he performed "a lightning dive . . . and a sensational flight through space" for the circus, until he hurt his back and returned to Chicago.[51] The Rocky Mountains and news of ample work in Denver drew the Flying Norseman to Colorado in the spring of 1909, where he joined the Denver local of the Bricklayers and Masons International Union.

As he explored the mountains in the region, this immigrant worker introduced recreational skiing to Denver and its surrounding mountain towns. In December 1911, Howelsen and friend Angell Schmidt took the Moffat Railroad to the top of the Continental Divide and set out on skis to look around. They talked with a Swedish rancher in Fraser — Doc Susie's stomping ground — and skied on to Hot Sulphur Springs, where they met John Peyer, a Swiss immigrant who was eager to get winter sports going in Colorado. He had helped organize Hot Sulphur's Winter Sports Club that fall, and its first winter carnival was to be held the day after Howelsen and Schmidt arrived. After a quick demonstration and tales of the Holmenkollen, the two Norwegians added skiing to the planned events and showed local residents as well as visitors from Denver the novelty of ski jumping. The *Denver Post* exclaimed, "Sulphur Springs Successful Winter Sports Awaken Interest for Skiing Carnival in Denver" and "Former Residents of Norway Give Exhibition that Pleased Spectators."[52] The carnival was such a success that the Winter Sports Club planned a larger, three-day carnival for the coming February, in which Howelsen and Schmidt agreed to participate.[53]

Shifting smoothly from circus to carnival, the Flying Norseman lived on. Howelsen and Schmidt knew of eight or ten "good ski jumpers" living in Denver, and at least two of them became great promoters of the sport in 1912.[54] Turning and jumping distinguished nineteenth- from twentieth-century skiing in Colorado technically, giving the sport a new meaning for mountain communities and their visitors. No longer the product of necessity, skiing became recreational for participants as well as spectators. Europeans like Peyer and Howelsen understood it as a leisure activity appropriate for the whole community and worthy of celebration during winter carnivals. Town residents in early-twentieth-century Colorado redefined skiing as a possible attraction for visitors. Instead of enabling the now-defunct business of mining to continue in winter, skiing itself represented potential business. And Howelsen became a new kind of heroic skier, one defined by the novelty and spectacle of his feats as well as by the strength, bravery, and expertise with which he performed them.

With all this in mind, John Peyer set out to find as many competitors and spectators as he could for the next carnival in Hot Sulphur. He invited ski clubs from the East and the Midwest as well as people from all over the West, asking experts on skis, sleds, and skates to attend. The *Rocky Mountain News* wrote that entries were coming from "nearly all the States of the Union where snow and ice are to be found," as well as from Canada, western Colorado, and Denver. Afterward, the *Denver Post* declared the three-day event a "huge success" and announced that Hot Sulphur Springs had better natural conditions for winter sports than Switzerland, Norway, and Europe as a whole.[55] The carnival continued to grow the next year, featuring the Norwegian sport of skijoring, where skiers race across the flat pulled

Hot Sulphur's 1912 winter carnival incorporated European sports into community tradition. Norwegian Carl Howelsen is pictured holding a trophy; Swiss John Peyer is in the white sweater. (Grand County Historical Association)

by galloping horses, and a contest pitting Howelsen and Colorado jumpers against two of the best ski jumpers from Red Wing, Minnesota. The *Daily News* proclaimed that "Cracks of East and West Will Meet in Program of Daring Feats," advertised a special round-trip on the Moffat Railroad for $7.40, and predicted that attendance would far outnumber that of last year.[56] The success of this second carnival was guaranteed when Howelsen, the local favorite, emerged victorious over the visiting jumpers. The news coverage represented the first effort in a long tradition of associating Colorado with the country's best skiing and skiers. Like the early mining camp competitions, the carnival helped strengthen Hot Sulphur's and Denver's community identity. It also brought business to a struggling town during its quiet season. In their efforts to bring visitors to town and promote winter sport, recent immigrants to Colorado wound up turning skiing from a novelty to an anchor of winter mountain culture.

Nor were the residents of Hot Sulphur alone in their aspirations for skiing. A group of Denverites decided that they would like to hold their own winter carnivals. With the help of Howelsen and a collection of Norwegians, they formed the Denver Ski Club in late 1913 and the Denver–Rocky Mountain Ski Club a year later. They built a 100-foot-long jump, appropriately at Inspiration Point, where the Denver Press Club sponsored an exhibition by Denver's own Flying Norseman. This ski tournament would be, the *Denver Post* said, "A spectacle worth seeing."[57] Observers remarked at the "novelty of it all, the daring," and "the enthusiasm of the contestants." One newspaper estimated that 20,000 spectators watched "as the form of Carl Howelson [*sic*] shot with bullet-like speed from the apex of the bump and rose thirty feet in the air . . . negotiating great distances."[58] The sport seemed to catch on, and so did the draw of big competition. The National Ski Association agreed to hold its championships in the West for the first time since its founding in 1905, and an estimated 40,000 to 50,000 came to watch the 1921 meet. Local crowds went home happy when Howelsen won the national professional championship, but they were even more excited when the city secured the national championships again for 1927.[59] Denver boosters expected contestants from every ski club in the country, champions from Canada and Norway, and 15,000 to 20,000 spectators. They planned a week of events, including "street stunts, floats, folk pageants, and a carnival ball, besides skiing and skating contests," and they appropriated $1,500 for improvements to the

Genesee Hill jump and clubhouse.[60] They turned the national championships into much more than a competition.

The event became a performance akin to Howelsen's circus act. Flying Norsemen, Flying Swedes, and Flying Americans, first in Hot Sulphur and later in Denver, sought to best one another at what most observers considered daring yet outlandish behavior. They acted out the significance of Scandinavian culture to the American West at the same time that they introduced a new sport to its inhabitants. By drawing attention to their Nordic feats, these performers embodied the national origins of skiing and articulated their hopes for its rising popularity. Each time Carl Howelsen emerged victorious, he reemphasized the notion that while it may have come from Scandinavia, skiing — like himself — now resided in Colorado. Winter carnivals and national championships became social events of the winter, drawing locals together in ski clubs and townwide celebrations with dances and parades. Promoters lured photographers and moving picture cameramen to these events so that they might report the promise of winter sports in Colorado to the nation. By advertising skiing to locals and the community to spectators, competitors and ski club members helped develop winter tourism as they influenced Colorado's winter culture.

But skiing in Colorado was much more than a spectacle. Howelsen's main goal — and that of the ski clubs — was to get more people out in the snow skiing. To that end, Howelsen and other experts became instructors as much as heroic performers. Howelsen himself taught hundreds of people to ski between 1912 and 1921, including individuals from Denver, Estes Park, Leadville, Yampa, Craig, Clark, Breckenridge, Golden, and Hayden.[61] Fellow Norwegian Peter Prestrud moved to Colorado in 1910, became the postmaster in Frisco, and organized the Summit County Ski Club. By introducing their sport to Denver and isolated mountain town residents, these men wove together Scandinavian and American, urban and rural, working- and upperclass traditions into a ski culture that would ultimately support Colorado's ski industry.

That ski culture, like its nineteenth-century predecessor, was community oriented and participatory, as well as fun to watch. More recreational than its earlier version, however, the sport crossed the boundaries separating work from leisure in new ways. Ski clubs formed to support winter carnivals and wound up becoming local institutions. In Steamboat Springs, where

Howelsen moved in 1913, skiing gradually took over the town every winter. The weekend picnics and day trips he led encouraged young and old to take up skiing, and residents were quick to establish a tradition of winter carnivals. The town's first one in 1914 featured the now standard cross-country races and jumping contests, as well as events geared toward community participation. Although only a few spectators made it from Denver on the train, "everyone in town fit for boots and mittens was there, and ranch families from miles about hitched up sleds and were on hand." Events included amateur and professional ski jumping, a shooting match, cross-country races, and street events such as the Boy Scout fire race, the wheelbarrow race, a hazard race, a log-sawing relay on skis, and skijoring.[62] Separate contests for local, regional, and boys' amateur jumpers offered a forum for all levels of homegrown skiers, and nightly dances gave even those with an aversion to snow a chance to join in the festivities. Putting the carnival on became a job in itself. As with most rural ski clubs, Steamboat's was rooted in the town's working-class population. Howelsen himself, along with a few other Norwegian immigrants nearby, continued to earn their livings through manual labor.[63] With its ladies auxiliary and a high school affiliate, Steamboat's ski club — and the carnival it put on — stood out as larger and more well known and boasting a broader community base than any other carnival and club of the time. Rather than a sport for elite outdoor recreationists, the kind of skiing Howelsen brought to Steamboat Springs represented a locally based sport that continued to blend work with play.

These characteristics enabled mountain town women to continue skiing. Within the community context of winter carnivals, women could bend even their already loose local restrictions on feminine behavior to include outright competition. Colorado's first winter carnival in 1912 at Hot Sulphur Springs, where Carl Howelsen demonstrated his jumping skills to an enthralled crowd, also featured a jumping exhibition by the women of Hot Sulphur.[64] Steamboat Springs' first carnival in 1914 included a "ladies' free-for-all" race across a half-mile course and street events for everybody — man and woman, boy and girl — but women's roles remained distinct from men's.[65] Two years later, town residents declared that they would crown a carnival queen each year to lead the carnival parade and "reign as queen of beauty for twelvemonth."[66] Through the figure of the carnival queen, local women and men integrated notions of femininity and community power

with winter sports, while relegating women's participation to a fairly super-
ficial level. Other women chose to be more engaged, forming their own ski
clubs. Women in Steamboat Springs established their own S.K.I. Club in
1917 "to create, develop and sustain interest in ladies' skiing and in all outdoor sports; to encourage the formation of local ski clubs throughout the
country; to assist in defraying the expenses of the annual Mid-Winter Sports
Carnival; and to aid and foster the carnival spirit." Many of these same
women established the Ladies Recreation Club in 1920 to support young
women athletes.[67] In this way, Steamboat Springs women linked their desire to enjoy outdoor sports with the cause of the sport nationwide and their
support of the community. They established skiing as a female activity in
their own terms, as both part of community "spirit" and an acknowledg-
ment of female athleticism.

As celebrations of winter and sport imported from Norway, Colorado's
local winter carnivals served important cultural purposes. They brought together groups of people who were otherwise separated by residence, class, and
ethnicity; they engaged women, men, and children in games and sporting
competitions; and they provided some mountain communities with their
biggest social events of the winter. During carnivals, people of different classes
and backgrounds mingled on equal terms, and cultural restraints on women
were temporarily lifted.[68] In this context, wealthy CMC members from Denver cheered lustily for their local champion Carl Howelsen, whose fame over-
rode his working-class immigrant identity. Women and children competed
in their own events — including jumping contests and events with ambigu-
ous names like the "ladies' free-for-all."

Through winter carnivals, skiing joined men and women from different
backgrounds in the interest of sport. Howelsen formed a long-lasting friendship with founding CMC member and Smith graduate Marjorie Perry after
she saw him jump at Hot Sulphur. They skied together at Steamboat Springs
and in the mountains near Denver. At the same time that Colorado mountain town women participated in community ski activities, some upper-class
Colorado women cultivated a more general freedom of movement by driving cars, traveling overseas, and donning skis. Generally urban residents educated in the East at colleges such as Smith, these "New Women" of the 1910s
and 1920s established new roles for women, supported by the opportunities
for leisure that their class and education afforded them. Marjorie Perry moved

Smith graduate and Colorado resident Marjorie Perry exercised the freedom of movement characterized by the early-twentieth-century "New Woman." She is pictured here practicing the Scandinavian sport of skijoring. (Tread of Pioneers Museum, Steamboat Springs, Colorado)

freely between Denver and Steamboat Springs on the train, on horseback during the summer, and on skis in the wintertime.

The appeal of moving through winter landscapes under their own power, combined with the spectacle and accessibility of carnival skiing, helped spread the sport to other urban skiers. The CMC began sponsoring annual winter outings near Estes Park in 1916, four years after Denver outdoorsmen and -women founded the club. Members packed in their equipment, clothes, and provisions for a weekend and spent the days skiing and the evenings socializing. In this way, one member explained, "mountain-clubbers first began to make the most of Colorado's glorious mountains in winter, and began to realize the thrills of skiing for real pleasure and enjoyment."[69] By the mid-1920s, the popularity of these trips had spread; the Boulder branch of the CMC and the University of Colorado both sponsored winter sports and cross-country trips in February 1925.[70] Meanwhile, Denver–Rocky Mountain Ski Club members practiced their technique on their land at Genesee, outside Denver. With perhaps a less lofty attitude toward their endeavors than the CMC, they sang "Ski-i-n-g, wonderful ski-i-n-g — You're the only spo-r-t that I adore. When the snow falls over the hillside I'll be bumping down the hill till I'm sore."[71]

Skiers outside Denver, too, responded to the growing enthusiasm by forming their own clubs and hosting their own events. Just as the Hot Sulphur carnival brought Howelsen and Perry together, this circuit of carnivals and competitions united men and women who lived in mountain towns with those who lived in Denver. In addition to the ski clubs in Hot Sulphur Springs, Steamboat Springs, Dillon, and Denver that started before 1920, the Denver–Rocky Mountain Ski Club held its first annual Fourth of July Ski Tournament on St. Mary's Glacier in 1923. Jumpers from Denver, Allens Park, Hot Sulphur, Dillon, and Steamboat all made the trip, and the contest continued to attract competitors and spectators through the 1930s.

Between the development of skiing in Denver and nearby towns and the increasingly public space women occupied in sports during the 1920s, Colorado women found many opportunities to enter competitions. The Denver–Rocky Mountain Ski Club tournament in 1922 offered girls' sliding, ladies' sliding, and ladies' jumping contests, for instance, along with boys' and men's jumping, cross-country, and "fancy skiing." Girls and ladies also jumped at St. Mary's Glacier in 1923, by which time the Allens Park Ski Club, the Rocky Mountain National Park Ski Club, and the Pikes Peak Ski Club held tournaments as well. Still other clubs joined in the local tournament circuit soon after, including the Homewood Ski Club out of Denver (1926), the Pioneer Ski Club of the University of Denver (1928), the Woodbine Ski Club (1931), and the Silver Spruce Club of Colorado Springs (1931). These organizations and the events they held drew Colorado skiers together and made Nordic skiing and jumping available to a growing group of enthusiasts, both women and men.[72]

By the twentieth century, Colorado skiing had moved from the realm of skiing mail carriers and isolated communities to the ski clubs of Denver and local winter carnivals. As Colorado's unstable economy boomed and busted, the meaning of the sport and its place in mountain communities changed. Norwegian snowshoeing rose out of Colorado's distinct economy, landscape, and population. The sport represented work as well as play for the men and women who lived in mountain towns. Physical isolation and economic uncertainty bred John Dyer's kind of skiing, vital to the local economy and society. Howelsen's feats, in a more developed if less exciting social and economic landscape, defined the sport in more recreational terms without erasing its immigrant, working-class roots. But participation in the sport —as a spectator or ski club member — began to unite people across class and gender lines rather than distinguishing between them.

Although skiing spread to new groups of people in the early twentieth century, and hurling oneself through the air to attract crowds contrasted sharply with skiing across the mountains to deliver the mail, flying Norsemen and snowshoe itinerants practiced a similar version of the sport. Theirs was a clearly Scandinavian activity. Gold miners and carnival spectators alike respected the techniques and expertise that Norwegian, Swedish, and European skiers brought to their communities. Both men and women took up the sport consistently, associating skiing with either bravery, strength, and skill or family, community well-being, and a love of sport. As a means of mining, ranching, or getting around in the winter, or as a social diversion and attraction during slow times, the tradition of skiing that men and women established in Colorado blended work and play.

By the 1920s, snowshoe itinerants, flying Norsemen, and their neighbors had established the origins of Colorado's ski industry. The sport took hold in local town "snowshoe parties" and races from Aspen and Breckenridge to Crested Butte and Steamboat Springs. Expert skiers from abroad who moved to the Rocky Mountains established a wide base of local interest, first out of necessity and then for fun. As the economic and social context of Colorado changed, skiers redefined their sport. If mining camps gained important connections to the outside world and life-saving (albeit also life-threatening) mobility from skiing, Denver and twentieth-century mountain towns benefited from the spectacle of winter carnivals. These events gave a boost to stagnant economies by bringing visitors to town; they brought rural people together and introduced them to city skiers, and they became annual rituals reaffirming the vitality of mountain culture. Towns ranging from Hot Sulphur Springs and Allens Park to Denver and Colorado Springs developed a winter culture in which skiing took center stage. This level of enthusiasm and support, combined with an annual schedule of carnivals and competition, set the stage for the growth of Alpine skiing and winter tourism in Colorado.

2

The Romance of Downhill
Alpine Skiing and Resort Culture in the United States

In 1939, Friedl Pfeifer gazed across Sun Valley's ballroom and noticed a beautiful young woman. He asked her to dance and fell in love. The Austrian ski instructor courted Hoyt Smith and captured her heart, but her parents would not agree to the marriage. President of the largest chain of banks in Utah and part of Salt Lake City's high society, Fred E. Smith recoiled at the thought of his daughter marrying a ski instructor and consented to the wedding only after she threatened to elope. Otto Lang empathized with Pfeifer, his friend, countryman, and fellow ski instructor. A year earlier, Lang had also fallen in love, with the beautiful daughter of a rear admiral. Upon meeting her well-respected Texan parents, Lang "could sense immediately that [they] were not too happy about their daughter's fast-developing attachment to an itinerant *sportsmeister,* such as I was."[1] These men, their future fathers-in-law quickly noticed, knew little of high society. Indeed, they shared more with Carl Howelsen, the high-flying immigrant bricklayer, than with their intended brides. Pfeifer had grown up in an Austrian farming village and Lang was from Salzburg, and both had faced economic hardships. They wound up teaching skiing at St. Anton, Austria, with other rural men — including one instructor who had to leave early every day to milk his cows — before coming to America in search of work. Their European national identity, modest economic status, and obsession with the sport of skiing linked them to Howelsen at the same time that it distanced them from their wives and in-laws. When these men skied, however, they acted out a very different identity than Howelsen did.

Howelsen's spectacular leaps made him a local hero; Lang's and Pfeifer's skiing brought to mind images of elite European resorts and a suave, authoritative masculinity that proved irresistible to women like Hoyt Smith and Sinclair Gannon.

Friedl Pfeifer and his fellow Austrian instructors also skied differently from Howelsen. Although the earliest origins of Colorado skiing came from Scandinavia, another thread came out of the Alps and a tradition of European tourism. In St. Anton and St. Moritz, resorts supported the local economy, and professional mountain guides and ski instructors earned a high degree of respect. These skiers used shorter skis, two poles, and a different style of turning than Nordic skiers, and they concentrated on going downhill rather than touring across country or jumping. These differences signified more than a change in athletic practice. Alpine skiing brought visions of the Alps and a cosmopolitan social world to America in the 1920s and 1930s in the form of European ski instructors. These men taught skiing technique as they conferred their masculine authority, elegant style, and European expertise on their students. Skiing in America became a kind of consumption, not only as skiers purchased the latest fashion and equipment but also as they sought out the skills, qualities, and associations available from their instructors.[2] Famous instructors and urban ski clubs invited such consumption, and they made Alpine skiing accessible to new groups of Americans in the 1920s and 1930s. In Colorado, they introduced Alpine skiing to local ski clubs, whose members embraced the sport and incorporated it into their own ski culture.

Teaching and consuming Alpine skiing created strange power relations within resort culture. Farm boys, by virtue of their athletic skill, skiing expertise, and good looks, wound up exercising authority over the European kings and Hollywood stars who were their clients. This teacher-pupil relationship that could invert class identities also came loaded with gendered meanings. Although people took ski lessons for different reasons, most enjoyed the suave masculinity of their instructors. For some women, their instructors' expertise transferred easily from the slopes to the bar and even the bedroom. For a few other women, associations with European instructors helped them create a new expertise of their own as they competed in international competitions and became instructors themselves. Each, in their own way, sought more than technical advice. In the context of Sun Valley, where ski instructors epitomized a cosmopolitan masculine ideal and wealthy socialites went to find a touch of European charm, it made perfect sense for Friedl Pfeifer to ask Hoyt Smith to dance, and it made sense for her to say yes. The story behind Pfeifer and Smith's romance — and the romance between Americans and Alpine skiing — begins with the development of the sport in Europe.

Alpine Skiing in Europe and Its Masculine Ideal

Friedl Pfeifer grew up in St. Anton am Arlberg, Austria, the birthplace of Alpine (or downhill) skiing. The skiing style that had caught on across Europe and America during the nineteenth century was designed for traversing Scandinavia's rolling landscape. When skiers attempted to negotiate a different topography — the steep mountains of the Alps — they had to make a few adjustments. Austrian Mathias Zdarsky read of Fridtjof Nansen's ski trip across Greenland and invented a different style of "stem" turn while experimenting on his local mountain west of Vienna. Zdarsky began teaching people to climb and descend mountains on skis before the turn of the century, and he trained troops to ski downhill and wage mountain war in the southern Tyrol during World War I. Mountain climbers throughout the Alps adapted mountaineering techniques to work with skis in the late nineteenth century, opening up the mountains to winter recreational enthusiasts and creating new jobs for guides.

Because many alpine towns were both farming communities and resorts, downhill skiing developed hand in hand with the local community and its tourist trade. Local ski clubs such as the Ski Club Arlberg in St. Anton organized the town's youth and sponsored competitions between neighboring clubs as early as the 1890s. Resorts offered alpine ski tours to their winter guests and provided guiding jobs to local skiers with enough expertise. Skiing icon Hannes Schneider, for instance, took a job as a guide at the Hotel Post in St. Anton when he was seventeen, after which he went on to win so many competitions that he became recognized as the best and fastest skier in Austria. Already a center for alpine ski tours due to its Hotel Post, great scenery, snow, and train access, St. Anton am Arlberg capitalized on Schneider's reputation by advertising "permanent classes of instruction by the Austrian champion" in 1910.[3]

During World War I, few people vacationed in Austria. After the war, tourists began to return to St. Anton, where they could enroll in Schneider's new ski school and learn his "Arlberg" system, a carefully planned progression of turns that resulted in a smooth, fast style of skiing. He had students use two poles and the shorter, narrower, more maneuverable skis that World War I mountain troops had adopted, and his new technique allowed students to learn, and racers to race, faster than ever before. By 1922, wealthy tourists were raving about Schneider's system, and he had starred in a classic instructional ski movie — starting a trend that would spread the sport's popularity through a new visual mass culture. More action-oriented movies quickly followed, ensuring the success of skiing and of Hannes Schneider. After the release of *Fox Chase in the Engadine,* Pfeifer recalled, "almost overnight, skiing became a social phenomenon."[4] Pfeifer and Schneider crossed paths in 1925, by which time Pfeifer had made a name for himself as a talented young racer and Schneider had decided to recruit him as an instructor in his prestigious ski school. Pfeifer's tenure there coincided with international recognition for Schneider's ski school and his Arlberg system, the evolution of a ski resort culture, and the growth of downhill racing in Europe.

As St. Anton was gaining an international reputation for its winter tourism, it also claimed a leading role in international ski competition. Skiing had become so popular throughout Europe by 1910 that Norway, Austria, Switzerland, and Germany joined the first international ski association, which sponsored its own competitions.[5] After World War I, Alpine skiing joined the Scandinavian-style cross-country races and jumping contests as part of this international competition. "Downhill" races tested who could get from the top of the mountain to the bottom fastest, and it allowed racers to choose their own paths. The difficulty of negotiating trees led British skier Sir Arnold Lunn to develop a separate race called slalom, in which skiers raced down through a series of poles.[6] Although downhill races often accompanied Nordic events in competitions, the first Alpine-only competition did not take place until 1927. Sponsored initially by the Ski Club Arlberg, this race would later be known as the Arlberg-Kandahar. The club awarded prizes in a slalom race, in a downhill race, and for the fastest combined time. Soon resorts throughout the Alps — in Switzerland, Germany, Austria, France, and Italy — were holding similar races, establishing a circuit of Alpine contests through which the sport would spread.[7]

Downhill skiing and tourism in St. Anton and more famous towns, including St. Moritz and Davos in Switzerland, blossomed in the 1920s. Resort towns organized ski clubs, sponsored races, and financed traveling teams precisely to improve their tourist business, one of their few economic opportunities during the 1920s and 1930s. The skiers who represented these towns in races and taught in the resorts' ski schools became the locus of fame and fortune. Hannes Schneider, Friedl Pfeifer, Otto Lang, Luggi Foeger, and Rudi Matt introduced Alpine skiing to eager students in Europe and America, and they all began their careers at the same place: Schneider's ski school in St. Anton. These skiers helped create a distinct masculinity and style through their expertise in the mountains, their skill in competition, and the beauty of their skiing style.

Many of St. Anton's ski instructors took extensive exams that qualified them to be mountain guides and join what Pfeifer called "a select brotherhood."[8] Alpine guides had led tourists through the Alps for decades — Pfeifer's father was one — and in the 1920s and 1930s, trips on skis grew quite popular. Without the benefit of ski lifts and designated trails, tourists who wanted to ski difficult terrain had to first climb up it and cope with the dangers of avalanches, snowstorms, and cold as well. As Pfeifer explained, "Skiing the Valluga [the highest mountain above St. Anton] was a wilderness experience that called for a protecting leader to intercede between the skier and raw nature. The St. Anton instructor was expected to be that leader."[9] One American's "cherished memory" was of a July 1931 ski trip up the Breithorn in Switzerland, during which his group's guide cut quite a figure. Rousting skiers at 3:00 A.M., setting "a terrific pace" up the mountain, and breaking trail in thigh-deep snow, the guide protected his reputation by reaching the summit with his group first, ahead of another guide from outside the district. Once on top, the group "looked forward with great anticipation to a five or six-mile coast down the glacier."[10] This guide's leadership and control — even his reputation and rank in the world of ski guides — helped make the group's trip both memorable and enjoyable. Skiing in the Alps was no easy task; it took strength, endurance, and competitiveness on the way up and on the way down. Leaders had to know the terrain, the weather, and the snow — they had to know nature — better than anyone else. And mountain guides embodied an ideal that their group members could only hope to emulate. As guides, these men defined a masculinity based on a particular way of interacting with the mountains that was central to the experiences of tourists and to resort culture in general.[11]

Alpine racing offered a critical venue for forming these masculine identities. Friedl Pfeifer and Rudi Matt made names for themselves on the European racing circuit, while others competed on lower levels. Pfeifer, representing the Ski Club Arlberg, won the very first Hahnenkamm race in 1929, and two years later he won Austria's national championship. Although Schneider's ski school served as a training camp for its local instructors and racers, its main business was attracting tourist dollars. These goals were not mutually exclusive, however, or even in conflict. Pfeifer explained, "My sphere of interest was managed by the authoritative but benevolent Hannes Schneider, whose fame had reached almost mythic proportions. An instructor's job was to teach skiing and to convey that authority and benevolence to our students."[12] Having well-known racers as instructors certainly helped business, and racing victories only added to the masculine authority that instructors already exercised as mountain guides, group leaders, and skilled ski technicians.

European ski instructors melded their overt authority in the mountains and their competitive skill on the racecourse with a style that tempered the ruggedness of their masculinity and incorporated them aesthetically into mountain landscapes. Some skiers understood their sport as an act of raw power and masculine dominance over feminine nature. "The great thrill of skiing," one male author explained in 1938, "rises from the mastery of the individual . . . over the forces of nature — her treacherous snows, her vast space — over the forces of gravity, over the pull of speed. It is the feeling of being completely in control when in contest with these forces . . . [that] is the enchantment of skiing."[13] Alpine guides and racers demonstrated their skill in this regard. They tempered this kind of masculinity, however, with a certain style.

One author wrote that "beauty is the very essence of skiing . . . it could not be escaped if one were foolish enough or dull enough to try, for skiing is an esthetic experience compounded of the magnificence of nature and the form, grace and symmetry of a sport which is at the same time an art."[14] As much as ski instructors exercised mastery over mountains and racecourses, they also demonstrated skiing as art and cultivated elegant form. Hannes Schneider and Rudi Matt appeared in a popular ski film called *The White Ecstasy,* made in 1931 and shown all over Europe, which featured an elaborate ski chase that highlighted both the style and the excitement of downhill

Hannes Schneider became a symbol of alpine authority and style after he established his ski school. Resorts such as St. Anton embedded skiing expertise within a gendered consumer culture (expressed here through adoring snow bunnies) that European ski instructors re-created in the United States. (New England Ski Museum)

skiing.[15] The multiple and interdependent aspects of ski instructors' identities came out in one U.S. ski team member's description of Friedl Pfeifer. She introduced him in her memoirs as the team coach, "a native of St. Anton [and] a beautiful stylist who had won the Arlberg-Kandahar."[16]

The expertise, skill, and style that Pfeifer and his fellow instructors embodied gave them status in resort towns that attracted an elite clientele. One resort a few hours by train from Vienna, Semmering, had been a popular playground for affluent merchants, aristocrats, and celebrities of the Austro-Hungarian empire before the war, and it balanced its postwar clientele of tubercular summer visitors with a ski school in the winter. Even after the war, Otto Lang explained, "there was a sizable population of healthy nouveaux riches who looked for ways to spend their money in an environment of prewar luxury."[17] Other resorts in Switzerland enjoyed a similar clientele, mainly of British ski enthusiasts. Schneider's fans swelled Kitzbühl and the little town of St. Anton. By the early 1930s, when Lang had moved to St. Anton to teach in Schneider's school, Pfeifer's family had opened a hotel of its own, and "celebrities, nobility, millionaires, and even royalty [were] all lugging their skis to the ski school meeting place."[18] From there, students hiked up the mountain as a group and dutifully followed direction from their instructor on the way down. Even King Albert of Belgium came to St. Anton for ski lessons, although on one very rainy occasion, the instructors convinced him to retire to the bar in the Hotel Post instead.[19]

Although not every student wore a crown, they generally took part in a resort culture that merged skiing with associations of wealth, consumption, and socializing. "With a new fall of snow there came a change in the town of St. Moritz," one American skier noticed in 1931. "From everywhere came people. Sleighs jangled down the curved streets. The store windows, filled with soft woolen things and smartly tailored skiing suits, were irresistible," and "smart people from all the world filled the hotels."[20] A group of American skiers vacationing in 1926 noticed that skiers in Switzerland tended not to retire early, despite the physical demands of skiing. "In Switzerland," one wrote, "the social life is as attractive as the skiing. We change wet clothes for evening dress, and dine, dance, and make merry in the bar."[21]

As the business of resort ski schools grew intertwined with that of local hotels and ski clubs, instructors became more than guides, competitors, and teachers. They infused their students with alpine expertise and style, and they acquired some of the cosmopolitan cachet of their clients in return. In doing so, these men came to embody all the associations of resort culture itself, leaping across the class lines that divided elite tourists from service employees. And they made such strides self-consciously. Most began their careers as simple country boys. They had to learn, as did Pfeifer, not to come to the ski school in clothes that smelled like the barn. Schneider insisted that his instructors be clean, neat, prompt, and polite. He wanted their classes to be fun and safe, so he taught them to build relationships with their students and to develop camaraderie by discussing the mountains around them while they climbed. In order to improve his status in the ski school and the impression he made on his students, Pfeifer copied the German diction of a more educated colleague and then took English lessons. This also helped him earn more money, since Schneider paid instructors double for teaching in a foreign language.[22] When Otto Lang joined the ski school in 1929 from Salzburg, his cosmopolitan image and his fluency in French and English proved a great asset. Pfeifer noticed this, and in 1933 he took up the study of French.

Both men cultivated a cosmopolitan image and became favorite instructors of influential people in the process. Initially reluctant to do so, Schneider eventually allowed his instructors to relax after class with their students. Guests and instructors alike enjoyed unwinding over a glass of beer at the end of the day, and they sometimes made dinner plans as well. Instructors often found themselves dining in quite distinguished company, meeting important people and so enhancing their own images. Occasionally, relationships went even further, as the status and worldly image of Austrian ski instructors came to outweigh their modest origins, educations, and bank accounts. According to stories spread through the ski school, "Some of the instructors, handsome by nature and bronzed by the sun, developed an amazing aptitude for sexual encounters."[23] One American heiress apparently fell so in love with an instructor that she stayed for the summer and built a house, leaving when she finally realized that he would not return her affection.[24] The camaraderie that skiing fostered both on and off the hill contributed to a resort culture where handsome, tanned ski instructors became escorts and sex symbols, as well as authorities on the sport. In some cases, ski instructors made social connections at St. Anton that established their reputations among America's rich and famous. One winter morning, for example, an American movie star appeared at the ski school meeting place seeking a private instructor. So began the friendship between Friedl Pfeifer and Claudette Colbert, a relationship that would subsequently ease Pfeifer's transition to living in America. Pfeifer also met one of his future employers in St. Anton — Alice Wolfe. The daughter of distinguished conductor and musician Walter Damrosch, she was an enthusiastic skier and mountaineer and had been visiting St. Anton since the 1920s. She hired Pfeifer as a mountain guide in 1935 to see if he would do as a coach for her pet project, the U.S. Women's Ski Team.

Otto Lang also met future friends and sponsors through Schneider's ski school. After rescuing an injured man he had found with his ski class and easing the distraught wife's fears, Lang made the formal acquaintance of Larry Dorcy (the injured man) and Maud Hill Dorcy (the distraught wife), plus two of Maud's brothers, who proved to be grandchildren of railroad magnate James J. Hill. Lang became close friends with Jerome Hill and learned from him to appreciate music, literature, painting, theater, and films. The Hill family practically adopted Lang, urging him to travel with them abroad, stay with them, and accept their financial support. Through the Hill family, Lang would cultivate a cosmopolitan life and meet his future American employer, Katherine Peckett. She joined the Hill entourage in St. Anton from Franconia, New Hampshire, where her family owned an inn that would soon be open for winter guests. She had come to St. Anton in search of ski instructors, and in December 1935, Lang started work as the first St. Anton instructor in America. Many others would follow. These "Arlberg" instructors from St. Anton — and instructors from other European ski schools as well — served as emissaries of Alpine skiing to countries all over the world during the 1930s. They brought their enthusiasm for the sport, familiarity with resort culture, knowledge of mountainous terrain, and experience as both teachers and competitors to America, where skiers embraced them as experts.

Alpine Skiing in the United States and the West

By the 1920s and 1930s, news of Schneider's Arlberg technique had spread around the world. Introduced by tourists who had visited Lunn in Mürren and Schneider in St. Anton, downhill technique came to the United States in the late 1920s and concentrated, at first, in the Northeast.[25] College outing clubs and urban clubs such as Boston's Appalachian Mountain Club (AMC) popularized downhill skiing during a period of urbanization, economic boom, and unprecedented leisure time. Nature grew at once more appealing and more accessible. These national trends made it both possible and desirable to participate in recreational sports. These trends also underscored changes in gender identities that made sports popular. A bigger and more consumer-oriented economy meant an increase in white-collar jobs for men, who sat behind desks all day and sought new outlets to express their masculinity after work. The "flapper" image that was popular in the 1920s, though not a realistic view of their actual behavior, still gave women a new degree of power over their bodies that quite a few expressed through athletic pursuits.

Unlike many favorite sports in the 1920s — baseball, basketball, track, and football among them — outdoor recreation appealed largely to wealthy urbanites who had the time and money to acquire expertise, purchase equipment, travel to the mountains, and practice. Though emanating from the cities and a few accessible resorts, however, Alpine skiing also attracted residents of mountain towns, for whom the sport required little financial or temporal investment. Downhill skiing gained new cultural associations during the 1920s that made it popular, but climbing up and skiing down scenic mountains was fun no matter who you were. During the 1930s, western skiers who could afford it (usually from Denver) embraced European ski resort culture; those who could not welcomed downhill skiing without its elite trappings and incorporated it into their communities. For each, Alpine skiing proved irresistible.

As with the spread of Nordic skiing during the nineteenth century, immigrants brought Alpine technique with them to America. Unlike Howelsen and his compatriots, however, these immigrants shed their working-class roots, sought work as professional ski instructors, and spread images of elite resorts. In America's new consumer-oriented culture, European ski instructors became export commodities in high demand. They emerged as minor celebrities in a nation where the mass media were making Hollywood stars and sports heroes increasingly visible and popular. Their specific brand of masculinity, though a mystery to steelworkers, farmers, or meat cutters, proved attractive to white-collar and upper-class urbanites, who appreciated the rugged outdoorsiness, athleticism, and elite style these men represented.

Some ski instructors acted as catalysts for the explosive growth of American skiing in the 1930s, and others arrived in response to that growth. Both sets came, in part, because their employers guaranteed them jobs and (relatively) handsome salaries. Of the European "experts," Otto Schniebs was one of the first to arrive. He came from Germany, instructed Boston's AMC on the Arlberg technique during the 1928–29 season, and took over as coach of the Dartmouth Outing Club ski team in 1930.[26] In 1935, Otto Lang was the first St. Anton instructor to come to America, where (along with Sig Buchmayr and Kurt Thalhammer from Salzburg) he instructed at Peckett's on Sugar Hill in New Hampshire.[27] After that year, European skiers seemed to arrive in droves. Walter Prager, a well-known Swiss skier, took over as Dartmouth's coach in 1936, and Austrians Hannes Schroll, Sigi Engl, and Otto Tschol also made names for themselves.[28] Hans Hauser set up a crew of Austrians in the Sun Valley ski school, which Friedl Pfeifer would take over two years later. At least three more of Hannes Schneider's instructors established their own ski schools in America: Otto Lang started an Arlberg ski school at Mt. Rainier; Benno Rybizka started one in Jackson, New Hampshire, and brought eight others from St. Anton to help him run it; and Toni Matt ended up at Whitefish, Montana. These men found work across the country — in established mountain resort areas, wherever outdoor clubs had formed, and at new resorts built explicitly for skiing, from New Hampshire to Washington State.

For many, the promise of work and status as ski instructors in America was enough to bring them across the ocean. Other skiers, however, came to America for political reasons. Conflicting sentiments over Hitler's rise to power in the 1930s divided Schneider's ski school, and Hitler's occupation of Austria in 1938 wreaked havoc in the town of St. Anton. After the Anschluss, a group of strong Nazi supporters in St. Anton emerged, and one of them became the new mayor. "Several ski teachers, known to be anti-Nazi," one American there remembered, "were smuggled across the border to Switzerland."[29] Among them was Friedl Pfeifer, who made it to Australia and taught skiing there for a season before heading to America. Pfeifer wound up, on the recommendation of his old student Claudette Colbert, in Sun Valley, Idaho.[30] Instructor Luggi Foeger also fled Hitler and ended up teaching skiing in Yosemite, California. Hannes Schneider had a more difficult time. An outspoken critic of Hitler among what turned out to be some ardent Nazis in his ski school, Schneider was pulled from his bed and thrown in jail. According to Otto Lang, "a cadre of loyal townspeople, other ski instructors, and legions of influential former ski school students in Europe and abroad

... tried everything in their power to set [Schneider] free."[31] The U.S. and British ski teams were among many that withdrew from the Arlberg-Kandahar race in protest of his imprisonment.[32] Finally, a longtime friend and skiing companion called in a favor from Hitler and was able to bring Schneider to his home in Germany. From there, Harvey Gibson — a skiing enthusiast, president of Manufacturer's Trust Company in New York, and chairman of the American Banking Committee, which negotiated loans with Germany — stepped in to help. Gibson made a deal with Hitler's exchequer to free Schneider and his family, and then arranged for him to live and work at a resort Gibson owned at Mt. Cranmore, New Hampshire. Schneider, his wife, and their two children finally arrived in North Conway on February 12, 1939.[33]

The Anschluss mobilized the growing international ski community and brought new talent to ski slopes all over the United States. Encouraging the growth of skiing in America with their enthusiasm, experience, and skill, these instructors established themselves as experts and infused American ski culture with alpine references. In addition to establishing ski schools at mountain resorts across the country, they taught skiing in cities, where the heart of America's skiing population lived and spent their money. Though the depression hit Americans hard, those with enough cash welcomed opportunities to indulge in some alpine culture, glamour, and sport. Department stores in Boston and New York, interested in selling ski clothes and equipment, orchestrated giant indoor ski shows and quite literally made European experts into commodities on display. Otto Lang starred in the first indoor ski show, sponsored by the department store B. Altman and held in December 1935, where he demonstrated the Arlberg system by skiing down a short slide on synthetic "snow."[34] He was such a success that the next year organizers planned mammoth shows in Boston and New York, recruiting Lang, Benno Rybizka, and Hannes Schneider himself to demonstrate their technique. American ski enthusiasts filled both Boston Garden and Madison Square Garden — according to Lang, 80,000 people saw the show in New York alone. The December 11 *New York Times* reported, "Skiing hysteria has seized New York with a tremendous grip."[35] These shows continued for at least a few more years, bringing Alpine skiing and all its associations to urban residents hungry for an outdoor respite from the city and a taste of Europe's glamorous resorts.

Alpine skiers also demonstrated their expertise in smaller arenas. Europeans appeared as guest speakers and instructors at ski clubs all over the country, and Americans proved receptive to all that these men offered. Otto Schniebs gave his first talk in Boston to an audience of about forty people. Three hundred came to his second one. One follower said, "Otto, the brilliant apostle of the religion of skiing and camaraderie, combined with his classic way of picturing his ideas in a vivid mosaic of English and German, seemed to ignite all New England." His influence on Dartmouth College, where he coached from 1930 to 1936 and consistently led the ski team to championship victories, seemed equally profound. The same author, who raced for Dartmouth, wrote that "skiing has claimed more enthusiasts than football or Smith [College]; there are more skis in Hanover than dogs, an unprecedented situation; and Dartmouth's ski consciousness has threatened to replace the old life blood — the 'Beat Yale' complex."[36] Schniebs became a ubiquitous figure in America's Alpine ski world. He established and taught a ski school workshop for eastern ski instructors and took his show on the road, well past the confines of Boston and New York.[37] He, and other European instructors like him, helped Americans fall in love with Alpine skiing.

The sport proved so appealing because of all the associations attached to it. Schniebs told everyone, "skiing is not just a sport; it's a way of life!" For those enamored with European resort culture, his claim referred to a specific leisure experience rendered especially attractive in the 1930s. Downhill skiing's "way of life" was tinted with ethnic signs pointing to the Alps, at a time when financial troubles and Hitler's rise made those mountains inaccessible, and gender signs pointing toward a particular masculine ideal, at a time when American men felt economically disempowered. By the 1930s, these signs had become so attractive that European skiers such as Schniebs, transplanted Arlberg instructors, and famous racers found themselves in the center of an expanding American world of alpine references. Terms such as *schuss* (to ski straight down without turning) and *sitzmark* (the hole you leave after a fall), and calls of "Ski Heil!" (an insider's hello and affirmation of the sport), peppered skiers' speech, and students listened extra hard to instructors with German accents. The status of European skiers had reached the point, one author noted, where imposters could simply say "bend zee knees, two dollars pleez."[38] Usually, however, European skiers who came to America earned the respect and admiration of their colleagues and students. When the Swiss ski team participated in ski races throughout America and Canada in 1937, one college racer characterized their presence as "an intoxicant from which our ski spirit may hope never to recover."[39] In the world of Alpine skiing, Europeans reigned supreme, and Americans recognized it through the enthusiasm with which they embraced that world at home.

Alpine skiing and all it represented sold as well in Colorado as it did in the East. Downhill skiing spread from Denver to surrounding ski clubs and more isolated mountain towns throughout the state. Although each group adopted the trappings of resort culture to differing degrees, they all responded to the influence of European experts. One of the earliest Europeans to bring downhill skiing to Colorado was Marquis "Bend More the Knee" Albizzi, who "revolutionized" Colorado skiing in 1923 by teaching some members of the Colorado Mountain Club (CMC) to turn and stop without the hitherto obligatory sitzmark.[40] A succession of these skiers came to Colorado in the 1930s, including the ubiquitous Otto Schniebs, and job opportunities for instructors with an accent expanded. "It seems as though," one resident of Climax remembered, "I learned to snowplow and counterstem in seven different languages."[41] Swiss mountaineer Andre Roch and his Italian colleague Gunther Langes made the long trip to Aspen in the fall of 1936. By the time Roch returned to Switzerland the following June, he had designated the best spot for a resort, taught locals and visitors from Denver to ski, helped establish a popular downhill skiing club in Aspen, and set club members to cutting the soon-to-be-famous Roch Run on Aspen Mountain.[42] A group of CMC members spent a week skiing in Aspen and wrote, "Two European guides were there, and they proved themselves to be high-class experts, both in skiing and teaching. We plan to go again next year."[43] In Denver and in more isolated towns such as Climax and Aspen, Alpine skiers from Europe introduced their sport and their expertise to approving crowds.

These men found a wide variety of skiers in Colorado. In old mining towns such as Aspen, locals who had skied during mining days continued to do so after the decline of that economy in the late nineteenth century. Farm and ranch kids skied "straight down on homemade skis" or went touring through the valley.[44] Kids in Aspen climbed up the back of Aspen Mountain and skied into town or down the upper end of Aspen Street. "We tied boards on our feet and went for it," one local remembered. "We would slide off a pile of snow from the shed roof [and follow] cow paths on Aspen Mountain."[45] Locals continued to ski in Gunnison as well, despite the early demise of its nineteenth-century ski club. Like Aspen's East End crowd, Gunnison's

Western State College students had few diversions besides skiing once winter set in. The college established skiing as a regular sport in 1916; students and locals skied around town and rode the train to Quick's Hill near Crested Butte.[46] The skiing legacy of miners, the cultural memory of Scandinavian immigrants, and the reality of long winters kept young people skiing in distant mountain towns through the early twentieth century, until Alpine skiers from Europe and Denver taught them new techniques and revived local ski clubs.

People in Denver and more accessible surrounding towns continued to ski throughout the 1920s and early 1930s in a more organized fashion, joining the growing number of ski clubs. Carnivals and competitions held in the 1920s fanned interest in Nordic skiing and jumping and incorporated the sport into local winter culture from Denver and Colorado Springs to Allens Park, Dillon, and Steamboat Springs. These competitions and carnivals united wealthy skiers from Denver with mountain town residents and established a structural framework through which Alpine skiing could spread throughout Colorado in the 1930s.

European experts and urban outdoors people introduced Alpine skiing to the rest of the state from Denver, where they tended to gather. Members of the CMC played an important role in attracting skiers to this new sport. From their ranks emerged the Arlberg Club, Colorado's first explicitly Alpine ski club and the one that most faithfully reflected the sport's resort culture. Members came from Denver's social elite, and though deeply enamored with downhill skiing itself, they fully embraced the social culture surrounding it. The group came together when Graeme McGowan, a "gentleman skier from Denver," discovered the potential of the West Portal area for skiing and built a small clubhouse there. The Moffat Tunnel offered dependable railroad access to the area from Denver in 1928, opening up a new playground for Denver skiers that would eventually become Winter Park.[47] The Arlberg Club came into being on the train ride home from West Portal after a day of skiing in 1928. The original members chose its name from a magazine article that featured Hannes Schneider and his ski school in St. Anton. Although they got the name from an article in *Vogue,* chances are that these skiers were already familiar with Schneider and his Arlberg system. They were all members of the CMC; some had attended college in the East at schools with ski teams, such as Williams and Yale; and many had leisure time and money to spare.

Even if they had not been to European resorts themselves (McGowan learned to ski from books written by European experts), this group successfully transferred the cosmopolitan and social image of European resort culture to Colorado. By adopting the Arlberg name, they expressed their desire to be associated with European resorts, Schneider's school, and their accompanying expertise and style. The club, members agreed, was to "encourage the development of downhill skiing in Colorado, encourage desirable persons to take up skiing and learn it by club standards, and to assist the development of Colorado resorts."[48] Their bylaws thus embraced the sport, its elite participants, and its resort culture — and re-created it in Colorado. The Denver businessmen who formed the club worked toward their goals by spending weekends skiing at their clubhouse in West Portal, hosting and promoting annual slalom and downhill races there starting in 1929, and developing the area as a ski center. To complete the picture, the club also hired its own professional instructor from Grenoble.[49]

Other Denver skiers incorporated Alpine skiing into the activities of their city ski clubs during the 1930s and made the sport accessible to a broader public. The Denver Winter Sports Club conducted a free school for general touring and downhill skiing taught by the best local skiers in 1932. Five years later, however, the *Ski Bulletin* reported that "the club has given up this activity . . . now that professional coaches are available."[50] The CMC followed a similar path. Downhill ski enthusiasts in the CMC made frequent group trips to Rilliet Hill on Lookout Mountain or traveled to West Portal and Berthoud Pass. Experienced local skiers volunteered their services as instructors until 1936, when the CMC hired Robert Balch, originally from the East but now "one of the leading skiers in our part of the country," to give lessons for 50¢ each on Berthoud Pass.[51] Balch, by virtue of his eastern training, skill, and professional status, represented a version of the masculine expertise embodied most completely by St. Anton instructors. Both clubs deemed professional instruction more appropriate than local volunteers, and they agreed that such instruction was worth paying for. As Alpine skiing spread throughout the West, then, so did the sale of Alpine expertise.

And Colorado ski clubs did more than offer this expertise for sale. They incorporated downhill skiing into local tournaments and carnivals, thereby transplanting those images of international competition common in European resort culture and repositioning them in Colorado. As a result, Scandinavian and alpine references converged in the Rockies and gave local culture a new flair. After Grand Lake's first annual winter carnival in January 1932, the *Denver Post* referred to the town as "a sparkling, snowy, Norse Mecca — a St. Moritz right in Denver's backyard."[52] The second annual ski carnival in Grand Lake featured, in addition to skijoring, snowshoeing, hockey, jumping, and cross-country competitions, a down-mountain race on a course almost two miles long with more than 2,000 feet of vertical drop. Spectators could look forward to Arlberg members demonstrating "the Austrian style of down mountain skiing" in this event, the first one held outside of West Portal, and one in which "unprecedented interest [was] being shown."[53] A week later, the Hot Sulphur Springs Ski Club took up the mantle, explaining in its carnival program: "The Down Mountain Race was first entered as an event in U.S. Western Ski Ass'n tournaments by the Grand Lake W.S. Club. The H.S.S. Ski Club is the first club to enter the Slalom Race. A formal challenge has been issued by this club to the Ahrlberg [*sic*] Club, for honors in this event."[54] Downhill and slalom races gave towns a hint of Alpine flavor, and they helped develop local experts in the sport who could compete against elite Arlberg Club racers.

The combined influence of European experts, professional instructors, the Arlberg Club, and carnivals that featured Alpine events tipped the balance of skiing in Colorado away from its Nordic roots and toward the Alps. New downhill ski clubs sprang to life in Denver in the 1930s, including the Zipfelbergers and the Colorado Ski Runners.[55] These skiers attended races, independent of local carnivals, which provided new forums for developing Colorado skiers and identifying the state with Alpine skiing.[56] In 1938 and 1939, Aspen's club broadened its scope further, hosting the Rocky Mountain Downhill and Slalom Championships and then the National Championships in 1941.[57] Even in Steamboat Springs, Carl Howelsen's hometown and a bastion of Nordic skiing, residents could not stay away from downhill skiing. Graeme McGowan demonstrated new techniques to skiers there in 1931, and Robert Balch taught lessons there in 1936. By 1937, Balch wrote that the town was experiencing "that evolution now so familiar, out of Scandinavianism into Alpinism."[58] Towns distant from Denver and its growing circuit of competitions also took up the new sport. In 1938, the San Juan Ski Club formed with about 100 active skiers from Ouray, Montrose, and Grand Junction. Also in the southwestern part of Colorado, the San Luis

Valley Ski Club made "a fine ski course" on Wolf Creek Pass, where more than 5,000 people skied in 1938.[59]

By the late 1930s, Americans across the country had taken up Alpine skiing. European instructors who immigrated to the United States wound up in eastern cities and colleges, mountain resorts, and even department stores, advertising their sport and their own images at the same time. Cosmopolitan Americans familiar with alpine resorts and eager to escape the city for the outdoors took up downhill skiing in droves. This dynamic held true in the West as well, where a few St. Anton instructors established ski schools and other experts visited to share their knowledge and enthusiasm. The CMC, as Boston's Appalachian Club had before it, became an avid fan of the new sport, and its members helped spread it across the state. New downhill ski clubs formed in Denver and surrounding towns, established ski clubs added Alpine events to their winter carnivals, and both supported a growing number of Alpine competitions.

In their use of professional instructors, their celebration of European experts, and their incorporation of Alpine races, however, Colorado ski club members were not simply changing their technique. They adopted — albeit to different degrees — important images of European resort culture. They accepted the ideal of European expertise embodied by Alpine ski instructors and worked to emulate it. Towns that put on Alpine races and winter carnivals took on a hint of European charm that redefined them as Scandinavian–Alpine–Rocky Mountain places. The change from Nordic to Alpine skiing thus represented the establishment of a new ski culture in the United States and the American West, now linked with the act of consumption and leisure. The price of a lesson bought skiers a host of images originating in European resort culture, including a particular brand of masculine expertise, cosmopolitan wealth, and Alpine style. These images changed the meaning of the sport and helped make Alpine skiing popular in the United States.

Alpine Women

Once they hiked up, Alpine skiers could make elegant turns down the mountain. This aesthetically pleasing and simultaneously masculine activity encouraged skiers to identify with suave European instructors. Students who could pay for lessons or otherwise mix and mingle with experts hoped to emulate them. Formalized through professional ski schools, this student-teacher relationship could give European farm boys authority over railroad magnates, Hollywood stars, and even kings. It had equally transformative power over the people who took lessons. For men, this usually meant the opportunity to acquire some of the expertise, authority, and style embodied by their teachers.

Women students — of which there were many — had a more complicated relationship with their instructors and the sport. By virtue of their gender, skiing offered them a collection of transformative experiences that differed from those of men. The elite trappings and social orientation of resort culture tended to define women skiers as wealthy consumers of fashion whose presence on the slopes said more about their wealth than their athletic abilities. Indeed, some women used these associations to demonstrate social status, to find wealthy husbands, or both. Not all women skiers, however, actually fit that description. Women across the economic spectrum found themselves enamored with skiing downhill, which could offer them a liberating taste of speed, exhilaration, and danger. This physical freedom, and the expertise they could gain from instructors and coaches, led some women to join the international racing world as well as Colorado's ski clubs. Skiing down mountains thus offered women physical freedom and empowerment at the same time it emphasized their roles as consumers, social beings, and objects of beauty.

These women fell under the contemporary category of the "New Woman." Referring in the late nineteenth and early twentieth centuries to college-educated suffragists and Progressive reformers, by the 1920s, the designation cut across class lines and described women who occupied public, urban, and modern spaces. By the 1930s, "new women" had set aside political demands for equality, in exchange for lives that included interests outside the home as well as marriage and children. Such women enjoyed being chic, heterosexual, and feminine rather than political, and they focused on individual rather than collective goals. It is within this context that many women embraced the sport of Alpine skiing.[60]

For many Alpine enthusiasts, male and female, the sport's main draw was the companionship that developed among skiers. Skiing was essentially an individual sport, but during hikes up the slope and pauses on the way down, and over refreshments at the end of the day, skiers shared their common interests and experiences with one another. The mix proved intoxicating for some. "No bounds can restrain the joys of freedom and forgetfulness, of independence and intimacy, of companionship," one skier explained in 1937, "which at once drug and stimulate the threadbare senses of the metropolis-refugee who has at last found the solace of mountain solitudes."[61] As a setting for sport, winter landscapes had drawn people together since the nineteenth century, but during the 1930s, they took on a more overtly social cast because of skiing's association with European resorts, leisure, and nightlife. Socializing was key to this scene. Indeed, the German-language term for après-ski congeniality became central to Alpine skiers' vocabularies. "A skier loves company," a CMC member wrote in 1938, "this is the root of the 'gemutlich[keit]' which is skiing's final justification."[62]

Although certainly possible among a single-sex group of skiers, *gemütlichkeit* implied men and women socializing together. This was especially true in the 1930s, when popularized Freudian psychology stigmatized same-sex relationships, the depression shifted American society toward more conservative values, and even feminists cast themselves as more feminine, heterosexual, and social than before.[63] More than simply a sport, skiing helped bring men and women together. One author noted that in skiing there is "a large element of romance of the boy-meets-girl type, not to be overlooked." "This aura of romance," he continued, "is the 'special introductory offer' which inspires a great many people to take a first fling at skiing."[64] When seen in this light, skiing could define skiers simultaneously as romantic objects, social beings, athletes, and outdoors people. At ski hills throughout Colorado and the nation, men and women shared stories of their day and relaxed together over drinks in clubhouses, restaurants, and hotels. Early skiers in Aspen frequented the Hotel Jerome, where they could drink highly alcoholic "Aspen cruds" and socialize. Arlberg Club members encouraged women to go skiing with them, even though the club did not allow them to join until 1938, almost ten years after its inception.

If dating and après-ski sociability expanded the meanings connected to Alpine skiing, so did its opportunity for consuming fashion and appreciating skiers' bodies. America's growing consumer culture in the 1920s reinforced these connections established at European resorts and offered an increasing array of clothing and equipment that could mark their wearer as stylish and attractive. Department stores such as B. Altman were among the first to advertise Alpine skiing to Americans through live ski shows in Boston and New

York. By the early 1920s, Americans were accustomed to using ski slopes as a stage for fashion display, and women usually claimed the most attention. "Altho [sic] it had not been announced that a style show would be held in conjunction with the skiing," one reporter commented of a Denver event, "the brilliant display of sporting toggery was all of that, and caused many eyes to wander frequently from the tournament itself in the direction of some fair maid or matron."[65]

As Americans invested increasingly in the emerging consumer culture of the 1920s and skiing slowly grew more popular nationwide, image-makers discovered the aesthetic value of women skiing, and pictures of them began to appear. Such images emphasized the streamlined and modern female body, a nod perhaps to the independence and mobility skiing represented during a time when women were moving more freely through public spaces than ever before. They also described women in more limiting terms, however, by portraying them as passive, with their skis by their sides or standing under the protective wings of their male companions. One magazine cover spoke directly to the ties among sociability, fashion, and sport with its image of a woman on skis busily applying her makeup. The text, perhaps with tongue in cheek, reminded readers to "look before you leap." Just who is supposed to be looking at whom is not clear, and consumption — of clothes, makeup, and men — took precedence in these images over the physical act of skiing down mountains. Magazines depicted women skiers above text spouting "new spring fashions" and "exclusive style notes from Paris," the "luxurious smoothness" of a new automobile, or the seemingly incongruous slogan of Lucky cigarettes: "They taste better." In depicting women skiers in this way, the popular press emphasized women's role as consumers while it defined women skiers as passive objects of desire. The ability to spend money helped establish these women as elite and therefore as desirable components of Alpine skiing's resort image. Women bought fashion through magazines and department stores; they consumed images of European resort culture and perhaps even the instructor himself, along with their ski lessons; and in doing all that, they presented themselves as objects available for (male) consumption within that culture. [66]

This phenomenon helped establish a long-standing stereotype of women skiers. One author in 1939 argued that the "Ski Rabbit" (a.k.a. "ski bunny") used skis merely as "a vehicle of support for a glamorous female whose main

Because skiing combined physical thrills with the potential for romance, it was important commercially. This woman is both consumer and consumed, displaying her fashion, gear, and style so that she can attract a male audience. (Gary H. Schwartz, The Art of Skiing, 1856–1936 [Tiburn, Calif.: Wood River Publishing, 1989], 46)

interest in the out of doors is to dazzle and not to ski." This image, she implied, relegated women skiers to the status of sex objects. Indeed, some women
reveled in such dazzling, and in doing so, they established themselves firmly
within Alpine skiing's elite, social, consumer-oriented culture. But there were
other ways into that culture, and other appeals of the sport that centered on
its physical, outdoor experience. This author's suggestion was that young
women learn to ski not for social reasons but for the fun and power of making good turns.[67] She wrote during a time, one historian noted, when physical educators and promoters of women's sports worried that women would
become masculinized by their athletic behavior. So women's sports advocates
helped promote two ideals to ease the conflict between sport and femininity: the athlete as beauty queen — the ski bunny that this author scorned —
and the wholesome, modest athlete that she endorsed.[68] Both ideals allowed
women some room to ski with abandon.

The rising popularity of skiing during the 1930s suggests that women took
advantage of that room and even created more by flocking to the mountains in spite of these conflicts over feminine behavior. Only some women
skiers, after all, actually fit either of those dominant ideals. Outdoor enthusiasts in the CMC, elite Arlberg socialites, and mountain town residents alike
donned Alpine skis and took up the sport with gusto.[69] Back East, one skier
remarked on the "girls, who, fired by Otto [Schniebs's] ski talks, have abandoned silks and fragile shoes for ski clothes and battleship boots, and have
fled to the ski country." In Denver and Colorado mountain towns, local
women joined ski clubs and took on new levels of leadership. Within the
CMC, women assisted with or led ski trips themselves and even volunteered
as ski instructors.[70] In some ways, they outdid their male counterparts. "That
skiing is a woman's sport as well as a man's," one man wrote in 1937, "was
very clearly indicated here at Aspen when, during this difficult summer,
Aspen Ski Club's active women members outnumbered the men, and their
total efforts in helping to finance the construction of the Roch Run was
certainly equal to or greater than the total accomplished by their men companions." The CMC's list of new members for the same year demonstrated
a similar trend.[71] Some women — especially in places where local traditions
tempered elite resort culture — found a new degree of power and authority through their ski clubs. In leading ski trips, instructing classes, financing local development, and simply signing up in record numbers, women

defined their skiing outside the images of the beauty queen and the modest athlete.

Women Alpine racers went even farther outside those images and placed themselves in the very male context of competition. There were not as many women as men racers in Colorado, and their decision to plunge down often frightening courses — with no control gates or groomed snow — put them in a curious position within Alpine ski culture. Women's racing first began in Colorado within the festive atmosphere of winter carnivals. It took a few years from the first downhill race to attract enough competitors for a separate women's race, but by 1937 at least, Hot Sulphur's Girls' Down Mountain Race and its Ladies' Down Mountain Race had become part of the winter carnival program.[72] Downhill skiing caught on faster for women in Denver than in local clubs; at least four clubs in the city encouraged the sport and sponsored women-only races. Five Denver women raced in the CMC slalom competition at Berthoud Pass in 1937, representing Denver's Colorado Ski Runners and the CMC. Louise White claimed first place at the Berthoud race, which was no surprise, since she was the defending regional champion. She kept her streak for years, beating nine others to win the 1939 Rocky Mountain Ski Association Championships for downhill and slalom and the 1940 championships as well.[73] White's competitive skill gave her a degree of expertise and authority that, though comparable to Alpine visions of masculinity, seemed quite at odds with the beauty queen and modest athlete ideals put forth for women at the time. Sports journalists reflected this tricky situation by describing her in a multitude of ways, including "the conqueror," "the masterful maneuvering Louise White," and, more simply, "Mrs. White."[74]

A few women racers developed an even higher level of competitive expertise than White. Because the best women racers competed internationally, however, they spent every season in European resorts that most American skiers in the 1930s could see only in postcards. These athletes participated in authentic alpine resort culture, which tempered their athleticism with images of class and status. Indeed, it took a woman immersed in such a culture to organize the U.S. Women's Ski Team. Illustrative of the upper class, Alice Wolfe was the daughter of Walter Damrosch, famous conductor of the New York Philharmonic Society, the Metropolitan Opera, and the New York Symphony Society. She had vacationed in St. Anton since the 1920s and, according to Otto Lang, knew everybody in *Who's Who*.[75] Upon learning that the International Olympic Committee would allow Alpine events in the 1936 Olympics, she took it upon herself to organize and finance a women's team. She chose twelve women and sent them off to Austria, to practice in St. Anton.[76]

These skiers included world travelers, college graduates, and experienced competitive skiers. They found themselves at home in St. Anton, where expert skiers and the "international set" mingled, and they quickly became part of the town's resort culture. The group's coach from Zermatt, Switzerland, and his assistant from St. Anton taught them technique and gave them a kind of authority on the slopes. In town, the women socialized regularly. Betty Woolsey was asked to dinner just about every night and met, she said, "almost every interesting person there at parties." Those people she noticed included the Duke of Kent; the Duke of Hamilton; dress designer Elsa Schiaparelli; Marina Challiapin, daughter of the great Russian basso; Aus-

These athletic women from the 1936 U.S. Women's Ski Team came together in St. Anton, Austria, where they trained with famous coaches and dined with the cosmopolitan elite. From left: Lillian Swann, Mary Bird, Ellis-Ayr Smith, Grace Carter, Otto Furrer, Hannes Schneider, Herman Tcholl, Helen Boughton-Leigh, Clarita Heath, Elizabeth Woolsey, Marian McKean. (New England Ski Museum)

trian foreign ministers; Prince Starhemberg; many Dutch, Belgians, and Hungarians; and a Balkan king or two.[77] Far from manly athletes, these women participated in the social whirl of St. Anton as much as they skied. Though many came from wealthy families, these women entered St. Anton's resort culture through their close association with their European coaches, their skiing expertise, and their ability to socialize with international elites in the evening — a mix of characteristics summed up through their membership on the U.S. Women's Ski Team.

Their status as competitive athletes opened new social worlds for them, and it also allowed them to revel in skiing's physical challenges wholeheartedly. Downhill skiing typically attracted those who enjoyed the exhilaration of the sport and rent the air, as one person put it, "with [an] inevitable whoop."[78] These women went one step farther. Betty Woolsey wrote, "I took to downhill [versus slalom] immediately, loving the speed, the sense of danger, and its classical simplicity." She studied courses to see where she could cut time by taking extra risks, reveled in the intense physical effort of racing, and described her teammates as "competitive" and "determined."[79] Such behavior put women racers in danger of injury, and they sustained quite a few. Dot Brewer broke her back after slamming into a gully while practicing in St. Anton, Woolsey broke her leg while training for the Federation Internationale de Ski (FIS) championships in Chamonix, and Miggs Jennings wound up in the hospital with a concussion after taking a fall in Sun Valley.[80] Countless other women racers shared the experience of getting hurt, and most returned to competition. In embracing the sport's speed and exhilaration, these women accepted the possibility of injury and defined themselves as women skiing on the edge.

In doing so, they, like many female athletes of the 1930s, ran the risk of appearing too masculine for society's taste. One female author argued that despite the excitement and thrills that international competition offered, it was not clear that women skiers could compete without temporary or permanent injury. She went on to argue that the level of training necessary to compete against the German "Amazons from beyond the Rhine," if possible at all, would put women in constant danger of getting hurt, and it would mean giving up any social life for that one goal. Finally and worst of all, she concluded, it would be the demise of their "feminine charm." As her last piece of evidence, the author produced a photo of the women's FIS team and declared them unattractive.[81] According to this reasoning, members of the U.S. Ski Team, Louise White, and other women who competed at high levels placed their femininity in question and ran the risk of turning into manly women.

The "wholesome, modest athlete" ideal helped mitigate the tension between femininity and competitive skiing, especially for women who could be described as cute or pretty. In an article with the tag line "Ski Moppet," the author emphasized one female racer's youth. "No ski slope is too steep or too tough for nineteen year old Barbara Kidder — Colorado's own pigtailed wonder," he wrote. "Although she's America's number one skier, her charm and modesty make her seem like somebody's kid sister."[82] Kidder could ski fast without seeming masculine because, as a cute kid sister, she could indulge in tomboy activities like ski racing and still grow into a woman. Pigtails symbolized this wholesome, athletic identity for Kidder, as they did for Gretchen Kunigk Fraser, who won America's first winter Olympic medal in 1948. Unlike Kidder and many other members of the U.S. Ski Team, Fraser was older (twenty-eight) and married. That did not diminish the symbolic importance of her chosen hairstyle, however. After her gold-medal slalom performance, the media dubbed Fraser "the Pigtailed Housewife" and played up her good nature and humility rather than her competitive drive. At her victory parade in Sun Valley, she remembered, "every horse and dog wore pigtails," and so did "half the girls" in her hometown of Vancouver, Washington. Fraser eventually got so tired of the fuss that she cut her hair, but by then she had retired from competition to raise a family with her husband.[83] Youthful pigtails and modesty helped the public understand the athletic pursuits of Kidder and Fraser, but this did not work for all women skiers — especially those who blended their athleticism with a more mature, authoritative style.

Resort culture was so focused on fashion, socializing, and romance that women who skied fast and hard during the day could reaffirm their femininity and sexuality in the evenings. This held true in the United States to some extent. As much as groups like the Arlberg Club may have wanted to emulate European resort culture, they could not re-create St. Anton or St. Moritz. Only one place in America came close. Sun Valley in Idaho drew more international skiers, wealthy vacationers, and movie stars than any other resort before World War II, and it illustrated the purest form of European resort culture in America.

Sun Valley, carefully created by Averell Harriman and his promotional wizard Steve Hannagan, incorporated European resort images in its instructors, clientele, accommodations, and social setting. Hans Hauser initially ran the ski school, with a group of lederhosen-clad instructors from Salzburg. Otto Lang came every year as Nelson Rockefeller's personal instructor, and Friedl Pfeifer arrived after Claudette Colbert recommended it to him, taking over the ski school soon after. Other regular guests from Hollywood included Norma Shearer, Clark Gable, June Allyson, Darryl Zanuck, and Gary Cooper.[84] The Lodge, with its Duchin Ballroom, offered luxurious accommodations. A group of skiers from Denver, Colorado Springs, and Albuquerque went to see the

Sun Valley brought Austrian ski instructors to the American West, where they embodied European resort culture and masculinity. (Sun Valley Resort)

spectacle in 1938 and described the new, less expensive, but visibly European Challenger Inn as "picturesque pseudo-Swiss, neo-Austrian, [and] quasi-Bavarian." A festive atmosphere added to the physical setting and collection of people. Visitors reported "skating festivals, bal en masque swimming in the hot pools, Bavarian music, the Austrian instructors schussing down Dollar [Mountain] with red flares — never a dull moment there," they said.[85]

These events and their setting, combined with skiing and its own *gemütlichkeit*, helped re-create the sensuality of Alpine skiing in America. Friedl Pfeifer remembered Sun Valley as a "romantic oasis." "The social whirl," Pfeifer explained, "that centered around the Duchin Room in the Sun Valley Lodge, where an orchestra played every night, made Sun Valley a never-never land where everyone was rich and young and all invited to the dance."[86] Women in this world who flew (or tumbled) down the slopes during the day changed into their dinner clothes ready to eat, drink, and be merry. As fashion plates and dinner dates, they obeyed the imperative to consume that created the social, sexual, resort culture. They kept up with the latest ski fashion, frequented the best bars, and boasted the handsomest, most masculine escorts — Austrian ski instructors. When Pfeifer instituted an 11:00 P.M. curfew for his ski instructors in the interest of establishing some discipline, he said, "I found some opposition to my changes. Not from the instructors but from the guests, particularly from the starlets who flocked to Sun Valley."[87] Pfeifer could not complain too much, since it was here, dancing in the Duchin Room, that he met his bride Hoyt Smith.

But what happened if the ski instructors were female? Though few and far between, they had graced the hills of American ski resorts since at least 1939, when Pfeifer hired Clarita Heath, Marion McKean, and Elli Stiller to teach for him at Sun Valley. Unlike the CMC and probably other club women who volunteered their expertise locally, these women were professionals. When they entered the elite group of masculine European instructors, they took on the authority and power that their roles as teacher, leader, and expert commanded. This expertise empowered them, especially in relation to their students, who, by definition, needed help. The instructors' skill, combined with their assigned role as leaders and teachers, gave them authority over students who were feminized and infantilized by their inability to negotiate the mountain. Beginners took their lessons — and still do today — on "nursery slopes" and "bunny hills." This power relationship between teacher and student gave farm boys authority over royalty in St. Anton, and it gave women athletes authority over men in Sun Valley. Through their skiing, some women could turn traditional gender relationships on their head.

Just as a European name and accent qualified many skiers as "experts" in American ski clubs, associations with Pfeifer, periods of training in St. Anton, and places on international racing teams granted these instructors power and authority at Sun Valley. Of the three women Pfeifer hired in 1939, two had competed on the U.S. Women's Olympic Team and had trained with Pfeifer in St. Anton; the other, also coached by Pfeifer, had been a member of the Austrian women's team. Despite the fact that this expertise centered on their potentially "masculine" ability to ski fast, these women retained a certain kind of femininity based on the aesthetics of skiing and a tradition of elite women being able to operate outside normal gender constraints. Men as well as women wanted to learn how to ski with elegance and beauty. European "stylists" such as Pfeifer could do this without compromising their manhood, because their reputations were based on expertise in forbidding mountain landscapes and success in international competition. For female instructors, however, long-standing associations between femininity and beauty made it seem perfectly natural for them to teach others to ski with grace. Women instructors, moreover, quickly developed the ability to exercise authority on the slopes with tact. For those students more interested in après-ski life than technique, women instructors may have filled a role as objects of beauty and sex — a role comparable to that played by male instructors for their starlet pupils. Their inclusion in Sun Valley's ski culture, finally, placed these women instructors in a context that encouraged others to see them as women first and athletes second. This held true for competitive athletes as well. Indeed, when Betty Woolsey and the rest of the U.S. women's team went to Sun Valley to train for the 1940 Olympics, she "settled down to a pleasant routine of skiing and partying," she said, "with the emphasis on the latter."[88]

In this social whirl, Alpine skiing offered much more than the chance to skim down a snowy mountainside. It combined sport with the consumption of fashion, après-ski socializing, and instructors, all of which promised to confer Europe's good life on fortunate Americans. So in Sun Valley, women skiers acted out different kinds of femininity that could include competitive athleticism as well as flirting on the dance floor. Containing these disparate behaviors grew less and less problematic as Alpine skiing and its culture spread across the United States. Skiing had become such a socially acceptable sport for upper-class women by the late 1930s — and so inseparable from social gatherings — that the sport itself sometimes fell from view. "Skiing has now reached the point," one woman from Smith College wrote in 1939, "where participation in the sport has become a social asset. Most modern girls want to be able to swim and play a fair game of tennis or golf. Now skiing falls in line with these sports in being an activity which men and women may enjoy together." The thrills and exhilaration of skiing still mattered, the author conceded, but they were an added bonus to its primarily social benefits.[89] During the 1930s, women and men found Alpine skiing attractive in a multitude of ways, as socialites and athletes, consumers and objects of desire, and usually some mixture of each.

In this context, Friedl Pfeifer and Hoyt Smith made the perfect couple: he the stylish, romantic, Austrian head of the ski school, and she a beautiful, wealthy young woman on vacation in Sun Valley. Although separated by class and national origin, Pfeifer and Smith represented the masculine and feminine ideals of European resort culture. They were counterparts in a complicated set of relationships that bound instructor and student, rural European and urban American, man and woman. Smith fell for Pfeifer for the same reasons so many Americans fell for the sport of Alpine skiing: he and the sport represented much more than technique or physical exhilaration — they represented a glamorous, sophisticated, and cosmopolitan world. And he fell for her because, by simply appearing in the Duchin Room at Sun Valley, she transformed into much more than a banker's daughter — she became part of the elite, athletic, and feminine collection of women that flocked to Alpine skiing and reveled in its resort culture. It made perfect sense that they would fall in love, marry, and have children together. They could not live their entire lives in Sun Valley's never-never land, however. And once outside the culture that created and affirmed their relationship, Pfeifer and Smith grew apart. She would ultimately return to her parents in Salt Lake City; he would make a life for himself in the tiny, depressed town of Aspen, Colorado.

3

A Shack and a Rope Tow
Colorado Skiing through World War II

In the fall of 1936, mountaineers Andre Roch and Gunther Langes arrived in Aspen expecting to plan a large, European-style ski resort in Colorado's Rockies. They found, instead, a depressing, isolated town surrounded by steep, dangerous, or otherwise inappropriate skiing terrain. "You will understand," the Swiss Roch wrote, "that we were not exactly in a skier's paradise and that we did not look forward with enthusiasm to the winter we were to spend here." After six months of exploring, they discovered Mt. Hayden and the area around Ashcroft, a peak and an old mining town above Aspen that could, they believed, be a winter sports center beyond compare. Roch and Langes planned a resort that included a Swiss village in Ashcroft with hotels for 2,000 skiers; a lift servicing ski trails, jumping hills, and sled courses; and a cable car up Mt. Hayden leading to more trails and a hotel that would offer spring and summer skiing.[1]

The European mountaineers left Aspen in June 1937, by which time Roch had acquired legendary status in the town's history, but not for the grand resort he envisioned. Instead, Roch wound up becoming famous for work he did on a much smaller scale. In December 1936, he helped organize about thirty Aspen residents into the Roaring Fork Winter Sports Club, which would soon become the Aspen Ski Club. Familiar with old mining camp skiing traditions, club members quickly adopted the Alpine techniques they learned from Roch, raised money to buy equipment from Denver, and held their first competition that February. In addition to drawing spectators from nearby towns, the races reflected a growing interest in the sport locally. "Maybe thirty people started skiing [that season]," Roch remembered, "but the year after we were off, I think everybody who could walk started to ski."[2] Roch used his status as a European expert to instruct local people rather than wealthy socialites; he also showed them how to build a small ski area for themselves. Before he left town, Roch walked up Aspen Mountain and marked out what he thought would make a good ski run — a downhill racecourse that would attract publicity to Aspen skiing as well as provide recreation for town residents. Volunteers from the ski club cut the trail that summer and pieced together a short tow from an old Studebaker motor, two old mine hoists, and a couple of sleds that could carry about ten people each. Skiers could ride this "boat" tow for about 10¢, but if they wanted to reach the very top of the Roch Run, they had to hitch a ride with the miners headed to work and hike the rest of the way. It was this bare-bones ski area, not the deluxe resort in Ashcroft, that flourished and won Roch his place in Aspen's history.

During the 1930s and 1940s, Alpine skiing took hold in a similar fashion throughout the state of Colorado. The resort culture of St. Moritz, St. Anton, and Sun Valley, while fueling the reputations of European experts such as Roch and Langes and attracting new students to the sport, altered its shape drastically once it was established in Colorado. Skiers simply could not maintain the kind of culture that defined skiing as a form of elite leisure and consumption. Daunting mountain passes, limited financial resources, and the war effort kept the focus of Colorado skiing local and small-scale through most of the 1940s. With no clear model to follow, Colorado skiers tested different avenues of support, ranging from their ski club friends to the U.S. Forest Service and federal relief agencies, and wound up with a sport characterized more by cooperation than by private investment or upper-class leisure. An intimacy with the mountains through volunteer labor became an accepted part of the package. Once it was set down in the mining and ranching landscape of the Rocky Mountains, Alpine skiing became associated with local skiers, local businesses, and tentatively with the federal government. It developed into a sport that melded cooperation and work with recreation and leisure.

A Study in Contrasts: Sun Valley and Colorado's Local Scene

Alpine ski resorts as they appeared in Europe never made it to Colorado before World War II. The closest resemblance was the resort in Sun Valley,

Idaho, and only a special effort on the part of Averell Harriman and the Union Pacific Railroad ensured its success there in the Rocky Mountain West. When Harriman became executive chairman of the struggling Union Pacific in 1932, he sought to boost the railroad's passenger service and define the company as a constructive force during the depression by developing a winter resort somewhere along its lines. It became his personal dream to build "the American St. Moritz," and his access to the railroad's extensive resources allowed him to do so to a remarkable degree.[3] Ultimately, Harriman's desire to create a celebrated alpine resort overshadowed his hope that it would turn a profit, and Sun Valley's fame and reputation grew largely because the Union Pacific could afford to let it.

Harriman took careful and often expensive steps to ensure the success of his venture. He hired a member of an Austrian banking family, Count Felix Schaffgotsch, to ride the Union Pacific and its subsidiary railroads around the country in search of an ideal resort site. After settling on an area near Ketchum, Idaho, Harriman bought up ranch land in the area and used $685,000 of the company's money to build a lodge there. "It was a relatively small investment for the railroad," he recalled, "a great big railroad with a great big income."[4] Harriman hired the architect responsible for designing the North Rim Lodge at the Grand Canyon to build his lodge in Idaho, and he hired Steve Hannagan — who ran one of the nation's leading public relations firms and had made Miami Beach popular — to design, advertise, and promote it.

Hannagan's vision was to create a million-dollar palace in the wilderness, and the Lodge ultimately cost $1.5 million to build. It boasted its own Saks Fifth Avenue store, the Duchin Ballroom, a "physiotherapy unit" complete with X-ray machine, a glass-enclosed outdoor pool and ice skating rink, a bowling alley, a billiard and game room, a barber shop and beauty parlor, and a bachelor's lounge; each room had its own telephone. On opening day, it was equipped to house 288 guests and 170 employees.[5] To emphasize the resort's image as a beautiful land of leisure, Hannagan gave it the name Sun Valley. He loaded that landscape with alpine sexiness when he settled on its central promotional image: a young man on skis, stripped to the waist and glistening with sweat, looking athletic, virile, suntanned, and incredibly satisfied. Harriman spared no expense to develop images of alpine luxury on the ski hill, as well. Rather than ask his guests to climb up mountains and actually work for the thrill of skiing down, he gave Union Pacific engineers the job of finding a way to carry skiers up the hill in comfort. After lots of experimenting, they adapted a lift designed to carry bananas to create the country's first chairlift. Having solved the problem of getting people up the mountain in style, Harriman then set out to get them down. For this he hired a cadre of ski instructors from Salzburg, Austria, headed by Hans Hauser and later Friedl Pfeifer. These men were fully equipped to teach skiing and otherwise educate visitors in the joys of alpine resorts. To round out the picture, Harriman brought Alpine skiing competition to the slopes of Sun Valley by sponsoring the Harriman Cup. This annual race pitted America's best racers against those of Europe, who traveled to Idaho at Harriman's expense. "Harriman was determined," said famed U.S. racer Dick Durrance in reference to the Harriman Cup, "that Sun Valley would match anything that Europe had to offer."[6] Hosting such an elite race encouraged further comparison between Sun Valley and European resorts and gave the place an added cachet.

Sun Valley's ideal customers, Hannagan and Harriman planned, would reinforce the resort's image. "Although the very nature of the community . . . makes it selective," Hannagan wrote, "it will be necessary to further restrict clientele through careful perusal of reservation requests. We must be careful to get our style . . . from the very first."[7] They sought members of the New York social register and Hollywood stars, inviting guests with names such as Pabst, DuPont, and Rockefeller to the opening and attracting Hollywood's David O. Selznick, Claudette Colbert, Samuel Goldwyn, and others. Lowell Thomas broadcast the opening extravaganza to 20 million listeners on his weekly radio show, and newspapers on both coasts touted the resort as the new hot spot on the social circuit.[8] Celebrities including Colbert, Bing Crosby, Gary Cooper, Ernest Hemingway, Norma Shearer, and producer Darryl Zanuck became associated with Sun Valley through publicized visits or prolonged stays. Generally unable to make the trip themselves, the public participated in Sun Valley's image and romance when they read the society pages and watched movies filmed there, including *I Met Him in Paris* (1937) starring Claudette Colbert, *The Mortal Storm* (1940) with Margaret Sullivan, and *Sun Valley Serenade* (1941) with Sonja Henie.[9] The images captured in these films represented concrete success for Harriman and his dream, despite the fact that the resort never paid for itself. Sun Valley's sumptuous amenities, mountain setting, reputation for downhill skiing, and association with celebrity effectively created an elite alpine resort culture in the American West.

Resort developers who shared Harriman's dream but not the backing of a company like the Union Pacific had a much more difficult time creating such places. Colorado's failed Highland Bavarian Lodge is a case in point. At a party in Pasadena in the spring of 1936, T. J. Flynn struck up a pointed conversation with two-time Olympic bobsled champion and Cambridge graduate Billy Fiske. At first the charismatic Fiske was put off; he was not interested in buying Flynn's mining claims in Aspen, Colorado, where Flynn had spent much of his youth. After Flynn described Aspen's beautiful, high mountains and the local tradition of skiing, however, Fiske took more notice, and they found themselves deep in conversation. The two ultimately teamed up with New York banker Ted Ryan to develop a winter resort in Aspen. They wanted to build an American version of St. Moritz, a Colorado resort to rival Idaho's Sun Valley. Flynn had local connections, Fiske had an unquenchable enthusiasm for winter sports — as well as an influential circle of friends in Europe and America — and Ryan had financial know-how. Together the group created the Highland Bavarian Corporation (HBC) and constructed a small lodge in the Castle Creek Valley, seven miles from the town of Aspen.

They, like Harriman, chose a name that would elicit images of alpine leisure and sought to establish their Highland Bavarian Lodge as a destination for upper-class vacationers and expert skiers. They brought Andre Roch and Gunther Langes from Europe to make recommendations on the resort's development and to instruct its first clientele. They convinced Dartmouth ski coach Otto Schniebs to visit with his annual coaching school and included Schniebs's positive evaluation in their public relations packet.[10] Fiske and Ryan talked up their resort to their friends in Hollywood and back East, and one of them, *New Yorker* humorist Robert Benchley, wrote a promotional brochure that compared the Highland Bavarian favorably with European resorts. Flynn also filmed a short movie highlighting the scenery and expert skiers to show at travel expositions in Chicago, St. Louis, and Cincinnati. The Highland Bavarian Lodge drew immediate attention. It hosted guests from Denver's Colorado Mountain and Arlberg Clubs, soon-to-be-senator Stephen Hart, famous Colorado skiers Frank Ashley and Thor Groswold, and radio personality Lowell Thomas. The nascent resort was also written up repeatedly in the eastern-based *Ski Bulletin* — all in 1936–37, its first season.[11]

Despite its advertising, its well-connected clientele, and Roch's plans for a large alpine resort, however, the HBC would not last. The lodge's image, its visitors, and its level of development fell well below the bar Harriman and Hannagan had set with Sun Valley. Lowell Thomas and the occasional European expert appeared, but resort clientele represented regional rather than national celebrities, and much of the area's publicity focused on the fact that no one really knew where Aspen was. To ski at the Highland Bavarian, guests had to ride the train to Glenwood Springs, drive from there to Aspen, and then meet a sleigh that would carry them to the lodge, a modest development that could accommodate sixteen guests in the main building and about thirty more in four other cabins. Roch considered the skiing that was immediately accessible from the lodge unsatisfactory for an elite resort; he taught beginners there but took experts to the distant slopes above Ashcroft. By the start of 1941, the company's plans to build an aerial tramway up Mt. Hayden and a resort village in Ashcroft remained unrealized. Negotiations for funding the project through the government's Reconstruction Finance Corporation had finally come together, only to be overshadowed by America's impending entrance into World War II. To make matters worse, Billy Fiske, the charismatic force driving the HBC, was killed while flying for the RAF in the Battle of Britain. After America's entrance into the war, Flynn and Ryan gave up on the project.[12]

Aspen's isolation, the HBC's lack of resources, and World War II all prevented their ideal resort from taking physical shape. Those same factors that worked against re-creating alpine resort culture in Colorado, however, helped foster a different kind of skiing there. They created an alternative version of the sport focused on individual towns and ski clubs rather than corporate entities. For local officials, ski club members, and boosters of the sport, skiing was not the romantic leisure sport that Harriman and the HBC founders tried to cultivate; it was the traditional winter pastime of mountain town residents. Coloradans discarded the exclusive, glamorous, and European images associated with alpine resorts and embraced instead the image of a winter playground designed for everyone from local kids and ski club members to visiting competitors and tourists. In adopting this image, Denver and other Colorado towns promoted a kind of Alpine skiing geared toward improving local economies — one that remained largely local and regional in scope, and one that encouraged active participation through ski club membership and competition.

This kind of skiing had a larger audience than elite resort-goers and a wider set of beneficiaries than one company or group of developers, so it generated broad support in many Colorado communities. In hosting ski competitions and defining their towns as winter playgrounds, newspaper writers and ski boosters hoped to draw business to their areas and revive the flagging economy that characterized much of Colorado from the 1910s through the 1930s. Denver residents articulated this optimism as early as 1915, and it grew after the Denver–Rocky Mountain Ski Club hosted the national ski championships in 1921. Publicizing regional and national meets in 1923 and 1927, respectively, newspapers crowed: "Annual Ski Tourney Will Clinch City's Fame as Winter Sport Center" and "National Ski Meet Is Coming to World's Playground in Rockies." In 1927, the *Denver Post* noted that it "ha[d] enlisted the cooperation of every service and athletic club and every civic organization in the state in its extensive plans for making Colorado the winter sports headquarters of the world."[13] These Coloradans understood skiing as a sport for everyone rather than an elite few, and they saw it as a business opportunity as much as a form of leisure.

Nor were Denver residents and journalists the only ones who saw the advantages of defining skiing in these broad and participatory terms. Small mountain towns all over the state, hurt by the decline in mining and trying to fight off the "ghost town" label, embraced skiing and the winter visitors it would attract. "This spirit of developing the asset of the sunshine-tempered winter in Colorado," one journalist noted in the mid-1920s, "has manifested itself from Fort Collins thruout [*sic*] the state, touching Durango, Grand Junction and Glenwood Springs."[14] The Durango Exchange, which would become the Chamber of Commerce in 1930, marketed the city as a "complete vacationland," promising local businessmen and prospective visitors alike that people who "Come to PLAY" will "Want to STAY."[15] From the 1910s through the 1930s, local towns and ski clubs advertised winter carnivals and ski competitions, fun community events that would also put them on the tourist map. For its first gala winter carnival, Grand Lake opened private cabins, hotels, and camps, devoting all "its excellent accommodations to the festival."[16] Steamboat Springs' entire community helped finance and organize its annual winter carnival, which had been popular since 1914. Colorado Mountain Club (CMC) member Henry Buchtel wrote, "perhaps the best reason to go to Steamboat is that the residents are so glad to have you and so anxious to have you enjoy yourself."[17] By 1940, residents had turned this fact into a public relations message: the *Steamboat Pilot*'s annual recreation edition encouraged readers to "Do Your Vacationing Friends a Favor — Tell Them About Steam-boat Springs." As Buchtel had noted, local residents and businesses welcomed the development of winter sports in their sleepy ranching town. The Steam-boat Springs Winter Sports Club, the Lions Club, and the American Legion all "used their influence and funds to further the cause of winter recreation in a town that seems destined to rank among the first ski resorts of our state."[18]

Other Colorado towns fought for that honor. After Flynn, Fiske, and Ryan announced their plans to open the Highland Bavarian Lodge outside Aspen and brought in Roch and Langes to help them, residents latched on to skiing and tourism with vigor. "A determined, enthusiastic and coop-erative effort on the part of the citizens of Aspen and Pitkin County should be given to both Mr. Fiske and Mr. Flynn in putting over this, the greatest economic boom that this community will enjoy since the early '90s," the *Aspen Times* declared.[19] The town concurred. The Aspen Band, professional and amateur skiers, Mayor Willoughby, and state senator Twining joined hundreds of local residents and Denver skiers for the Highland Bavarian Lodge's gala opening in December. It was then, one Aspenite noted, that "the town got so excited about skiing." As one man put it, "mining was faltering and people felt they had a new thing going."[20] A few years later and forty miles down the river, the Glenwood Springs Winter Sports Club and Chamber of Commerce were also "[doing their] utmost to encourage skiing and winter sports in western Colorado."[21] Local skiers, journalists, and businesspeople supported the development of skiing to put their towns on the map for winter recreation.

Despite dreams of national notoriety, most of Colorado's skiers during the 1930s and early 1940s participated in a local, community skiing tradition. Mountain town residents — especially young ones — skied in their back-yards, around town, on whatever mountains were most convenient.[22] For Aspen kids, hiking up Aspen Mountain and skiing down after school made much more sense than trying to get to the slopes of Mt. Hayden or the High-land Bavarian Lodge. And residents supported local ski clubs in part for the opportunities they provided for children.[23] These young skiers had neither the economic resources nor the inclination to travel and take part in resort culture. Instead, they joined clubs, competed against kids from neighboring towns, and, if they were good enough and got financial help from their clubs, traveled to regional or national races.

Such races brought visitors to Colorado towns, they reiterated the importance of clubs in supporting Colorado skiing, and they turned local competitors into sources of pride. Hot Sulphur Springs, Steamboat Springs, and Grand Lake hosted elaborate carnivals throughout the 1920s, 1930s, and 1940s, and ski clubs from Colorado Springs, Idaho Springs, Allens Park, Estes Park, Dillon, Aspen, and Denver put on ski competitions and tournaments. Local Aspenites still attribute their town's later success in part to the fact that it hosted the Southern Rocky Mountain Skiing Championships in 1938, 1939, and 1940 and the National Downhill and Slalom Championships in 1941. Race results from across the state peppered the Denver papers, and Colorado skiers such as Frank Ashley and Thor Groswold (in the 1930s) and Barney McLean, Gordon Wren, and Barbara Kidder (in the 1940s) became regional heroes when they did well in national races. In fact, they became heroes because of their modest backgrounds rather than in spite of them. Hot Sulphur, Steamboat Springs, and Denver skiers, respectively, claimed McLean, Wren, and Kidder proudly as their own.

Local businesses, newspapers, and community organizations supported carnivals and competitions to give their economies a boost; they celebrated Colorado skiers, who rarely came from privileged backgrounds; and they developed a regional and local skiing scene in the process. Their goal of becoming some form of St. Moritz remained tantalizing yet elusive, and wealthy resort-goers found few reasons to visit Colorado until after World War II. Despite the efforts of the HBC and the hopes articulated by many communities, they were all hard pressed to find resources on a scale comparable to Harriman and the Union Pacific Railroad. By depending on local support and smaller-scale development, however, Coloradans established an alternative model for skiing based on community participation and pride rather than outside private development.

Getting Places

Coloradans' understanding of skiing as a local and participatory sport was partly a reflection of their mining and ranching economies, which established little towns in high mountain ranges, built the physical framework for transporting their resources to outside markets, and gave them a common need for an economic boost when those economies declined. Towns' search for some extra income through skiing and tourism added another layer to their economic landscape and created a new use for old transportation networks. The system of roads and railroads built in nineteenth-century Colorado directed the movement of people and resources through the mountains and so determined which towns would grow and which would bust.[24] When Averell Harriman was looking for a site for his resort, he consciously limited the hunt to places accessible by Union Pacific lines. He created Sun Valley to promote the railroad, but he also realized that the only way his dream resort would take shape was if members of New York high society and Hollywood stars could actually get there. The existing skeleton of transportation routes similarly influenced the development of skiing in Colorado. But this is not a story of economic determinism. Alpine skiers and summer auto tourists used existing roads and railroads, but they also developed them, added to them, and appropriated them for a new purpose: recreation.

Physical remnants of an earlier mining and ranching economy — the roads and railroads — limited where most Coloradans could travel for work or play. The advent of the automobile in the 1920s enabled throngs of Bostonians and New Yorkers to travel to small ski resorts in New Hampshire and Vermont on the weekends. Colorado mountain passes, however, were much more difficult to negotiate than New England roads. Most were closed to automobile traffic during the winter until the 1930s. For skiers who lived in mountain towns, this situation posed no particular threat — they skied at home. For those who lived in Denver, it limited their skiing to places either near the city or accessible by train. By World War II, road and railroad networks had improved tremendously, but not to the point where skiers could get across the state for a competition or a carnival. The pattern of these routes, improved by recreational clubs, still encouraged the growth of a limited regional skiing community with Denver at its center and distant mountain towns on the periphery.

Efforts to improve automobile transportation within the state began at the turn of the century and increased through the 1920s as leisure and recreation grew in economic significance, but Colorado's weather and geography limited their success. The road from Denver to Middle Park over Berthoud Pass, built as a wagon road in 1874, had been "improved" in 1911 and again in 1918 to allow automobile traffic. By 1918, 40,000 cars had crossed the pass, but only in the summer and autumn months. Heavy rains and unsafe bridges often

Ski towns and paved roads, 1940

closed the road, which reached 11,300 feet in elevation, and it was not until 1931 that the Highway Department even tried to keep it open all winter.[25] Improvements in the 1930s made automobile travel in the mountains more feasible, if still challenging. Construction began on the road over Loveland Pass in 1928, providing another main link between Denver and the Western Slope. But the road reached an elevation of 11,992 feet and was, as late as 1939, still dirt.[26] Between 1928 and 1939, workers completed the road over Loveland Pass and covered it with gravel, and they paved Highway 40 over Berthoud Pass and most of the way to Steamboat Springs. "Only yesterday," one skier noted in 1937, "all mountain roads were little better than narrow, winding footpaths . . . [and] any summer cloudburst rendered them impassable." "Today," he went on, "a few places are accessible by magnificent broad highways, safe and easy any day in the year."[27] The operative word here may be "few." Colorado highways crossed the Continental Divide in at least thirteen

Berthoud Pass reached 11,306 feet and proved a challenge for early motorists. This 1920s view shows a building meant for summer tourists that skiers made use of in the winter. (Denver Public Library, Western History Collection, Harry Lake, L-398)

places; only three of those passes, however, were paved, and little funding or manpower was available for further improvements after America's entrance into World War II.[28]

While skiers limited their trips to accessible slopes and applauded the development of Colorado's highways, they also made creative use of existing routes. Recreation offered ski clubs a new way to consume the roads and railroads initially built to support the state's mining and ranching. In the case of Berthoud Pass, it encouraged skiers to reinterpret the road as a kind of ski lift. Denver skiers most often drove to Berthoud Pass and, after skiing down, drove back up to the top so they could do it again. This ritual required someone willing to shuttle friends rather than ski. In response to "the great demand for such transportation," the CMC financed and operated Berthoud's first ski bus, which began operating on January 5, 1936. The CMC ski bus not only brought skiers from Denver to Berthoud but also shuttled them up the pass at regular intervals. The price: $1.75 for the round-trip from Denver, 15¢ for each ride up the pass for members, and 25¢ for nonmembers.[29] By February, the CMC emphasized the regularity, dependability, and reliability of its bus to Berthoud Pass, although skiers seemed more interested in using it as a ski lift once they were there rather than riding it from Denver. The increasing patronage of skiers riding the bus to the top of the pass just a month after it started, one member noted, "proves conclusively that the bus is indispensable on the Pass itself."[30] The CMC and its bus illustrate a larger state trend. Local clubs and their members literally and figuratively drove skiing in Colorado, and they did so largely by reinterpreting old roads and mountain passes as recreational landscapes.

Railroads were not immune to this treatment. Established routes continued to support a local and regional model of Alpine skiing, but recreational passengers did more than simply use the trains to get to the mountains — they appropriated trains for a use their builders had not imagined. In doing so, they inscribed a new meaning on Colorado's network of railroads and its economic landscape. Initially built to support the state's mining economy, the Denver and Rio Grande (D&RG) Railroad moved ore from Leadville, Durango, Gunnison, Crested Butte, Silverton, and Dillon in the 1880s and from Aspen, Ouray, and Telluride a few years later. Even older lines connected Denver with the mining districts around Breckenridge and Como, where Father John Dyer had made his living carrying the winter mail. In opening access to these mining towns, the railroads put mailmen like Dyer out of business and encouraged others to hang up their Norwegian snowshoes for good. After that, skis functioned more as toys than tools, and recreational skiing spread along railroad routes as the old utilitarian version of the sport was fading away.

Scandinavian immigrants and Denver ski enthusiasts in the early twentieth century rode trains into the mountains so they could ski. Carl Howelsen and Marjorie Perry, for example, spread their winter sport gospel along the Moffat Road. Formed in 1902, David Moffat's Denver, Northwestern and Pacific Railway went up Rollins Pass and crossed the Continental Divide at Corona, 11,660 feet above sea level. The Moffat Road reached Hot Sulphur Springs in 1905, Steamboat Springs in 1908, and ended in Craig in 1913, after Moffat died and the railroad went bankrupt.[31] The costs of maintaining the railroad outweighed its income from carrying coal, lumber, and cattle over Rollins Pass to Denver. Clearing snow and blockages off the highest railroad in North America ate up 41 percent of the Moffat Road's operating expenses. Reorganized as the Denver and Salt Lake (D&SL) Railroad Company, the Moffat Road kept up operations and enjoyed new importance during World War I when it transported coal and oil from northwestern Colorado.[32]

Despite frequent stoppages at Corona — even because of them, at times — the Moffat Road encouraged the spread of recreational skiing in Colorado. Howelsen first visited Hot Sulphur Springs after riding the train to Corona in search of skiable terrain. Marjorie Perry met Howelsen when she was on her way home from Steamboat Springs and got off the train at Hot Sulphur to see him jump. Perry, Howelsen, and friends from Denver took advantage of delays at Corona by hopping off the train, strapping on their skis, and meeting up with the train sixteen miles later in Tolland. More important for Hot Sulphur and Steamboat Springs, the Moffat Road carried Denver skiers to their carnivals. Competitors and spectators filled local hotels, turned out in big numbers for carnival events, and recounted their adventures to friends after they went home. From the 1910s through the 1920s, the Moffat Road helped Hot Sulphur and Steamboat Springs earn regional fame as centers of winter sport.

Alpine skiers refined this practice of riding trains to ski in the late 1920s, even as the Moffat Road struggled to earn revenue from other sources. Using the transportation infrastructure of earlier economies made sense for skiers because, like the miners and ranchers before them, they found value in inaccessible landscapes. The Moffat Road's efforts to solve the problems presented by Rollins Pass wound up opening new terrain for Denver downhill skiers as well as keeping the railroad in business. In the summer of 1923, work began on a tunnel under the Continental Divide. The 6.2-mile Moffat Tunnel opened for business in the end of February 1928, representing an investment of $18 million and twenty-eight lives.[33] Not only did the tunnel improve transportation from Denver to Hot Sulphur and Steamboat Springs; it also helped promote a new downhill ski area. Denver skier and U.S. Forest Service consultant Graeme McGowan had identified the West Portal area of the tunnel as ideal for skiing, so he turned a staff building into a clubhouse, bought a placer claim called Mary Jane, and established Portal Resorts.[34]

He and a group of Denver skiers rode the train to West Portal regularly as soon as the tunnel opened and, united as the Arlberg Club, practiced Alpine skiing at what would become Denver's Winter Park resort. In doing this, Denver skiers successfully appropriated the railroad for their own recreational purposes. And what began as an informal arrangement with the conductor to drop skiers off and pick them up again soon became more significant. A CMC member arranged for the first special train to carry skiers to West Portal in February 1930. The railroad company allocated an entire car to the skiers, which it left on a siding while the passengers enjoyed their day on the slopes. In rallying forty to fifty skiers for the trip, the CMC earned a discounted fare for its members, won recognition of skiing as a legitimate use of the rails, and turned West Portal into one of Colorado's best-known downhill ski runs.[35] Regular ski trains ran to West Portal for several years afterward, until the automobile road over Berthoud Pass opened year-round. The growing relationship between local ski clubs and the Moffat Road demonstrated the energy with which ski clubs pursued their sport, as well as the significance of transportation routes to the development of regional skiing in Colorado.

This relationship would continue to grow during the 1930s, along with skiers' cultural and economic influence. Local businesses embraced winter sports as a viable use of the railroad and recognized the sport's potential for their bottom line. In 1936, the *Denver Rocky Mountain News* sponsored Denver's first snow train to carry passengers on the 172-mile round-trip from Denver to Hot Sulphur Springs for the twenty-fifth annual ski tournament

and winter sports carnival. "You can get a nice ride on a railroad train —
which a lot of Denver folk haven't done in years," the newspaper promised.
"You can watch the thrilling snow and ice games! You can use your own skis
and skates and toboggans! And," the paper went on, "the whole day's outing, including round-trip rail fare and admittance to the carnival, will cost
you an even $1.75."[36] The *News* could not have wished for better success. Tick-
ets sold out; Denver department stores placed ads for ski equipment and fashions in the paper; the whole city (they said) got involved. More than 2,200
people rode the trains to the carnival — some coming from as far away as
Cheyenne. In Hot Sulphur, they met up with 500 others, including fifty jumpers and a forty-two-piece high school band, who had ridden in on another
train from Steamboat Springs. In all, Hot Sulphur counted 7,000 visitors for
the day.[37]

   The success of this campaign sparked others. Just six days after its Hot
Sulphur train, the *News* sponsored a special D&SL Pullman snow train with
overnight service to the winter carnival in Steamboat Springs. Its snow train
to Hot Sulphur became an annual event. Other Denver businesses, including Safeway Stores, the *Denver Post,* and Montgomery Ward, jumped in and
sponsored other snow trains, working with the railroad company and organizing trips in return for publicity. As railroads from Boston to Seattle had
learned, ski trains attracted business.[38] Even when no train catered to a specific event, skiers made good use of the railroads. By 1938, railroad pamphlets
advertised regular Sunday snow train service to West Portal on the D&SL
through the Moffat Tunnel, as well as D&SL and D&RG service to other
"Western Winter Playgrounds" in Aspen, Hot Sulphur Springs, Steamboat
Springs, and Marshall Pass.[39]

   Winter tourism and skiing had sprouted up along the routes of Colorado's
railroad system, expanded that system to include ski trains, and altered its winter
advertising campaigns. The railroads, in turn, welcomed skiers and opened
access to some winter sports centers. Colorado's system of highways and railroads grew hand in hand with recreational skiing during the 1920s and 1930s,
responding to the growing popularity of the sport and guiding the growth of
winter tourism along its routes. Local clubs and their members attached new
meaning to the roads and railroads they traveled, replacing ore and cattle cars
with trains of outdoor enthusiasts and turning mountain passes into makeshift
ski areas. Their power to turn Colorado into the country's winter wonderland,

*Skiers commandeered the railroads for recreation rather than ore during the 1920s and
1930s, especially along the route from Denver through the Moffat Tunnel. (Colorado
Historical Society, F26970/1002700)*

however, remained limited by the state's physical and economic characteristics. The difficulties of winter travel still isolated many communities from the
Denver area and reinforced skiers' local identities. Dreams of St. Moritz mate-
rializing in Colorado rested on a scale of financial backing that remained elusive. Instead, Coloradans hoping to build ski areas relied on one another, local
businesses, and a growing relationship with the federal government.

Making Trails and Building Tows

During the 1930s, the sport progressed to the point where skiers sought specific, developed places to ski. Increasingly associating their sport with leisure,
recreational skiers grew less willing to trudge uphill for every run down. They
invested skiing with a different sort of work instead, clearing trails and building lifts in cooperative efforts to maximize the fun and exhilaration they

sought on the way down. Ski lift technology was in its infancy in the 1930s, and most skiers appreciated rope tows, despite the feats of strength and coordination necessary to ride them.[40] Even simple rope tows cost money, though, and required a place to set them up.

Where to put them was easy; national forests covered most of the Rocky Mountains, and the U.S. Forest Service became an early supporter of Alpine skiing. Upon the organization of the Forest Service in 1905, the federal government established that it would promote and control "wise use" of national forest resources rather than preserve the land as wilderness. Since then, loggers have cut timber and livestock have grazed on forest land with the government's permission, and often with the benefit of government-built improvements. Recreation fell under this rubric of wise use, and during the 1936–37 season, winter sports participants made almost a million visits to America's national forests.[41] Federal employees tended to encourage this use. During the 1930s, "the personnel of the U.S. Forest Service, long accustomed to skis, snowshoes, and toboggans for timber cruising, wildlife estimates, snow surveys, and other administrative duties," one Forest Service representative wrote, "observed this growing interest in winter recreation with a sympathetic personal understanding of the fundamental appeal of adventure in a winter wonderland."[42] Graeme McGowan was a case in point. Besides being a founding member of the Arlberg Club and an avid outdoorsman, he also worked as a consultant for the Forest Service, surveying skiable terrain, recommending improvements to develop it, and promoting skiing from Berthoud Pass and West Portal to New Mexico and Arizona.[43]

Ski clubs had a difficult time raising money and recruiting labor for cutting trails, building cabins, and operating tows. Most got help from a combination of sources, including the New Deal's Civilian Conservation Corps (CCC), Works Progress Administration (WPA), and Public Works Administration (PWA), as well as the Forest Service, local businesses, and sometimes town or city governments. President Franklin Roosevelt's CCC, WPA, and PWA helped develop and finance small ski areas where interest dictated across Colorado, hoping to employ unskilled workers as well as improve the civic and recreational landscape of the country. The CCC often carried out plans formed by the Forest Service to cut ski trails, and the PWA and WPA helped local communities and ski clubs finance tows they wanted to install.[44] Although it is unclear exactly how well New Deal government agents understood skiing, the financial support and physical labor they offered almost certainly represented a commitment to the development of recreation and tourism. At the very least, funding the development of local ski areas gave jobs and economic support to Denver and many of Colorado's rural mountain communities. Colorado's two largest early ski areas grew out of this local and federal cooperation.

Ardent CMC members had been practicing their downhill technique on Berthoud Pass since the early 1930s, and this area within Arapaho National Forest became quite popular once the road over the pass was open through the winter. The trail from the summit to the highway, built in 1934, represented "the best efforts of the CCC and a chilly party of local surveyors"; Forest Service employees cleared stumps from the practice hill. The next year, CMC members spent "long, hot summer Sundays planning and marking the trails" that CCC recruits would build under supervision of the Forest Service.[45] This system of trails attracted regular skiers from Denver in increasing numbers. The group of skiers had once been so small, one man recalled, that everyone knew one another by their first names. Just a year or two later, "the top of Berthoud Pass, crowded Sunday after Sunday with four to five hundred cars, became so that there was scarcely room for comfortable skiing."[46]

To oversee the development of local ski areas such as Berthoud Pass, a dozen or so ski clubs and communities came together and formed the Colorado Winter Sports Council in November 1936. This organization continued development at Berthoud Pass, building trails, improving parking, and installing Colorado's first rope tow. Funded in part by the May Company department store in Denver, the tow opened on February 7, 1937. By charging a small fee for rides, the CMC recouped $500 the next season, about one-fifth of the tow's cost. Not to be left out of the picture, the Forest Service financed the construction of a new three-story lodge, complete with telephone, water, and toilet facilities. By 1941, the area at Berthoud Pass offered skiers lunch or refreshments at the lodge, plus six different trails, two rope tows, and parking space for 600 cars.[47] The second-largest ski area in Colorado at the time, Berthoud Pass typified a model of development based on local participation and cooperation with the Forest Service and New Deal agencies.

Winter Park, the state's largest ski area, built on this model and added a couple of new twists. West Portal attracted skiers from Denver, especially when the road over Berthoud Pass proved impassable. Arlberg Club members, CMC members, their friends, and other enthusiasts rode the train there and skied on "the old sheep driveway," cut by the Forest Service in the 1920s to connect grazing areas and known more popularly as the Mary Jane trail. The Arlberg Club, which regarded West Portal as its home turf, leased land and a makeshift clubhouse from McGowan's Portal Resorts. Instead of asking the Forest Service to build a public lodge on national forest land, however, the Arlberg Club built its own lodge on private land adjoining the Arapaho National Forest in 1933, financed primarily through a large donation from one wealthy club member. A few years later, the CMC also built a cabin near West Portal for its members and guests, with seventeen bunks and meals available.[48] This practice of developing lodges on private land adjacent to ski trails on public land, though it would come to characterize resort development after World War II, represented an unusual step away from the government-built public lodges that had become the norm during the 1930s. In their scale and local club orientation, however, the Arlberg and CMC lodges reinforced Colorado's model of small-time and cooperative ski areas. So did their relationship with federal agencies. Because the skiable terrain lay on Forest Service land, the Arlberg Club worked together with the Forest Service and the CCC to clear and improve the Mary Jane trail in 1933. That relationship continued the next year when the CCC built a steep, straight, downhill racing course on which the club held its annual competitions.[49] The Forest Service thinned and cleared three more trails in the West Portal area in 1936 and 1937 (one of which led skiers there from the top of Berthoud Pass) and made plans to build a public lodge as well.[50]

When faced with the need to build tows, the fledgling ski area added another twist to the standard model by drawing the city government into its web of supporters. Tows represented a significant investment, one that few individuals or clubs wanted to handle on their own. The Colorado Winter Sports Council and the May Company had financed the ones at Berthoud Pass, and the city of Denver decided to take on West Portal. Manager of parks and improvements for the city and county of Denver in 1938 was George Cranmer, an outdoorsman who had learned to ski from Carl Howelsen and wanted to expand the city park system. He, along with some Denver businessmen and the *Denver Rocky Mountain News,* thought that "the fun of sliding over snow with a couple of boards tied to the feet may bring millions of dollars to Colorado."[51] Crowding at Berthoud Pass further convinced him that skiers could support more areas. After inspecting the West Portal area with experts, including Otto Schniebs and Bob Balch, Cranmer and the Denver Chamber of Commerce's Winter Sports Committee decided that "this area can afford pleasure for several thousand skiers every day after proper development" and determined that the city of Denver was just the organization for the job.[52]

After that, financial wheels started moving quickly. Cranmer got a Forest Service permit for 6,400 acres between Berthoud Pass and West Portal and incorporated the ski area into Denver's Mountain Parks System. The city council raised the $25,000 necessary to build tows and trails by applying for a WPA project that would cover 45 percent of the bill and soliciting subscriptions from local businesses and individuals for the remaining $14,000. The city's backing "gave this undertaking a permanence and stability formerly lacking in the eyes of business interests," encouraging Denver businesses and ski club members, as well as the Moffat Road, the Burlington Railroad, and the Union Pacific Railroad, to invest in the ski area.[53]

Although the city's support influenced the scale of its development, Winter Park still depended on a web of local and federal help. Nothing made this point more clear than the problem of labor. The city's resources were limited, and when Cranmer ran out of money to cut trails, he called for volunteers. Ninety people answered — Arlbergers, CMC members, and skiers from other Denver clubs, both male and female. In 1939, Bob Balch became the first manager of the Winter Park ski area, overseeing city employees who had volunteered to build trails and a J-bar lift there on the weekends. Its grand opening in January 1940 brought racers from ski clubs across the state, as well as some from Wyoming and Sun Valley. The next year it operated two T-bar lifts, a tractor sled lift, more than a dozen trails, a thirty-five-meter jump, a lodge with food concessions, a well-equipped racecourse, and accommodations located only two miles down the road.[54] Although tiny by current standards, in 1941, these facilities made Winter Park the biggest ski area in the state.

Farther from Denver's concentration of cash and recreational skiers than Berthoud Pass and Winter Park, a number of smaller ski areas throughout Colorado depended on similar support networks for their growth in the late 1930s. They, like the two larger areas, served local skiers interested in taking

This early 1940s view of Winter Park's J-bar lift and Hughes Trail shows the modest size of Colorado's then-largest ski area. (Denver Public Library, Western History Collection, X-14188)

day trips. One group of Denver skiers pooled their money and built a ski lodge in Empire called the Trap Door — named after the spider's nest the building resembled — from which they could ski terrain on Loveland Pass, Jones Pass, St. Mary's Glacier, and Fremont Pass.[55] A more ambitious group from Denver, ski club Zipfelberger, started to develop Loveland Basin. By 1939, the Forest Service had built a lodge there and four downhill trails, including the Zipfelberger racing trail. The club built a cabin just below timberline that same year and put up a small tow on the practice hill. By 1941, there were three rope tows in operation. To the south, Colorado Springs skiers frequented the area at Glen Cove, where the Forest Service built some trails and a jump and the Pikes Peak Ski Club installed a tow. Still other ski clubs across the state teamed up with the Forest Service and local businesses to build ski areas. Grand Junction skiers put up rope tows and built a lodge in the Grand Mesa National Forest, and the Continental Ski Club of Climax built a small area near Fremont Pass that stayed open for night skiing.[56] Steamboat Springs hosted slalom and downhill races and built a tow of its own in 1938. Along the D&RG line in Glenwood Springs, the Winter Sports Club, the Chamber of Commerce, officials of the White River National Forest, members of the local CCC camp, and high school volunteers all came together to build a downhill course in one of Glenwood's city parks on Lookout Mountain.[57]

Farther from Denver, and thus even more dependent on local skiers and local support networks, downhill ski areas grew up in the southwestern part of Colorado as well. Long connected with the sport, the Gunnison and Crested Butte region installed Colorado's first chairlift at the Pioneer area, offering skiers a rope tow and the well-known Big Dipper trail as well. Western State College had a practice hill in Gunnison itself. Telluride skiers followed Bruce Palmer's portable rope tow around the area and formed the Ski-Hi Ski Club to sponsor local competitions and raise money for a new rope each year.[58] Durango businessmen and civic organizations bought a rope tow, which the San Juan Basin Ski and Winter Sports Club operated twenty-five miles outside of town. Locals facetiously referred to Chapman Hill, closer to town and

In 1942, only local Colorado skiers frequented Loveland Basin, where the Forest Service welcomed them but few amenities existed. (Denver Public Library, Western History Collection, Z-3094)

funded in part by the WPA, as "Durango's Sun Valley."[59] The San Juan Ski Club of Ouray also used WPA funds — about $5,000 worth — to clear a course by its practice slope. The club got permission to do so in the form of a Forest Service permit, and membership funds financed a ski shelter. Salida, too, had its own ski area by 1941, when the Monarch Pass area opened for business with two rope tows and a ski club lodge. The San Luis Valley Ski Club drove to Wolf Creek Pass for its snow, where a Forest Service shelter, two rope tows, and long runs attracted skiers.[60]

These Colorado ski areas, built for the most part in the late 1930s, shared more than their mixture of local and federal support. They were small. They were simple. Amenities, if any, consisted of a ski shelter where it might be possible to buy lunch. Tows were prevalent, though many skiers hiked above the top of the lift to reach better terrain. Thirteen of the thirty-three Colorado ski areas listed in a 1941 brochure had no lifts at all. And local people skied there. People wanting to spend more than a day skiing had to travel to

Local ski areas such as this one in Hot Sulphur sprang up throughout the Rocky Mountains during the 1930s, a result of community, ski club, and federal cooperation. (Grand County Historical Association)

the nearest town with a hotel and return to the slopes the next day, or, if they were club members, they might opt to spend the night in a clubhouse bunkroom. Limitations in highway development, ski lift technology, and financing — despite New Deal support — kept Colorado ski areas and the groups that ran them locally oriented.

Even the HBC, with its European experts, Wall Street connections, and images of an American St. Moritz, could not buck the trend. While Flynn, Fiske, and Ryan tried to find financing for the tramway and resort village they envisioned below Mt. Hayden, the Aspen Ski Club's little boat tow and Roch Run on Aspen Mountain gained fame. Like other local ski areas across the state, Aspen's area opened and attracted skiers because a series of local networks supported it. Local businesses and governments joined their ski clubs to forge relationships with a willing Forest Service and supportive New Deal agencies. This combination of funding and labor reinforced a model of Alpine skiing in Colorado far different from the one Averell Harriman envisioned at Sun Valley, and it fostered the appearance of small ski areas throughout the state.

With America's involvement in World War II, the development of Alpine skiing changed course. Sun Valley became a navy hospital. In Colorado, Berthoud Pass closed down for the duration. Hopes for the HBC disintegrated. Materials for tows and lifts, money for construction and labor, and gas for travel all seemed to disappear overnight. The need for diversion and the local orientation of most ski areas, however, meant that Coloradans could and would keep skiing through the war. In fact, the war effort wound up having a strikingly positive effect on Colorado skiing. It brought a diverse group of outdoorsmen to Colorado, who volunteered to ski for the U.S. Army. These men expanded the notion of participatory skiing to include military service, and they came from across the country to create their own local skiing community at Camp Hale.

America's Mountain Troops in Colorado

The origins of America's mountain troops can be traced, rather appropriately, to a group of men accustomed to the volunteer work that was often connected with skiing. One evening after the Hochebirge Ski Club of Boston's annual races in 1939, a group of men started talking about the Russo-Finnish war.

They applauded the skill and tactics of the Finnish ski troops and came to the conclusion that America would need similarly trained forces to repel any attack on the northeastern coast. That night, Minot "Minnie" Dole and Roger Langely, presidents of the National Ski Patrol (NSP) and the National Ski Association, respectively, decided to offer their services and those of their organizations to the secretary of war.[61] A long series of letters, proposals, and meetings finally led to official cooperation between the War Department and the NSP on the issue of equipment development and the recruitment of volunteers. In November 1941, the army activated the 87th Infantry Mountain Regiment — the first of three regiments that would ultimately make up the 10th Mountain Division.[62]

With a national structure that united local ski patrols under regional chiefs, who were in turn responsible to division chairmen, the NSP could recruit skiers and outdoorsmen from all over the country. Minot Dole called for "men who have lived and worked in the mountains, such as rock climbers, trappers, packers, guides, prospectors, timber cruisers . . . if they ski, so much the better." "Good skiers without extensive mountaineering experience," Dole's bulletin continued, "if they are physically fit for rigorous winter and mountain training, will be acceptable." Volunteers had to fill out a questionnaire on their background and experience, as well as submit three letters of recommendation to verify their qualifications. The only civilian agency authorized to recruit for the army, the NSP recruited 10,634 enlisted men and 370 officers over the next four years for what would become the 10th Mountain Division.[63]

Through their efforts, Dole and the NSP effectively expanded the volunteer labor commonly sought by local ski clubs to include national military service. They brought people from local ski cultures together with Ivy League outdoorsmen and icons of European resort culture to form their own sort of ski club. Ski racers of regional, collegiate, national, and even international fame signed up for the 87th and headed to Fort Lewis, Washington. Charlie McLane, who had captained the Dartmouth ski team, was the first to arrive. Before long, he was only one outstanding skier among many. They included the head of the Mt. Hood ski school; head of the Mt. Rainier ski patrol; ex-coach of the University of Washington ski team; ex-captain and coach of the University of Vermont ski team; ex–New Hampshire State captain; an Olympic jumping coach; instructors from Sun Valley,

Mt. Hood, Yosemite, and Franconia, New Hampshire; competitors from Williams College, Dartmouth College, Denver, and Steamboat Springs; and a skiing mail carrier from the Sierra Nevadas. Foreign-born skiers also joined up, including Dartmouth coach Walter Prager; German national team member Peter Pringsheim; Wladyslaw Thomas Mietelski, a ten-year veteran of Polish army skiing detachments; Norwegian jumping coach Harold "Pop" Sorensen and jumper Torger Tokle; Italian Swiss-born mountaineer Peter Gabriel; Laplander Eric Wikner; and instructors Olaf Rotegaard and Hans Kolb.[64] This collection of men represented every aspect of America's ski history, from Scandinavian jumpers and European mountaineers to Austrian instructors and college outing club members. The 87th also attracted a weird combination of wealthy resort-goers and rural outdoorsmen. Minot Dole got to meet actress Norma Shearer when her escort came to volunteer for the mountain troops. George Frankenstein, son of the last German ambassador to England, also came to sign up.[65] The 87th brought these elites together with skiers, snowshoers, Maine woodsmen, dog-sled mushers, big-game hunters, Norwegian farmers, and more. "This remarkable collection of people," one member said, "was to have a truly distinctive stamp on the 10th Division."[66]

These men were not initially united, but they would be as their training brought them together in certain places and helped them coalesce as a group. During the winter of 1942, after the attack on Pearl Harbor, the men of the 87th Regiment moved to Fort Lewis and Mt. Rainier to train in earnest. After a day on the mountain, it became common for the men to break out guitars and sing. Besides supporting the characterization of the 87th as a kind of military ski club, their songs illustrate common perspectives and concerns. One titled "Oola" soon became a favorite. The first two (of many) verses are as follows:

I'm Oola, ski-yumper from Norway brought up on Lutefisk and Sil
Ay come to New York to find me some work but I guess I go vest right away.
Ay yomp on a train for Ft. Lewis to fight for the U.S.A.
Ay yoin up the Mountain Battalion and here Ay tink Ay will stay.

Each day and each night at Ft. Lewis, yee vhiss! how it would rain.
And if it vould keep up dis vedder, ay never go skiing again.
At last ve go up to the mountain. She's one doggone place you should see.
The minute I get there I'm happy. I run out and yomp on my ski.[67]

With its humor and stereotyping, "Oola" celebrates the ethnic diversity of the 87th and its identity as a volunteer fighting force; describes its activities as a mixture of work, fighting, and skiing; and expresses how training on Mt. Rainier created a common bond among the men. Mountain landscapes helped draw more men to the 87th and also became part of their identity.

In June 1942, the army decided to expand its Mountain Infantry and activate the 2nd and 3rd Battalions of the 87th Regiment. Because Fort Lewis fell short of the ideal mountain training facility, General Marshall appointed a team to find a new one. Of the four final possibilities, two in Colorado were too inaccessible, and the third (West Yellowstone) was home to the threatened trumpeter swan. So the winner was Pando, Colorado, a sheep-loading station just north of Tennessee Pass on the main line of the D&RG railroad, near Leadville on U.S. Highway 24.[68] Construction on Camp Hale was finished in November 1942. It would be home to 15,000 men of the 10th Mountain Division, formally activated in the spring of 1943 and made up of the 85th, 86th, and 87th Regiments.

Minnie Dole of the National Ski Patrol sent notices to all patrolmen asking for volunteers, and he toured colleges in the East looking for recruits to fill the new regiments. He found 3,500 men in sixty days.[69] Those men, combined with the 87th, made up one of the most highly educated — and correspondingly elite — military forces in the army. Some 64 percent of the enlisted men in the 86th Regiment, for instance, qualified for officer training school.[70] Quite a few members of the 10th Mountain Division knew one another from college. Gordon Wren knew a number of them from racing and ski jumping competitions he had taken part in across the United States. "It was a mixture of guys from everywhere," he remembered, "South, West, North, East — everywhere that anyone had heard of skiing."[71] Working-class athletes and wealthy men who wanted to become skiers joined elite skiers in the 10th, fostering an atmosphere and tone that existed in stark contrast to those of other military organizations.

The fact that this division operated as a collection of volunteer skiers tended to lessen — or loosen — military standards of discipline and behavior. This made some officers worry that the division was too much like a ski club, but it made the 10th even more appealing to its members and enlistees. One member joined specifically because he "disliked military organization, *per se*," and felt that he would have the greatest amount of freedom as a rifleman in the

Tenth Mountain Division soldiers earned a reputation as America's elite outdoorsmen. David B. Allen's pose at Camp Hale mimicked a drawing that graced the Saturday Evening Post *cover in March 1943. (Denver Public Library, Western History Collection, Tenth Mountain Division, TMD-757)*

ski troops.[72] Racer Steve Knowlton called the 10th "great," because "it threw me into a group of skiers that I had heard about who were probably the best skiers in the United States at that time . . . and I got to rub elbows with them."[73] This group included Sun Valley's Friedl Pfeifer and Florian Haemmerle and St. Anton natives Luggi Foeger, Toni Matt, and Herbert Schneider (Hannes's son), who declared their allegiance to the United States by becoming citizens and volunteering for the mountain troops.[74] These icons of international resort ski culture enhanced the reputation of the 10th and its character as a fraternity of elite skiers. The 10th Mountain Division would become the largest volunteer fighting force ever, with its appeal and reputation further cementing a group of men initially drawn together by skiing and outdoor sports.[75]

Of course, the 10th had its problems, too. Not all its members had volunteered for the mountain troops. Nor were they all familiar with the mountains. Their presence in the 10th resulted from stereotypical army mistakes and from the need to fill out the division's ranks. The 10th Cavalry Reconnaissance Troop from Meade, South Dakota, consisted primarily of cowboys,

and the 31st Dixie Division came to Camp Hale from Leesville, Louisiana —
one of the flattest, hottest, and lowest parts of America. One veteran recalled
a time when the division was short on numbers. "They sent out a bulletin
open to all military personnel to send their people to Camp Hale," and we
wound up with "a lot of the [army's] riff raff." Other disoriented soldiers
included men from disbanded tank destroyer units, many of them "from the
hoots and hollers of Appalachia." As one member of the 85th's C Company
put it, "Harvard could talk about Nietzsche and Einstein, but Harlan County
played a lot better poker." These men had a tough time adjusting to the cold,
high-altitude training exercises expected of them and to the division's unorthodox ski club atmosphere. Once they were out on the ski slopes at Cooper
Hill (Camp Hale's own small ski area), some officers were hard put to obey
their instructors of lesser rank.[76]

Training — sometimes even living — proved to be demanding in many
ways. "Life at Camp Hale was filled, as all army life is," veteran C. Page Smith
wrote, "with multitudinous small dramas and bits of high and low comedy."[77]
Their experiences drew the soldiers together and anchored their identity in
place, to the mountains of Colorado. Often referred to as "Camp Hell," Camp
Hale introduced members of the 10th to the problems of high-altitude living
as well as to the beauty of Colorado's Rockies. Built in eight months at an
altitude of 9,200 feet, Camp Hale gave a bad first impression. When the 87th
Regiment arrived there in November 1942, a coat of snow covered what turned
out to be a muddy quagmire studded with nails, glass, and tools left over from
its hasty construction. Their trucks did not get far that day. Troops arriving
later noticed an imposing cloud hovering over the camp, a result of 500 individual soft-coal-burning furnaces and frequent triple-engined steam trains
climbing the 4 percent grade between Pando and Tennessee Pass. This cloud,
trapped in the high valley and often reducing visibility to a city block, fa-
thered the ever-present cough known as the "Pando hack." Other troubles
plagued the residents of Camp Hale. Extreme cold led to dozens of cases of
frostbite, the altitude made marching more difficult than army manuals acknowledged, and the equipment they tested sometimes backfired. One set of
troops who had camped out at 12,000 feet woke up in the morning to find
themselves trapped in their sleeping bags, the zippers frozen. According to
one veteran, life at Camp Hale consisted of "strenuous activity conducted
always with some experimentation."[78]

If cold weather and high altitudes made life at Hale hell, they made training exercises worse. The infamous D-Series lasted about four weeks in the spring of 1944, and these divisional maneuvers proved to be the most rugged training exercise in the U.S. Army. Troops lived outdoors for the entire series, sleeping, marching, climbing, camping, and trying to keep their feet warm, often 12,000 feet above sea level in temperatures that reached thirty degrees below zero. "Designed to test our ability to operate in the mountains in subzero temperatures," one division historian wrote, "the operation succeed[ed] in pushing both men and machines to the limit of their endurance." "Looking back," another said, "it will be hard to realize that we actually went through that agony of cold, with clothes constantly wet and no way to dry them out, with no time for sleep, and with no time for more than a bite on the run." Being wet, cold, tired, and hungry characterized the D-Series for most. In one day alone, more than 100 men with frostbite had to be evacuated. "No one who took part in those maneuvers," one rifleman asserted, "will ever forget them."[79]

The very toughness of the D-Series bound members of the 10th Mountain Division into an even tighter unit than before. Conducting war games in snowstorms with only half an atmosphere to breathe required teamwork. "Through these past few days of hardship our squad had become a family," one man recalled, "closely knit, and concerned above all in the welfare of its members." This feeling applied to the entire division as well. The D-Series became understood as a rite of passage into the 10th, and stories of the maneuvers became part of the division's lore. "We of the ten thousand who went through the great experience," Harris Dusenbery argued, "had an elan that could have been acquired in no other way. Whatever the 10th Mountain Division was, it had its nucleus in the multiform and arduous experiences of our D Series."[80]

D-Series represented the culmination of a year and a half of work in the mountains surrounding Camp Hale. If the length and intensity of their training pulled members of the 10th together as a unit, its location wedded them to place. Skiing in winter and mountain climbing in summer gave soldiers an intimate knowledge of the landscape around Camp Hale. Even during strenuous maneuvers — or perhaps especially during them — men took time to notice the scenery. A volunteer from Wisconsin wrote about one winter bivouac near Cooper Hill, where the 2nd Battalion of the 86th was scheduled to train for two weeks. "Here, practically on top of America," he wrote, "we were high in the sky and it seemed as if we could reach out and help boost the moon up over the Divide."[81] Even during the D-Series, the landscape could enchant. One member of the 86th's C Company recalled a windy lookout. "I raised my eyes to the view that stretched out before me," he said, to "range after range of mountains, dazzling white peaks and long ridges, Holy Cross, Homestake, Elbert, Massive, and a thousand lesser peaks and mountain ramparts." "The majestic beauty of these ranges," he went on, "made me realize that there were some compensations for being in the mountain troops." Others noticed more than beauty. During the D-Series, Dusenbery and his squad saw terrain that they thought would make a great ski hill, and even plotted where the lifts ought to go.[82] Some foreign-born members of the 10th noticed, as wealthy tourists had since the nineteenth century, the resemblance between the Rockies and the Alps. Friedl Pfeifer recounted his first view of Aspen as he came down Hunter Creek while on maneuvers from Camp Hale. "The first look I had I thought I was home," he said. "The mountains reminded me of home."[83]

Living at Camp Hale and training in its surrounding mountains made Colorado feel like home for many; during the early 1940s, mountain troop soldiers effectively became Colorado residents. They added Cooper Hill to the network of local ski areas and visited others, participating in and supporting Colorado's version of Alpine ski culture. Trapped in a cycle of "training for two weeks," after which they "couldn't wait to get out of camp," soldiers from Camp Hale spent their free weekends with their wives, partying in Denver, skiing, or some mixture of each.[84] The practice of skiing recreationally on the weekends introduced the 10th's cohort of skiers to the community-oriented ski areas of Colorado. Steve Knowlton said, "we all went skiing on the weekends," even if it meant driving all night Friday to get there and all night Sunday to get back before reveille. (Knowlton represented a particularly enthusiastic group of 10th Mountain Division skiers.) Winter Park, Steamboat Springs, and Aspen were the favorites, though a trip across state lines to Salt Lake City and Alta was not out of the question.[85] Colorado ski areas that stayed open during the war and were accessible from Camp Hale found themselves inundated by soldiers on the weekends. Members of the 10th experimented with the best way to ride Climax's idiosyncratic rope tow, went home with friends like Gordy Wren to Steamboat Springs, and competed in races there and at Winter Park and Aspen. Winter Park sponsored a special "civilian race" in January 1943, pitting a team from the 10th Mountain Division against a team of other racers.[86]

Aspen, with its Roch Run and little boat tow, especially benefited from the soldiers' enthusiasm for skiing. In the words of one local, "every weekend the place was full of skiers and GIs that came over . . . there was a lot going on."[87] Those who had had enough skiing at Camp Hale came to socialize. A night at the Jerome Hotel cost $1 then, and meals were 50¢; the nightlife centered around the Jerome bar and an occasional community dance at the armory. Percy Rideout, an ex-Dartmouth skier who coached the college's team for a year after its European coach was drafted, said simply, "it was fun to come and hang around the Jerome Hotel and drink cruds." Composed of a vanilla milkshake with anywhere from one to six shots of whiskey, Aspen cruds were all the rage. "It was healthy," Rideout insisted, "and it made the weekend interesting."[88]

Fighting in Italy turned skiing in Colorado into a fond memory. Under the leadership of Major General George Hays, the division entered the war in February 1945.[89] Their main points of battle were on Riva Ridge and Mt. Belvedere, from which the Germans controlled the rich agricultural lands of the Po Valley. This position also gave the Germans observation of Highway 64, one of two main supply routes to the central Italian front, thereby preventing an Allied offensive up that road. The Germans had repulsed at least two earlier attempts to take Mt. Belvedere, and their position on Riva Ridge allowed them to direct artillery onto advancing troops. General Hays thus proposed an assault on Riva Ridge, which had previously been considered unclimbable. On the night of February 18, after hiding in nearby farmhouses and planning their routes of ascent, members of the 86th Regiment silently scaled 1,500-foot Riva Ridge, surprising the Germans above and taking control of the ridge the next day. While the 86th held Riva Ridge against seven German counterattacks in the next two days, the 87th and the 85th attacked Mt. Belvedere and the peaks nearby. It took four days to control Mt. Belvedere and longer to secure the surrounding ridge of mountains. During those days, the brutality of war made itself clear. More than one GI told another, "I wish we had that bastard Dole over here now." By the middle of March, the 10th secured the region. After a short rest, the mountain troops broke through the final German resistance in mid-April and spearheaded the 5th

Army's attack up the Po Valley. Moving so fast that they had no flank protection and sometimes led the 5th Army by thirty or forty miles, the 10th Mountain Division crossed the Po River and reached Lake Garda right on the Germans' heels. On May 2, a few days after the battle at Lake Garda, the German commander in Italy surrendered all his troops. Their celebration tempered with loss, soldiers of the 10th Mountain Division shipped out of Italy back to the United States in late July, 992 of their 14,300 members dead and more than 4,000 wounded.

The 10th Mountain was the last division sent to Europe and the first to be shipped home after the war's end. Some observers wondered why they had not been called on earlier; others believed that the war was effectively over by the time they arrived; and the respect they enjoyed as elite mountain troops did not seem fair to soldiers who had endured much longer stays on the European front. Still, members of the 10th led the 5th Army drive and helped bring a quick end to the war in Italy. In letters home then and in reminiscences well afterward, they showed intense pride in their division.[90] Regardless of how one interprets the strategic impact of the 10th Mountain Division, there is no doubt that its veterans experienced the full onslaught of war. Of the eight divisions in the 5th Army during the push up the Po Valley, the 10th suffered one-third of the casualties. The death of close friends, a landscape devastated by artillery and mortar shells, and the gruesome realities of battle all affected the mountain soldiers. Their experience of war isolated them — just as it has isolated soldiers before and since — and unified them as people who have seen too much. "Only a front line soldier can understand a front line soldier," William Douglas wrote to his uncle in March 1945. "I find it absolutely impossible to write home of the war. It is impossible to give the greatness of the whole thing. It is muddy. It is dirty. Nobody likes it. It can be funny at times. But above all, it is big."[91]

Once they were home and deactivated, members of the 10th Mountain Division spread out across the country. They left, however, a network of fellow soldiers crafted by a common love of outdoor activity, years of training together at Camp Hale, and combat experience in Italy. As one veteran put it, the 10th Mountain Division "was not an army, it was a fraternity. It was a brotherhood of outdoorsmen. It was a vivid life experience, and one we treasure, still."[92] Their group identity emerged directly from a specific set of physical experiences in distinct landscapes. It fostered a lively organization of veterans, and it had a large influence on Colorado's postwar ski industry.

Home for some and a second home to all, the Rocky Mountains attracted veterans after the war. Friedl Pfeifer wrote that upon looking down on Aspen, "I felt . . . an overwhelming sense of my future before me." And skiing offered an appealing future to veterans who cared more about the outdoors than getting rich. Fritz Benedict said, "the whole concept of living in the mountains was so appealing; whether you made money or not was not important."[93] Aspen became the jumping-off place for 10th Mountain veterans who decided to manage or start up ski areas of their own. Steve Knowlton, Florian Haemmerle, Dick Wright, Hans Hagemeister, Pete Seibert, Len Woods, Curt Chase, and John Jay all spent at least some time there before moving on to other skiing-related projects. In Colorado, 10th Mountain veterans opened Arapahoe Basin; managed Loveland Basin; managed Winter Park and ran its ski school; designed, opened, and operated Vail; started up Ski Broadmoor; and became involved in Powderhorn, Breckenridge, and Howelsen Hill ski areas. According to one estimate, about 2,000 veterans of the 10th became ski instructors across the country, and they founded, managed, or ran the ski schools of sixty-two ski resorts.[94]

Even though they had hardly used their skis at all in Italy, veterans of the 10th represented America's top echelon of skiers and outdoorsmen during the 1940s, and they embodied a corresponding ideal that merged the older European resort culture with one based on military experience. Membership in the 10th and training in Colorado connected these men to an American government and landscape; fighting for the United States and claiming victory over Germany further emphasized their American-ness. So, when they got involved in small Colorado ski areas, they brought a new kind of skiing culture with them, forged out of their physical experiences in the mountains. When combined with the transportation and economic infrastructures already established in the 1930s, the network and culture of 10th Mountain skiers changed the orientation of Colorado skiing. They expanded the focus of the sport from its local, working- and middle-class club roots to include skiers — wealthy and middle-class — from across the country. Their influence, when placed in the context of America's postwar economy and consumer culture, turned isolated mountain communities like Aspen into destination ski resorts.

"CARL HOWELSON" RECORD 171 FEET
STEAMBOAT SPRINGS SKI CARNIVAL
- MARCH 1-2-1917 -
-8-   -OUT WEST PHOTO- BOULDER-

Carl Howelsen poses after Steamboat Springs' 1917 carnival. Coloradans celebrated him as a Norwegian champion and an icon of early ski culture, but he was far from glamorous. Most days he worked as a stonemason. (Tread of Pioneers Museum, Steamboat Springs, Colorado)

Sun Valley's public relations expert Steve Hannagan wanted to connect the resort to images of beautiful people and outdoor leisure. He did it, in part, by spreading this photograph (taken inside a New York studio) across the country. (Sun Valley Resort)

These youngsters incorporated skiing into their daily winter schedules, as did many mountain town children during the 1940s and 1950s. (Grand County Historical Association)

This 1950 view of Aspen Mountain and the town below shows the landscape's natural beauty, the resort's modest development, and the community's rural nature — characteristics that future visitors both sought and threatened. (Denver Public Library, Western History Collection, x-6157, Charles E. Grover)

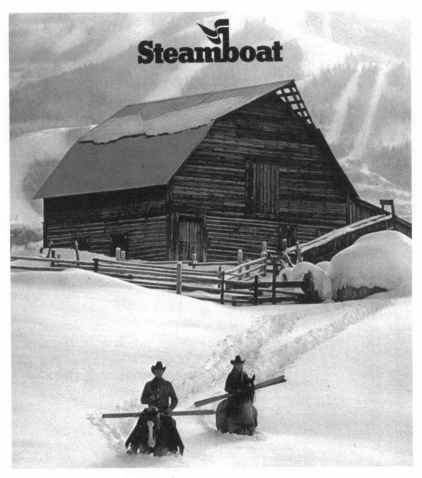

This famous poster, shot in 1973, highlights the combination of western myth, majestic scenery, and romance available at Steamboat. It does not show the housing subdivision that sprouted up in the neighborhood. (Steamboat/Gerald Brimacombe)

Naming a high-speed quad the "Vista Bahn" and calling its new terrain "Blue Sky Basin" are two of Vail's more recent efforts to impose notions of European style and untainted wilderness on rather obvious physical development. (Photo by the author)

This 1960 version of the snow bunny raised the possibility that women skiers could be predators as well as prey, though this "ski wolf" does not look very threatening. (Ski [March 1960]; photo by T. K.)

Female snowboarders expressed a brand of femininity that emphasized athleticism and daring over the feminine form. Here is Shannon Dunn trying out her first pro-model board at Mt. Hood in 1994. (Suzanne Howe, Sick: A Cultural History of Snowboarding *[New York: St. Martin's Griffin, 1998], 127; photo by Jeff Curtes)*

4

Call of the Mild
The New Ski Industry and Its Landscapes

Skiers visiting Aspen commonly rode partway up the back of Aspen Mountain in trucks headed for the Midnight Mine and climbed the rest of the way up the mountain. Reaching the top at lunchtime, they would rest, have a bite to eat and a look around, and then ski down into town. Elizabeth Paepcke's memories of such a trip in 1938 came infused with visions of the mountain landscape. "At the top we halted in frozen admiration," she wrote. "Mountain range after mountain range succeeded another, rising and falling like storm driven waves, crested with streamers of snow blowing straight out from each icy, perpendicular 14,000 foot peak." Intensifying the majesty around her was the impression that she and her group were completely alone in the mountains. "In all that landscape of rock, snow, and ice," she went on, "there was neither print of animal nor track of man. We were alone as though the world had just been created and we its first inhabitants."[1] Not only did the Chicagoan see herself as intimately connected to the mountains and snow around her; she understood that landscape as pristine, wild, empty, and natural.

Long hours of climbing let recreational skiers like Paepcke feel connected to the wilderness of the surrounding mountains, and many frequented ski areas that offered no lifts at all. Through the 1930s and into the 1940s, state ski area directories advertised areas such as Highland Basin, Montezuma Basin, Independence Pass, St. Mary's Glacier, Jones Pass, Hoosier Pass, Allens Park, Ouray, and Rabbit Ears Pass, where skiers were obliged to hike up whatever terrain they wanted to ski down. Indeed, one skier in the 1930s, referring to the increasing appearance of ski lifts, complained that "this way of skiing is so mechanical — you ride up in lifts, up and down, up and down — you don't get the feeling of what it's all about."[2] People continued to hike and climb for better scenery and longer ski runs even after short rope tows became available. More than mere visual beauty, the mountains offered snow, weather, and landscapes that skiers could feel as they moved through them.

During this period, Colorado skiing was a community activity for men and women alike, and successful competitors emerged as local heroes. Membership in the 10th Mountain Division and the experience of World War II translated veterans' skiing into an American act, and those same men helped introduce skiing to a broader slice of the American public after the war. The development of new ski areas with better lifts meant that it took less work to get up mountains — poma lifts and chairlifts, respectively, pulled and carried skiers up more easily than rope tows could — but the money, labor, and machinery needed to accomplish this feat transformed recreational skiing into a business as well as a sport. Postwar skiers shared feelings of exhilaration and a connection to the mountains with earlier enthusiasts, but they experienced the sport in an increasingly built and corporate setting.

The Aspen Skiing Corporation embraced lift construction with much fanfare. One sunny Saturday in January 1947, businessmen from Denver, Colorado Springs, Chicago, and Washington; famous skiers; 10th Mountain Division veterans; and the governor-elect of Colorado joined Aspen townspeople at the base of Aspen Mountain for the opening of Aspen's Lift No. 1.[3] Set in motion with the push of a button, it carried skiers a mile and a half through the air and up 2,200 feet, where, after a short hop on Lift No. 2, they could enjoy the scenery from the top of the mountain, have a snack at the Sundeck, and ski down the famous Roch Run. The world's longest chairlift at the time, and the fastest (moving 275 skiers an hour), Lift No. 1 introduced masses of people to the joys, thrills, and fears of skiing. Two locals guessed that a good skier, equipped with "a stout heart and seven spare legs," could ski 38,000 vertical feet in a day.[4]

With the development of chairlifts like the one in Aspen, Colorado's postwar ski areas offered skiing to far more people than ever before. Presenting an empty, pristine, wild, and natural landscape paradoxically became a business, with mechanization not just a necessity but a boon. This transition

Aspen's Lift No. 1 thrust machinery into a landscape that skiers imagined as natural and pristine, but it did not seem to spoil the view. (Aspen Historical Society)

placed feelings of freedom, exhilaration, and personal connection to the mountains — feelings central to the sport and responsible for its widespread appeal — in danger. Ski area developers and managers found themselves selling what had been an intensely personal experience to as many people as possible. The physical construction of lifts, lodges, and base areas directly altered Colorado's mountain landscape, and they attracted customers to such a degree that skiers' once fairly intimate relationship to mountain ski trails, scenery, and snow could not last. Area developers tried to restore skiers' cherished relationship to the landscape through an increasingly constructed and built environment, imprinting it with illusions of wilderness and selling it for the cost of a lift ticket. Doing so increased the tension between the physical experience of skiing, previously available to only a few, and the acts of consumption from which postwar ski areas made their money. When they skied such mechanized, managed, and commodified mountains, skiers experienced a different kind of freedom and exhilaration than their prewar counterparts — one that was individual and physical, but also one that the ski industry had crafted and packaged for sale.

Colorado's Postwar Ski Areas

"When the war is over," one skier prophesied, "youngsters will come streaming back, keened up for the sport far beyond anything we have ever seen in the past." Soldiers, too, would seek the limitless scenery, bright sky, and fresh air of skiing, this person argued. "When the lads begin shucking their olive drab and navy blues, . . . they'll want a pile of individual freedom, quite aside from that they are fighting for now to win for the nation. You'll see our hills thronged as never before."[5] He was right. Ski areas that had been closed for the duration reopened, along with brand new ones. Mountain residents, many of whom had skied throughout the war, approached the sport with renewed enthusiasm. Relieved of wartime stress and optimistic about good times ahead, Americans who had never worn skis traveled to the mountains for vacation and took up the sport.

National changes in consumption, leisure, and travel encouraged this trend, and American businessmen knew it. Without wartime demands on technology and materials, private enterprise had room to grow in new directions. After World War II, skiers who decided to turn the sport into their livelihood — often 10th Mountain Division veterans — sought and found investors willing to help them develop new areas or improve old ones. Armed with new leadership, financing, technology, and more potential customers than ever before, Colorado skiing developed from a community activity into part of a national industry.

The Aspen Skiing Corporation (ASC) first illustrated this change. The ASC represented an alliance among 10th Mountain Division veterans and businessmen from all over the country. Friedl Pfeifer first formed the ASC and tried to develop the area himself after the war, but he could not find sufficient financial backing until he won the support of Chicago businessman Walter Paepcke, who wanted to re-create Aspen as a cultural center.[6] In return for Paepcke's help in raising money to develop the ski area, plus 25,000 shares of stock and exclusive rights to run the ski school, Pfeifer gave up control of the ASC. The company attracted investors, including Paepcke's brother-in-law Paul Nitze of the State Department, future president of Denver's Colorado National Bank George Berger, Denver attorney William Hodges, Colorado Springs businessman and close friend of the Paepckes Eugene Lilly, and executive vice president of the Hilton Hotel chain Joseph Binns, as well as local landholder D. R. C. "Darcy" Brown and Minot Dole, founder of the National Ski Patrol and the 10th Mountain Division. Together they owned or sold $250,000 worth of stock in the company to build the chairlifts; by the end of May 1947, the ASC owned total assets of over $345,000.[7]

The ASC's corporate growth was accompanied by an influx of 10th Mountain Division veterans to Aspen after the war. John Litchfield and Percy Rideout ran the ski school, along with Friedl Pfeifer; Steve Knowlton helped cut new trails in the summer and trained for the 1948 Olympics in the winter; and Pete Seibert joined the ski patrol and monitored the slopes, hoping to learn enough in Aspen to start his own resort someday.[8] The businessmen and army veterans who converged on Aspen added their talents, money, and energy to that of the local community. Longtime Aspen residents, many from families who had moved to town during its mining boom, provided labor, technical knowledge, and community support for the ASC's projects.[9] Aspen Mountain's Lift No. 1, a huge cultural event organized by Walter Paepcke in the summer of 1949, and the World Alpine Championships, hosted for the first time in the United States at Aspen in 1950, won national media attention for the town and its young ski resort. Skiers from

Denver, Chicago, Sun Valley, and New York showed up to see what Aspen was like for themselves. With its organization, technology, management, and out-of-state customers, Aspen's ski area outgrew every prewar resort except for Sun Valley.

Other ski areas in Colorado adopted new financing and technology to support their own growth. Berthoud Pass reopened for business with only two rope tows, but by December 1947, the area's manager-operator had financed, installed, and opened the world's first double chairlift.[10] Similarly innovative was Steamboat Springs' Emerald Mountain lift, which interspersed chairs and T-bars on "the world's longest single-span ski lift." Financed by city revenue bonds and costing roughly $100,000, this lift officially opened for business in February 1948, with Colorado's governor, town dignitaries, and a large crowd looking on.[11] In response to its own ski area's growth and the accompanying need for greater financial structure, the city of Denver created the Winter Park Recreational Association, a nonprofit corporation that took over control of the area's planning, development, financing, mortgaging, and personnel.[12]

Brand new ski areas also took shape after the war. In May 1946, 10th Mountain veteran Larry Jump, along with his friend Sandy Schauffler, local property owner Max Dercum, ski legend Dick Durrance, and Denver ski manufacturer Thor Groswold, formed Arapahoe Basin, Inc. Financed by the original incorporators, the sale of 150,000 shares of stock, and a loan from the Reconstruction Finance Corporation, Arapahoe Basin opened for the 1947–48 season with two chairlifts, a rope tow, and a shelter complete with a lunch counter and a stall that doubled as the ski shop and the ski school office.[13] Without a town or overnight accommodations at their bases, places like Arapahoe Basin catered to day skiers rather than the destination skiers who traveled to Aspen and stayed for a week or more. Their directors and managers shared, however, the assumption that thousands of Americans would soon take up skiing. They were right. Americans flocked to Colorado on ski vacations. The number of visits to many resorts doubled and tripled in the decades after World War II. The most spectacular example was Vail, which entertained 310 skier-visits during its first season in 1962–63 and had reached 189,000 by 1966.[14]

Physical development both enabled and accompanied such growth. New and improved ski areas replaced rope tows with speedy chairlifts, T-bars, and poma lifts; areas with no tows at all disappeared from state listings. Between

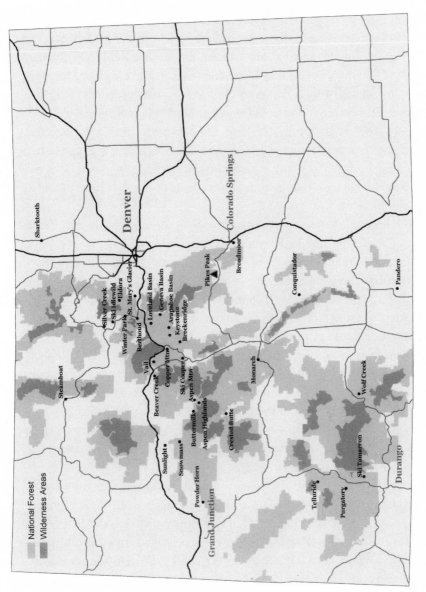

Major ski areas, national forests, and wilderness areas

1957 and 1961, such places as Aspen Highlands, Buttermilk, Crested Butte, Breckenridge, Ski Broadmoor, and Cuchara Basin opened for business. By 1966, Vail, Steamboat Springs' Mt. Werner, Eldora near Boulder, Purgatory outside of Durango, Sunlight in Glenwood Springs, and Meadow Mountain near Vail had added their names to the state's winter tourism and ski area directory; Snowmass-at-Aspen followed on their heels and opened in 1967.[15] These ski areas ranged from ritzy destination resorts to small areas targeting local clientele. Some opened only for weekends and holidays with one or two lifts; others operated as many as seven lifts all season long. Most, however, were new. By 1966, only seven of the thirty areas in the state had welcomed skiers in the 1930s.[16]

No longer was Colorado skiing only a local, community activity. Tenth Mountain veterans' national reputations, new financing and business organization, and the development of longer and faster ski lifts attracted more skiers than ever before. Residents from all over the state, as well as people from other parts of the country, took up the sport and came to Colorado. Out-of-state skiers spent an estimated $3 million in Colorado during the 1955–56 season and accounted for more than 30 percent of the state's ski business the next year; by 1966–67, their spending reached $41 million.[17] These numbers describe a sport increasingly accessible to people both outside of Colorado and outside of skiing's elite resort culture. Aspen ski instructor Fred Iselin remembered in 1968 that "in the 1940s people came to Sun Valley like they would go to Kenya on safari — it was new, challenging, an adventure. . . . It's better now," he explained, "because [skiing is] for the masses and then it was only for the people who were wealthy."[18]

America's postwar consumer culture and the nationwide growth of tourism, combined with the start of the ski industry, meant that people no longer had to belong to an elite club or live in a mountain town to ski. Most people had more money after World War II. The average American's income in 1960 was a third higher than it had been in 1945, and many had savings left unspent during the war. Americans bought new cars — 58 million of them during the 1950s — and they enjoyed more leisure time.[19] For many Americans after World War II, vacation meant getting in the car and seeing the country with the family. Visits to Colorado's national forests more than tripled from 1945 to 1947 and doubled again by the mid-1950s.[20] An accompanying "unprecedented flood of traffic" swamped Colorado's roads after 1945, forcing the state government to reorganize its highway system. By 1952, U.S. 40 and U.S. 6 swept cars over Berthoud and Rabbit Ears Passes and Loveland and Vail Passes, respectively.[21] In 1956, a federal act authorized and funded a system of divided, limited-access freeways across the country. The new interstate highways and the rise of air travel after the war made Colorado's Rockies a reasonable destination for middle-class Americans across the country, increasing physical access to ski areas and making ski vacations affordable to many. Cheap army surplus equipment meant that skiers could outfit themselves with skis, boots, bindings, and even pants and a parka for less than $25, and thousands did.

Outdoor recreation and leisure were not only easier after World War II, they were also morally sound. Buying cars, gas, and consumer goods supported the American economy and therefore the Cold War effort against communism; seasonal vacations featuring healthy, outdoor recreation strengthened America's nuclear families against foreign threats; and the growing popularity of sports such as skiing, tennis, and golf implied that (in contrast to the Soviet Union) America's middle classes were indeed upwardly mobile. Taking a ski vacation came to represent much more than physical exhilaration or membership in a particular community or club after World War II; it became an American activity in scope and in meaning, attached at least implicitly to notions of leisure, consumption, and liberation that appealed broadly to middle-class Americans of the time. According to one chronicler, "The socio-economic force of the leisure boom [in the 1950s] changed American skiing in less than a decade from a slightly eccentric preoccupation of a few thousand people to a mass participation sport with the number of participants exceeding a half million."[22]

Nor did they have to be especially rugged to enjoy the sport. After World War II, technological advances in ski equipment made the sport easier to learn. Army surplus skis and bindings were cheap, but aircraft engineer Howard Head drastically improved ski performance when he developed a metal ski in 1950. Lighter and easier to turn than wooden ones, metal skis found a solid niche in the American market by the early 1960s. A few years later, fiberglass skis hit the market, furthering the development and success of new ski equipment. Binding technology, too, advanced quickly in the decades following World War II. In the 1950s, cable "beartrap" bindings gave way to step-in "safety" bindings built to release during dangerous falls, easing the fears of timid skiers as well as improving their control over their skis. Similarly, new boots that were stiffer and higher provided more control than the leather lace-up boots typical of the 1940s. The first leather buckle boot sold in 1955. Plastic Lange boots appeared ten years later, earning kudos from European racers, who called them "les Plastiques Fantastiques."[23] By improving the connection between a skier's feet and the snow, the new equipment developed in the 1950s and 1960s helped people learn more easily, turn more quickly, ski faster, gain confidence, and ultimately have more fun skiing.

Ski lifts served a similar function, mediating skiers' relationship to the mountain and increasing access to the sport. As new equipment lessened the requirement for toughness while going down the mountain, lifts lessened it on the way up. Ski lifts and tows wiped hours of hiking off a skier's itinerary; chairlift and T-bar technology could make trips up the mountain downright relaxing.[24] Getting people up the mountain farther, faster, and easier thus became a main goal for ski area developers. In 1966, Aspen Mountain, then boasting seven lifts, could move more than 5,000 skiers in an hour, as could Arapahoe Basin, Aspen Highlands, Breckenridge, Loveland Basin, Vail, and Winter Park.[25] Whether as a cause or as a result of Colorado's growing ski industry — or more likely both — lift construction and ski area expansion did not slow down until the mid-1970s.[26] Technological advances in equipment and lifts attracted new skiers because they made the sport physically easier. Together with the consumer culture of the Cold War, they made the freedom that people associated with skiing more accessible and broadened its meaning. Beyond a purely physical and individual sense of freedom, skiing now included the freedom from hiking up mountains and the freedom to buy new products, take a vacation, and enjoy the outdoors.

Constructed Ski Area Landscapes

Ski area development and lift construction further changed how skiers experienced the mountain landscape. Owners could not replicate what it felt like to climb up mountains on foot and to ski down one or two runs in a day, nor did they want to. They built trails, lifts, and lodges to accentuate the attractive aspects of that experience and simultaneously make it accessible to as many skiers as possible. Skiers continued to feel exhilarated, free, and connected to the wilderness, but within a landscape that managers designed and controlled to remove the work, risk, and inconvenience that had once accompanied such feelings.

Successful ski resorts had to build lifts and fill them up with customers. These skiers could not actually be alone in undeveloped mountains, but resort designers could help them feel that way by offering them plenty of scenic views. Creating visions of presumably wild, empty, and pristine mountains thus became a priority at new ski areas. Lodges and restaurants sprouted up accordingly — even on mountaintops — featuring picture windows and architectural equivalents to the highway signs that announce "scenic overlook" to every passing vehicle. Arapahoe Basin built its Snow Plume Refuge atop a narrow ridge, so "its huge picture windows [could] . . . revel in the splendid panorama of the Gore Range, Tenmile Range, and the Mount of the Holy Cross far to the West."[27] Chairlifts and gondolas, too, offered riders aerial visions of impressive landscapes on every ride. Even the U.S. Forest Service, in its *Planning Considerations for Winter Sports Resort Development*, recognized that "lifts should be located to serve the best skiing terrain," and "seldom should the type of lift dictate the location of ski trails," but it admitted that "a lift intended to provide both ski trail access and scenic views for summer [and presumably winter] tourists is one exception to this principle."[28] Ski area planners had been noting that exception for some time. One developer of Snowmass attributed the resort's first-year success to its scenic appeal. By virtue of its terrain and lift placement, "even the weaker skiers . . . can get to the top of Elk Camp and the Burn, and it's almost as if they can get a Sir Edmund Hillary complex," he said; "they're on top of the world."[29]

Skiers — even those who had once hiked to ski — appreciated the views from lifts. "To be able to ride the lift at Berthoud," one CMC member recalled, "and get that view down the west side of the Indian Peaks, was a great thrill. I looked forward to each ride because I could get that view." Nor was that treat limited to skiing at Berthoud. "[It] was the same thing at Winter Park or any of the lifts. To be able to ski Aspen Highlands and get a look at the [Maroon] Bells and Pyramid at the top of the mountain, those are wonderful, important parts of the experience for me."[30] Lifts offered better and more frequent views than hikers could enjoy. They increased the impact of mountain scenery and transformed skiers' relationship to the landscape in the process. Skiers saw the mountains from a new and more comfortable position; dramatic "untouched" mountains became distant but real western wilderness.

Skiers still sought "wild" and "natural" landscapes, but few were willing to hike to reach them. Increasingly accessible by cars and then lifts, mountains' definition as wild and natural became more and more relative. The Forest Service encouraged ski areas to literally cultivate the image of a romantic, wild, "natural" landscape for summer visitors. "When they ride chairlifts or gondolas," the agency advised, "vegetation on ski trails should not only look as if it is not eroding, but should look natural and perhaps even be covered with native wildflowers."[31] Erosion itself was apparently not problematic, as long as mountain trails looked natural and healthy. City dwellers especially confused the image of pristine "nature" with that of "scenic mountain landscapes," sometimes with the help of the ski industry. One marketing director wrote, "The more hectic cities become, the greater the drive toward Nature, a reward for skiers." He went on to equate nature to "the vast sweep of snowbowls, the play of sun and shade, [and] the changing colors of the winter sky at dusk."[32] Even if skiers stood in a clearly developed ski area, at least they could see that a wilder and more pristine landscape existed on the other side of the ski area boundary.

Skiers experienced the landscape through their eyes, but they also connected with the mountains through their feet. Views from lifts mesmerized passengers on their way up the mountain, overpowering the visual impact of lifts, lodges, and access roads around them. Only on their skis, however, flowing through the snow and trees and transfixed by that feeling, could skiers believe that they were "in synchrony with the mountains and the snow," embraced by a "natural" landscape that, if they were to stop and look around, flashed "man-made" like a neon sign. The freedom, creativity, and exhilaration that skiers experienced through their sport created a dynamic and intense connection between skier and mountain. Ski area developers found themselves challenged to foster that connection — one of the most personal as well as appealing aspects of skiing — for large audiences.

In the years immediately after the war, there were few experts at cutting trails. Tools and techniques for clearing ski trails had yet to be developed, where to cut them seemed straightforward, and local skiers did most of the work. Andre Roch had laid out Aspen's famous Roch Run in 1937 and then left the townspeople to cut the trail. Tenth Mountain Division veterans helped Friedl Pfeifer and the local ski club clear two new short runs in honor of the grand opening in 1946. Two years later, Aspen Ski Club members continued to appeal to "members and friends of skiing" to help clear brush from the trails on Aspen Mountain.[33] These runs, according to ski instructor and 10th Mountain veteran John Litchfield, were "just plain a labor of love by the people that lived there."[34] Locals continued to pitch in when area manager Dick Durrance decided to open up the terrain and cut Ruthie's Run in 1949. "All we did," he said, "was simply go up to the top of the mountain and mark a very wide stretch and chop trees down."[35]

Simply cutting down trees was enough to build more trails, but planning them out took more thought. Roch Run had earned a national reputation among downhill competitors even before the war — Roch had designed it as a racing trail — but Pfeifer and Durrance knew that they would have to cut some easier trails to sell more lift tickets. Although Pfeifer designed some bypass runs so that less experienced skiers could avoid Roch Run's steepest sections, that was not always enough. Steve Knowlton recalled observing one woman descend the trail that first year the chairlifts were open. "She was sliding down the corkscrew with her hands out in front of her," he remembered, "and she was yelling, 'You son of a bitch, why did you bring me here!'"[36] This was not quite the experience that the ASC was hoping to foster. A few years later, ski instructor Fred Iselin convinced the corporation to bulldoze Spar and Copper Gulches into bowls, smoothing the terrain and opening it up to less experienced skiers. "Having done that," one ASC director recalled, "you couldn't keep the skiers away — it was the best damned skiing in the world."[37] Area developers caught on fast. People wanted nonthreatening terrain, one instructor and planner explained. Another instructor agreed: "Those intermediate slopes are really what pays the freight — those are the slopes that get people interested in the sport."[38] Building a ski industry, after all, required attracting new skiers to the sport and to Colorado; areas needed trails to accommodate their numbers and their skill levels.

Trail designers shaped mountains and skiers' relationship to those mountains. Cutting trees and brush and bulldozing new trails and access roads characterized most trail development until the 1970s.[39] Caught in the contradiction of selling a personal, intimate experience to as many people as possible, ski area developers tried to create trails that would lessen the impact of crowds. When Friedl Pfeifer cut the first new runs on Aspen Mountain for its grand opening under the ASC, he said that he "[removed] trees only when necessary [and] left much of the mountain untouched, so that skiing would feel like a backcountry tour."[40] Twenty-five years later, the U.S. Forest Service recommended such planning for all ski areas. "If a mountain is designed permitting inter-connecting, but separate ski run systems," the Forest Service pointed out, "a skier can have the feeling of isolation and freedom of congestion."[41] Efforts proved largely successful. "Despite thousands of new skiers annually who flood the [Colorado] mountains," one skier insisted in 1968, "there are still slopes and trails where a skier can feel almost alone in the white wilderness."[42] His comment spoke to the amount of space still open at Colorado resorts, but also to the slopes themselves. Designers consciously shaped ski trails to help skiers feel as if they were alone, personally interacting with the mountain. They wanted skiers to forget that they were in a designed, planned, man-made, and often crowded landscape. Ironically, they constricted skiers' vision in order to heighten the sense of freedom and unrestricted movement.

Trail designers tried to emphasize skiers' feelings of freedom and exhilaration through the shape of the trails as well as through their visual impact. Along with framing views or masking crowds, popular ski trails romanced skiers with their terrain. "Variety is key," Chet Anderson, designer of Purgatory, explained. Good trails needed steep and shallow pitches, room for cruising, and transitions between types of terrain. "That," he said, "is what can make it sensual."[43] One well-known instructor agreed, comparing such terrain to the human body and encouraging students to "caress the mountain, as you would a lover."[44] With mountains as their medium, good trail designers thus shared with artists the goal of creating a work that would elicit a flash of emotion, a work that people could return to again and again, experiencing it differently each time. A few of them became acknowledged masters. Pfeifer's design of Aspen Mountain "had a rhythm you would feel," remembered racer Steve Knowlton. More interesting than Aspen Highlands, Snowmass, or Vail, according to one well-traveled ski instructor, Aspen Mountain "is really a very romantic mountain." "Friedl did a masterful job in making runs and outruns and dips and changes in the terrain — where it would turn a little bit and romance [sic] and turn a little bit and go down, and you could have a rest." Big resorts such as Snowmass and Vail have more space, he continued, but "you don't feel like your blood is stirring up" there.[45] Different ski areas thus developed their own characters, based in part on how their trails felt.

Even skiers' connection to the snow itself changed with the advent of the ski industry. Before lifts dotted the landscape and skiers peppered the slopes, every day could be a powder day. No matter where one skied, there was usually room for more fresh tracks. On bad days, soft, heavy snow, perhaps rutted from earlier skiers, presented obstacles that skiers accepted as part of the sport. Racers who wanted a smooth course joined friends, colleagues, and volunteers arm in arm for a hike up the trail, "boot packing" the run. Once the general public began to frequent ski areas, the snow began to show some wear and tear. The holes fallen skiers left behind in the snow became a common problem. Roughly equivalent to divots on a golf course, these sitzmarks needed filling. Before the war, skiers tended to accept individual responsibility for such repairs. Many new enthusiasts, however, ignored such chores, since they increasingly understood the sport as distinct from and free of work. In 1948, one ski patrolman approached thirty-two fallen skiers and asked if they would help him fill up their sitzmarks. "Of the 32," he reported, "eight helped willingly; four grudgingly; and 20 blew [me] various and sundry types of 'birds' and pushed off to their next fall."[46]

With the introduction of better equipment and shorter skis in the 1960s, and the continual increase in traffic on the slopes, moguls overtook sitzmarks as the meanest snow hazard. These fields of snow mounds, created by skiers repeatedly turning in the same places, tripped up quite a few skiers and annoyed even more. As early as 1948, it became apparent that masses of skiers could not be let loose on the slopes without causing snow conditions to deteriorate.

As with other problems caused by increased participation in the sport, ski area operators discovered a way to mitigate, mediate, and manage the problem away. When lifts and lodges took away the "natural" feel of the immediate landscape, developers pointed skiers toward breathtaking views of the neighboring mountains instead. When crowds of skiers left holes and moguls behind them, the ski industry took up "snow grooming." Steve Bradley, manager of Winter Park after the war, invented the country's first snow grooming tool and accordingly became known as the "Father of Slope Maintenance."[47] His "Bradley Packer," which he designed in 1951 and continued to modify, smoothed the snow as ski patrollers pulled the contraption behind them. About ten years later, at Loveland Basin, Gordon Wren developed another early grooming machine pulled by an all-terrain snow-cat machine.[48]

Area owners and managers thus found themselves in the business of smoothing trails as well as designing and cutting them.

Postwar ski areas continued to take on new responsibilities in the interest of attracting more customers, solving — or at least changing — the problems that accompanied skiers' increasing consumption of the mountain landscape. By the late 1950s, ski areas had so much invested in providing a good experience for their customers that they could not afford to depend on the weather for their most valuable resource — snow.[49] One or two lean seasons could hurt even the most successful areas beyond hope of recovery. Ski area owners and managers knew this all too well. Consequently, when the Rocky Mountain Ski Area Operators' Association met in 1963, one member brought up "the question of starting our own weather modification program." He "suggested that some money be spent in investigating the effect of [weather modification] and the means to accomplish localized storms when conditions are right." The group agreed, budgeting $500 for cloud seeding and making plans to look into long-range forecasting as well.[50] Experts in the field, however, soon crushed their hopes. "No one can today speak with authority regarding the feasibility of cloud seeding to increase snow cover," a scientist from the National Center for Atmospheric Research wrote to the association. "The circumstances in respect to long range forecasts are not very much more helpful." "If I were in your shoes," he said, "I would regard the forecast as pretty much a random guess."[51]

Faced with huge financial losses should the snow refuse to fall, ski area operators turned to making snow for themselves. "Guaranteed snow! Think of it!" *Ski* magazine declared in 1957. An engineering firm in Massachusetts, originally involved in irrigation equipment, had developed a snowmaking system that one eastern ski area used profitably that year. "Snow-making promises to take the weather risk out of skiing," the article claimed, for skiers, area operators, and "everyone with a recreational or commercial interest in the sport."[52] Although this technology helped primarily ski areas in the East and Midwest (which were at relatively low elevations), Colorado resorts occasionally needed a few more inches than the weather provided. Magic Mountain outside Denver led the way in the late 1950s when Earl Eaton installed a snowmaking system there, followed by Ski Broadmoor, a small area that catered to skiers in Colorado Springs. In addition to boosting lower Front Range ski areas' snow cover, snowmaking could lengthen the season. By 1968,

Loveland Basin was using man-made snow to open in mid-October, a month before other areas.[53]

Bad snow years still caught most Colorado resorts unprepared, however. Vail and Purgatory each hired Eddie Box and his Southern Ute Ceremonial Dancers to relieve dangerous droughts by performing a "snow dance" for them. He and his group solved the areas' worries when their dances brought results — delaying, perhaps, the decision to purchase snowmaking equipment.[54] After the devastatingly dry 1976–77 snow season, however, most big Colorado areas invested in the technology. They had too much at stake, by that point, to do otherwise. The growth of snowmaking in Colorado represented yet another ski industry investment designed to ensure its continued popularity and growth. It also added another element to the built environment of ski areas, visible in snow guns, hoses, and the weird hills of snow they spewed (which people then used machines to groom). Finally, man-made snow altered human relationships to the weather. Ski area operators could manufacture a "natural" resource on which they depended, and skiers could plan their vacations, increasingly assured that the ski area would arrange everything for them.

Dangerous Landscapes and the National Ski Patrol

Skiers wanted snow under their feet. Great views and "romantic" trails were an added plus. Postwar ski areas provided these things in the interest of improving business. How skiers behaved at ski areas, however, remained up to them. Contemplative skiers cruised, glided, and stopped to admire the scenery. More adventuresome types sought that exhilarating high available only through speed. Quite a number did both, according to their mood. This caused yet another problem for the ski industry: crowds of creative and willful individuals on one mountain spelled danger. Complicating the situation was the fact that, for many, the appeal of the sport hinged on an element of risk.

Early skiers recognized the risks of playing in the mountains. "Death," outdoorswoman Dolores LaChapelle wrote, "is an ever present possibility in the powder snow world as the snow . . . when too deep or unstable, is drawn down by the gravity of the earth, and this mutual appropriation of the one to the other is called *avalanche*."[55] Mail carriers and nineteenth-century travelers accepted avalanches and extreme weather as dangers that they would face in their journeys, and occasional obituaries testified to the reality of those risks. Recreational skiers in the 1920s and 1930s, skiing on scenic mountain passes in small groups, similarly recognized the hazards of their sport. They accepted those risks in exchange for the chance to be outdoors in a rugged mountain landscape. Indeed, embracing danger helped define them as outdoorsmen and -women. They had to accept those risks, moreover, because there was no one else to do it for them. Elizabeth Paepcke had a guide on her 1938 trip down Aspen Mountain, yet the very act of hiring a guide showed that she acknowledged the dangers of skiing. She recalled that "it snowed silently as we followed the faint outlines of a logging road through forests broken by outcroppings of rock and an occasional meadow. When we came to a steep bank of snow," she continued, "our guide proceeded alone, testing every step with his ski pole. Only after crossing safely himself were we allowed to make the traverse, one by one. No one spoke or made the slightest noise in fear that the vibration of a voice should send us and the entire mass avalanching down the mountainside."[56] This real danger heightened the wilderness experience that skiing represented for city-bred Paepcke, adding a level of excitement that set skiing apart from other kinds of recreation.

For urban and suburban businessmen, skiing and its dangers offered an opportunity to get outdoors that contrasted favorably with their day jobs. When invited on a ski trip in 1933, for instance, Minot Dole wrote, "I was a family man, settled, a commuter, and so on. There was no reason at all why an expedition to the colds of Lake Placid should stir my blood a bit. But there it was," he remembered, "I could hardly wait." Trying to explain his feelings, Dole said, "That is modern man's dilemma: the occasion of security gives rise to the desire for adventure. That is something that the civilized American is not likely to have much of." He concluded, "The mushrooming of the sport of skiing owes a lot to the lack of adventure in the life of today's Everyman."[57] In this instance, skiing's exhilaration took on meanings associated directly with class. Men who worked outdoors, in "uncivilized" conditions or places, Dole implied, would not need to ski to take risks or prove their manliness.

Aside from avalanches, skiers had to worry most about injury from falls or collisions. Before World War II, one Denver skier remembered, "most skiers were conservative, experienced mountaineers." Accustomed to the local landscape and its dangers, these men (and some women) "were a very self-sufficient group." "As there were no *safety* bindings," he noted, "there was no false sense of safety."[58] These Denver club skiers performed necessary rescue work themselves, including transporting one friend with a broken femur. Skiers faced long, painful journeys before they could get medical help. It was sometimes possible, at popular places like Berthoud Pass, to find a doctor on the slopes to help out. Others were not so lucky. Minot Dole discovered this firsthand while skiing one morning at Stowe, Vermont. A tough fall left him lying in the snow with his ankle "not at the right angle for an ankle." It took until 3:00 for his friends to find help, drag him to the road, and drive him to a doctor, who told him that his ankle was so badly broken he should have it set in New York City rather than in the small Vermont hospital. Even after this harrowing experience, Dole recounted, he did not waver from "the standard fatalism that skiers had, at that time, about ski accidents."[59]

He took a more proactive stance two months later, when a friend who had been with him at Stowe was asked to enter a club race for which he was too inexperienced. Dole advised against it, "but Frank the explorer was too excited about this new possibility to think cogently." Frank died after running into a tree on the edge of the racecourse. His death forced a change in Dole's perspective that would ultimately result in the formation of the National Ski Patrol.[60] Initially, however, skiers argued that each must accept the dangers inherent in the sport. Perhaps attracted by the masculine implications of facing danger head-on, or overcome by the excitement of the sport's risks, a number of skiers responded to Dole's subsequent investigation into ski accidents by calling him and his committee "sissies, spoilsports, and frighteners of mothers."[61] These skiers consciously — and vigorously — defended skiing as inherently and appropriately dangerous.

With increased use of ski areas in the late 1930s, accidents and injuries became more visible. Some skiers behaved as if they would not get hurt no matter what they did. Although Colorado did not suffer its first recreational skiing fatality (other than by avalanche) until two years later, Denver skier Graeme McGowan observed in 1937 that if skiers had "a moderate amount of assured snow, mountains, easy access, and uphill transportation," they would "happily hurl themselves over cliffs or rip trails through jungles."[62] Ski area landscaping and trail design reduced the danger from avalanches and traffic congestion, but skiers' uncontrolled schussing caused most falls and collisions resulting in injury.[63] As more people hit the slopes made accessible by ski tows, a greater variety of skiers mingled there. Each savored the freedom to turn, stop, and schuss where they liked. Wide ski lanes cleared of all trees (common in the 1930s), McGowan argued, "are dangerous not only to the mentally deficient who career wildly down them at speeds far in excess of their ability to control but also to the timid soul who, with panic gripping his heart, 'stems like hell.' How often," he asked rhetorically, "have we seen collisions between these two opposites?"[64] Skiers sitting in the middle of the trail, rearranging their ensemble after a fall, unknowingly offered themselves as targets. Deep footholes left by hiking skiers and larger ones from sit-and-run culprits compounded the problem.[65]

Managing the snow and the shape of the trails could address some problems, but it became increasingly apparent that skiers themselves would need to be managed, too. Minot Dole noticed as early as 1948 that "a great number of mountains were suddenly opened up" by new lift technology. "Where previously only hardy and capable skiers had ventured," he continued, "now, every bunny or basher who had the price of a ticket found him or herself at the top of the mountain with no one to tell him where he could or could not go."[66] Even if someone were to accept that job, telling skiers what to do would prove difficult. "The average American," wrote one observer, "has a desire to enjoy the thrill, dash, and zip experienced in traveling at high speeds. This trait," he continued, "comes out strongly in the novice stage of skiing."[67] Organizing trails into beginner, intermediate, and expert slopes offered skiers guidance without forcing them to slow down, but the problem of skier safety continued to grow.

In response, ski areas relied increasingly on the National Ski Patrol. Established in 1938 by Minot Dole and his colleagues in the Amateur Ski Club of New York, the National Ski Patrol System (NSPS) trained volunteers who were willing to assist accident victims and transport them off the mountain. Local patrolmen who demonstrated "leadership, devotion to patrol work, tact in handling problems of skiers, and practical proficiency in first aid" were eligible for promotion to national status. A national structure and leadership hierarchy unified this volunteer organization: division (regional) chairmen oversaw section chiefs, who in turn took responsibility for local ski club patrols. Recreational skiers across the country quickly learned to look for the distinctive rust-colored jackets of NSPS patrollers when they ran into trouble. Ski area managers, too, appreciated the organization's work and handed out free lift tickets to any member willing to work for the day.[68] After the war, these patrollers were kept busy. The ski industry, in Colorado and elsewhere, embraced the NSPS as the solution to their safety problems. Resorts such as Aspen — too far from a city to depend on volunteers, as New England ski areas did — hired their own professional ski patrollers who were certified and registered with the NSPS. Aspen's 1947–48 ski patrol, for instance, consisted of thirteen men who packed, shoveled, and maintained ski trails; flagged, roped off, or otherwise marked danger spots; patrolled all areas in use; checked all trails at the end of each day for stray skiers; gave "any and all assistance possible to all skiers"; organized and ran recreational races; gave first aid; and evacuated all who suffered injuries.[69]

If that sounds like a lot of work, it was. Aspen's patrol that year sidestepped up and down each trail on their skis to pack a firm base of snow at least once; spent ten days cutting brush, filling holes, and building ramps for the Little Nell lift; put up more than fifty signs and three bulletin boards on the mountain; strung five emergency telephones; gave 121 injured skiers toboggan rides down the mountain; and treated thirty-four fractures, two dislocated shoulders, five lacerations, two knee injuries, and seven people who managed to get punctured by ski poles.[70] As Dole would have predicted, 75 percent of those who suffered fractures were novice skiers. Still, the accident rate was low — especially considering the sense of mounting danger that new postwar skiing crowds fostered. Fifty injuries out of an estimated 21,000 skier-days during the 1947–48 season gave Aspen a 0.2 percent accident rate. Even twenty years later, a report published in *Medical World News* estimated that of about 2 million American skiers, only 12,000 would injure themselves (a 0.6 percent rate). More injuries occurred in waterskiing or hunting, one reporter noted.[71] This level of safety was quite acceptable to ski area managers, who wanted to provide a thrilling but also a safe experience for as many people as possible.

To that end, area owners crafted increasingly managed landscapes for their clientele. They presented wilderness safely to skiers through scenic panoramas; they made and groomed snow to reduce risks from poor snow conditions; they paid attention to traffic patterns and safety concerns in their trail layouts; and they worked to control avalanche danger on their slopes. The NSPS grew along with the ski industry and worked hard to prevent and treat injuries, rescuing skiers from their own love of exhilaration and lack of judgment. Ski areas embraced this organization and its bureaucracy, introducing yet another mediating force between skiers and the mountain landscape. As early as the late 1940s, skiers could have the freedom to ski down mountains without the work of climbing up, the connection to wilderness without the inconvenience and danger of actually being there, and the thrill of skiing fast in a safe, "patrolled" environment.

The U.S. Forest Service and Regulated Skiing Landscapes

Postwar skiers thus enjoyed their sport in a landscape created largely by the ski industry and monitored by the NSPS. Still another layer of policy, bureaucracy, and control of the mountains affected skiers, however, because managers and ski area owners interacted with the U.S. Forest Service and its representatives. Colorado skiers did at least 90 percent of their skiing on federal land in 1946, with every one of the state's developed winter sports sites either on or adjoining national forest or park land.[72] That meant that along with the NSPS, trail designers, ski area developers, and lift engineers, the U.S. Forest Service (USFS) had a say in how skiers experienced the Rocky Mountain landscape.

The relationship between the Forest Service and the ski industry took shape slowly and changed from one of open support in the 1930s to one of control and regulation by the late 1960s. When skiers were few and far between, their use raised few problems, and the USFS signed on as a willing partner in developing small, local ski areas. But when their numbers grew in the late 1930s, the Forest Service began to wonder how best to handle them. "The planning, construction, and maintenance of sufficient facilities to meet the demand for the various forms of winter sports," according to one ranger in 1938, "present to the Forest Service an administrative problem of considerable magnitude." Even then, he noticed that self-reliant outdoors people were being outnumbered by an "increasing army of novices" that required improved skiing landscapes.[73] So the USFS got into the business of parking lot widening, ski trail cutting, and shelter building. "Fortunately," the ranger noted, "most winter sports that are enjoyed by the great mass of winter visitors require only simple facilities, which, if wisely planned, do not measurably mar the intrinsic winter beauty of the National Forests."[74] Within the context of Colorado's local club skiing, this argument rang true. After the war, however, and the subsequent increase in skiing's popularity, skiers would place greater demands on the national forests.

The USFS continued to support skiing despite its increased demands, but no one was quite sure how the Forest Service would figure into the postwar ski industry. "The few skiers in the Forest Service were also feeling their way in a little-understood use of National Forest land," another ranger explained. "In fact," he wrote, "those of us in the agency who skied were considered slightly crazy by the dominant timber and grazing resource-oriented personnel at the time."[75] If the Forest Service did not understand skiers, skiers did not know what to do with the Forest Service, either. Some argued that the USFS, rather than private ski clubs or commercial organizations, ought to administer ski areas on public land.[76] Others agreed that since the national forests were for all to use, and since skiers represented such a growing percentage of that use, the USFS should increase appropriations "to make possible more installations for the winter sports public," which would include clearing trails and slopes; building shelters, warming huts, and comfort stations; and hiring more trained personnel "to care for the throng."[77] One Rocky Mountain forest ranger pointed out in 1948, however, that "today skiing has definitely become [sic] of age; it can stand on its feet, and the need for being subsidized has passed."[78] While the Forest Service continued to plan ski area expansion and development, postwar ski companies such as the Aspen Skiing Corporation and Arapahoe Basin, Inc., took over responsibility for building lifts and making improvements. They developed lodges on private land adjoining national forests and placed the ski industry squarely within the private sector. "The change," the ranger noted, "has resulted in fine ski lifts, better tows, and vastly improved slopes and trails," not to mention "good resort facilities."[79] When the USFS relinquished responsibility for providing facilities for skiers on national forest land and turned it over to corporations, it encouraged the transition away from locally run and club-oriented ski areas and toward the development of a national ski industry.

Even though it stopped building ski lodges, trails, and parking lots, the Forest Service continued to promote skiers' use of the national forests through the 1960s. Policy required ski areas to apply for commercial special-use permits before they cut trails or built on public land. In the years immediately after World War II, the Forest Service made it simple for ski area developers to get the necessary permits and approval. Friedl Pfeifer negotiated the rights to build a chairlift on Aspen Mountain in 1946 with the local ranger. His initial permit was three pages long and set the annual use fee at $10.[80] As only

18 percent of the ski area lay on Forest Service land, subsequent development proceeded with little discussion. The USFS approved Berthoud's double chairlift and Arapahoe Basin's new area, as well as Aspen's lifts and others. Significantly, area managers hardly remember getting such permission. During the 1940s and 1950s, the permit process moved along so quickly and seemed so inconsequential that managers have largely forgotten about it. Dick Durrance, Aspen's manager in the late 1940s, recalled "no Forest Service regulations." When cutting a new trail, he said, "we didn't ask permission, we simply got rid of the trees." As far as lift construction went, Darcy Brown, director and later president of the ASC, recalled, "we just went out and built one — never thought about asking anyone."[81] Even at ski areas wholly on forest land, the USFS rarely interfered with development. Gordon Wren managed Loveland Basin and Steamboat Springs ski areas and remembered, "I never thought about [the area] being on Forest Service land. If we wanted to cut a trail, we'd cut a trail . . . put a lift in . . . that was all there was to it."[82] Even in the early 1960s, when Forest Service concerns rose along with skier populations, Chet Anderson got a permit to develop Purgatory soon after he wrote a slim three-page letter.[83]

The USFS did more to promote skiing on public land than simply granting permits quickly. As they had in the 1920s and 1930s, Forest Service rangers continued to scout out the best places to develop ski areas.[84] The USFS planned where ski areas ought to be for the same reason they planned where roads, logging activity, and grazing ought to be: to coordinate and control the forests' use. Locating the best ski resort sites was equivalent, for the USFS, to choosing the most appropriate grazing ranges or timber lots. Forest Service rangers had first discovered the skiing potential at Arapahoe Basin in 1941. It was about to call for bids on the site in 1946 when the members of Arapahoe Basin, Inc., submitted their proposal to develop the area. The company got its initial permit eleven days later.[85] The main reason to encourage specific projects was to balance demand with available facilities and to make sure that forest resources were not overloaded. Given the popularity of Aspen Mountain by the 1950s, the USFS sought to open another ski resort in the area. Local rangers approached Whip Jones, who had purchased a ranch at nearby Aspen Highlands, and suggested that he develop a ski resort there. Jones got some feasibility reports done, the Forest Service approved them, and Aspen Highlands opened for the 1957–58 season.[86] In the fall of 1959, the

Forest Service presented a comprehensive master plan for Colorado "to keep order in the state's booming ski business." According to USFS calculations, Colorado would need at least two new chairlifts each year to keep up with the current growth in recreational skiing. After surveying potential sites, the Forest Service presented a list of twenty-one that could be developed.[87]

As the ski industry boomed, however, USFS planning and promoting began to seem more like regulation than full-fledged support. The Forest Service set "a target date year by which skiing demand at the current rate will support construction of a new ski area" for each of the proposed sites.[88] Ski corporations, therefore, would not be allowed to build as fast as they might like. In the fall of 1957, snow ranger Paul Hauk field-checked six different proposals for new areas in the White River National Forest alone. Friedl Pfeifer had trouble getting a permit for Buttermilk to open the same season as neighboring Aspen Highlands, because the USFS had already committed to Jones's area and there was "no definite public need for another area" yet.[89]

Forest Service permit fees also became more complicated during these years. Aspen Mountain's permit fee, for instance, jumped from its original $10 in 1946 to $300 plus "one and a half percent of 12% of the net sales for the 76 acres of National Forest land" in 1957. By 1976, the Aspen Skiing Corporation (which by then owned and operated three areas in addition to Aspen Mountain) paid $278,277 to the Forest Service for its use of federal land.[90] Having initially welcomed the cheap use of national forest lands, ski area owners, managers, and developers faced a growing federal bureaucracy as their enthusiasm for new and bigger ski areas outpaced that of the Forest Service.

Once firmly established in the private sector and organized into corporate entities, Colorado ski areas actively sought new business. Colorado Ski Country USA (CSC) sprouted from the Rocky Mountain Ski Area Operators' Association in 1963. CSC got permission to use state funds allocated for advertising skiing and set its objective as "a mutual effort to promote, advertise, and sell skiing, lodging, transportation et al in this area to the world." "Everything I did," recalled CSC's first executive director, Steve Knowlton, "was to get more people to ski."[91] The National Ski Area Association, established in 1962, gave the industry more structure and power. The organization boasted 95 dues-paying members five years later and 554 by 1972.[92] The industry also spawned its own publications. *Skiing Trade News* started in 1964 and focused on business issues; *Ski Area News* enabled area managers to share ideas, technology, and solutions to common problems beginning in 1966.

As the industry gained momentum, its goals of expansion and development came into increasing conflict with a federal government interested in protecting its resources and a public afraid of losing wilderness. In its effort to address these issues broadly, federal legislation further complicated USFS policy for ski areas. First, in 1960, the government declared that no one interest group had priority on federal land — all users had to share. Then it said that some "wilderness areas" should be protected from everyone.[93] And after 1970, federal law required any development on federal land to go through a lengthy environmental review process.

The Forest Service had always influenced where ski areas sprouted up in the Rocky Mountains, since most of them were at least partly on federal land, but by the 1970s, the federal government's role in development had moved from promotion to restriction. This change accompanied Colorado's move away from local community ski areas, run with the aid of agencies such as the USFS, toward an emerging ski industry characterized by corporate ownership, technological advances, developed landscapes, and a national clientele, not to mention a profit motive. As the industry mediated skiers' relationship to the mountains through lifts, trails, snow, and the ski patrol, the Forest Service regulated just where and how fast all that development could happen. Federal policy recognized, moreover, the tensions emerging from the ski industry's efforts to sell freedom, exhilaration, and wilderness to an "army of novices."

Colorado's Destination Resorts

The success of Colorado's postwar ski industry came from its ability to market the experience of skiing to nonskiers. In doing so, the industry transformed the meaning of that experience. The feelings once associated with skiing alone in the mountain wilderness turned into the freedom of skiing down without climbing up, the thrill of speed without risking safety, and access to wilderness from a comfortable chairlift or lodge. The new industrial context for skiing made sense to new skiers because they understood skiing as part of a vacation experience.

What encouraged this transition — and made it possible in the first place — was the sport's corporatization. When 10th Mountain veterans, local skiers, and wealthy investors decided to make a living off skiing by selling it to others, they used new corporate structures, financing, and technology to create their ski areas. This relationship grew in scale during the late 1960s and 1970s along with Colorado's ski industry, and its momentum led to further changes. Ever larger corporations controlled ski areas, combining development of the mountains with that of the base area and the surrounding real estate.

Winter Park historians, for example, characterized the 1970s as a "new era of management refinement, sophistication, and expansion." The area changed its organization in 1975 when it assigned Jerry Groswold the new role of president and chief executive officer (CEO) of the Winter Park Recreation Association.[94] In the next two years, the area installed snowmaking systems worth $1.2 million and $1.4 million; celebrated the opening of its adjoining Mary Jane area, which included four new double chairlifts; and then built a new restaurant and bar, cafeteria, and nursery in 1978.[95]

During this transition, men with business degrees often replaced outdoorsmen and 10th Mountain Division veterans. As one manager put it, "Area managers and presidents [used to be] hard-core mountain men — they knew the mountains and they knew how to construct things on the mountain." Now CEOs and ski area presidents "are good businessmen, who . . . know all aspects of the business from marketing to engineering."[96] This new generation of managers constructed ski landscapes differently from their predecessors, emphasizing amenities above all else. At Steamboat Springs, 10th Mountain Division and Olympic team veteran Gordon Wren managed the Mt. Werner ski area from 1967 to 1970. Already condominiums, lifts, and a new airport studded the landscape. Development really boomed, however, when the Texas firm LTV Aerospace Corporation bought the area in 1970. Wren lost his job. "I think they were glad to get rid of me, and I was glad to leave," he recalled.[97] Able to invest larger sums than the previous local corporation, LTV installed a gondola, five double chairlifts, and three triple chairlifts within ten years. "From bottom to top it's a 15 minute ride," the Los Angeles Times travel editor wrote. Real estate and base area development accompanied new corporate ownership and investment. "Besides the ski rigs," the writer continued, "the Texans built a couple of shopping plazas, a rash of condominiums and a seven-story hotel which the locals call the 'Dallas Palace.'"[98]

Transformations such as this occurred at other Colorado resorts in the 1970s as well. Texas oil man Harry Bass bought control of Vail Associates in 1976, a move that led to the ouster of the original developer, 10th Mountain veteran Pete Seibert. The Aspen Skiing Corporation continued to grow in size. In addition to owning Aspen Mountain, Buttermilk, and Snowmass ski areas, it bought Breckenridge ski area in 1970. That transaction spurred plans to develop a $52 million "New Town" at the base of Peak 9 in Breckenridge. Even the ASC changed hands, narrowly escaping being bought out by a bowling alley corporation before it finally merged with 20th Century Fox Films in 1978.[99] This kind of conglomerate ownership became a pattern as the ski industry matured and corporate giants viewed it as a legitimate means of diversification. The Ralston Purina Company paired dog food with downhill skiing when it took over ownership of the Keystone ski area in 1973 and bought Arapahoe Basin five years later.

Corporate ownership and management turned Colorado skiing into a big business geared to sell leisure to vacationers. In some ways, it made sense that a film company and a food industry giant would be interested in ski areas, since skiing was becoming more about consumption and less about athleticism all the time. "The old image of the skier as a rugged individualist does not necessarily hold true today," a Denver attorney pointed out in 1972. Skiers demanded more man-made snow in times of drought, faster lifts, longer runs, and carpet-like groomed slopes. This changing public attitude toward the sport, the lawyer predicted, would affect how courts ruled on ski area liability cases. In the 1951 case of *Wright v. Mt. Mansfield,* which involved a fairly experienced skier who had broken her leg when her ski struck a five-inch stump hidden beneath the snow, the court said that ski areas could not be expected to guard against every hazardous condition and that Mrs. Wright had assumed the risk of the dangers of skiing, "so far as they are obvious and necessary." A snow-covered stump beneath a smooth trail, the court explained, was a normal danger. This decision would probably not hold up in 1972, the lawyer argued. By then, skiers — and resorts themselves — had altered standards for ski area landscapes as well as the level of service associated with the sport.[100]

With new expectations of their landscapes, skiers forced areas to invest increasing amounts of money in the built environment from which skiers enjoyed the "wilderness." Restaurants, hotels, bars, and retail shops in base areas and ski towns completed the skier-tourists' vacation experience and thoroughly encapsulated them in a planned, consumer-oriented landscape. As Vail's owner put it in 1989, "we're not selling just skiing anymore, we're selling entertainment! We're selling an entire entertainment experience."[101]

Vail and Snowmass, which opened in 1962 and 1967, respectively, represent the earliest culminations of mediated, planned, and constructed ski resorts. Although ski resort planners had long known that they must have hotel accommodations and adequate ski lifts to attract any customers, planners at Vail and Snowmass took the job a few steps farther.[102] Unlike local ski areas or those within a two-hour drive from Denver, Vail and Snowmass developed as "destination resorts," aimed at attracting customers for a week or more at a time. They shared characteristics that helped put them on the forefront of Colorado's — and the nation's — ski industry. They each seemed to grow, fully formed, from places that had previously only entertained summer livestock. At the junction of Gore Creek and Mill Creek along U.S. Highway 6, and up Aspen's Brush Creek, Vail and Snowmass combined on- and off-mountain development to embed the sport of skiing within a complete vacation.

Developers bought up the ranch land below the national forest and, once they had acquired the necessary Forest Service permits, built the base areas along with the ski areas. Vail quickly achieved what Snowmass developers planned from the start: an entire ski resort community. During Vail's first season, for instance, three hotels and four restaurants complemented the mountain's gondola, two chairlifts, lodge, and mid-Vail restaurant. By 1966, the town of Vail had incorporated, real estate sales were booming, and the base area had been transformed into the now-famous Vail Village. Swathed in European references, "every building is built with an eye to an entire architectural concept," one observer noticed. "Shops, apartments, lodges and homes all adhere to a plan to give the effect of a casual but unified village. Even the gondola house," he added, "conforms to the styling."[103] This writer went on to rave about Vail's vast bowl skiing, its great hotels, and its European restaurants — a tough combination to beat. Snowmass developers tried, however. After quietly accumulating 3,400 acres of local ranch land, developer Bill Janss signed a contract with the Aspen Skiing Corporation under which the ASC would operate the ski area and he would develop the base area. Janss hired architect Fritz Benedict to design a resort made up of separate villages — each to be "a balanced community of homes, shops, restaurants, lodges, swimming pools, tennis courts, stables and ice rinks" built with

Vail was established as an integrated ski area, resort, and town. This alpine-style building and the pedestrian street that leads visitors to the ski area give the place a coherence and image that people still enjoy. Vail consistently ranks among North America's best ski resorts. (Photo by the author)

architectural harmony in mind — to accompany a huge ski mountain with an extensive lift system. "The efficiency with which the area was studied, planned, developed, and sold," one reporter exclaimed, "was without precedent."[104]

Snowmass and Vail both reflected important changes in skiing landscapes. A carefully crafted resort, Vail was — and is — a landscape of leisure built expressly for large numbers of visitors. Far from the local community skiers that characterized the sport in the 1930s, Vail's customers came to Colorado from all over the country and even abroad. They sought an integrated experience, a package that included the physical and psychological benefits of skiing, plus shopping, dining, and socializing. They expected a vacation and were content for it to take place within a resort landscape constructed for their enjoyment. As these changes occurred, skiing took on new meanings not only for skiers but for town residents who welcomed these skiers as well.

5

The White West
Ski Town Image, Tourism, and Community

Where has Europe gone? To Vail, of course. According to this 1968 ad, Vail, Colorado, was much more than a well-panned resort village. It was European, Bavarian, "where everything comes off like it just came in from the Alps."[1] But it was also Coloradan. Vail combined Alpine skiing and Continental amenities with Colorado's snow, sunshine, friendly people, and nightlife to create an ideal world for vacationing skiers. The advertisement made this claim; Vail's resort landscape bore it out. Visitors coming from Denver approached the Vail Valley from I-70, crossing Colorado's Continental Divide at Loveland Pass (or the Eisenhower Tunnel after 1973) and the Gore Range at Vail Pass. Once into the valley and off the exit ramp, drivers parked their cars in convenient lots, gathered their skiing equipment, and entered Vail's Bavarian walking village. Narrow cobbled streets led skiers past shops, hotels, and beer gardens with German names and alpine architecture, then up a slight hill to the lifts that would whisk them to the top of the mountain and Vail's soon famous back-bowl skiing. The resort's alpine design created a landscape with such strong, European references that it might have made skiers wonder exactly where they were.

Vail's local past embedded the place firmly in historical themes familiar to Colorado at the same time it supported some European references. Although there had been no town before 1962, the historic presence of Ute Indians, the 1873 Hayden Expedition, homesteaders, sheepherders, and nearby Camp Hale defined the area as part of the Rocky Mountain West.[2] A French settler and two Greek

This 1968 ad sold European resort culture in Colorado's Rockies, a strategy that ultimately made Vail distinctly American. (Courtesy of Vail Resorts, Inc.)

sheepherders gave the valley ethnic diversity and ties to Europe. Skiing's own European roots and founder Pete Seibert's 10th Mountain Division experiences added to Vail's Continental past. Greek sheepherders and World War II combatants, however, failed to appear in the ski area's advertising campaigns. Instead, this resort — like others throughout the Rocky Mountains — crafted its image around a more appealing and romantic vision of alpine Europe, enhanced by western hospitality and snow conditions.

If Vail brought Bavaria to the Rocky Mountains, Steamboat Springs located the Wild West on its main street. Annual winter carnivals featuring sports such as skijoring, in which a horse and rider pull a skier through town, combined the place's ranching past with its skiing immigrant population. Although the town's history included homesteading, prospecting, and tour-

*Wild West references attached images of adventure, action, and
history to a town once characterized by its Norwegian influences.*
(Ski 40 [October 1975], courtesy Steamboat)

ism centered on the local hot springs as well as ranching, ad campaigns fash-
ioned Steamboat Springs as a Wild West cow town above all else. They pictured cowboys racing on horseback with skis in their saddlebags and a
handsome couple riding their horses through knee-deep powder, a barn and
the ski slopes in the background. The resort's spokesman, Billy Kidd, used
his name and an ever-present Stetson hat to illustrate his own wholesome yet
outlaw identity. In skiing down Steamboat's trails, walking its main street,

and appearing in advertisements, Kidd reinforced his own Wild West image and tied it to his chosen hometown.

Steamboat's local history, its ski resort, and its public image differed from Vail's, but they shared an economic transition to tourism that influenced each of those things. As Rocky Mountain ski areas grew into destination resorts in the 1950s and 1960s, their towns adopted the ski industry and tourism as mainstays of the local economy. Beyond creating planned, integrated landscapes of leisure, this required developing an image that consumers could attach to the place — a sort of branding. Residents and especially marketers had to choose what their resort would represent and what it would not, and making that choice had big consequences. Quaint Victorian communities such as Aspen, Breckenridge, and Telluride; Wild West cow towns such as Steamboat Springs and Jackson Hole, Wyoming; and alpine enclaves such as Vail and Taos, New Mexico, chose romantic aspects of their local past and ski history to define their towns. In focusing on these themes, such resorts built landscapes that reified all things stereotypically western and alpine while they concealed evidence of this construction.[3] They ignored the extractive industry, immigrant labor, and transient populations that connected ski resort towns to the western past and embraced the idea of real locals welcoming beautiful skiers to their home.

Alpine village and Wild West themes attracted skiers and tourists because they evoked an aura of sophistication or adventure that skiing embodied as a sport. They also lent a coherence to towns that made them easier to sell and more comfortable to experience — enabling visitors to inhabit cosmopolitan Europe without a transatlantic flight, for instance, or a Wild West without danger. These images acquired so much power that they did more than attract visitors and a constant influx of new residents — they convinced a staggering array of people that they were real. They defined skiing as a white and increasingly elite sport, effectively limiting access to racial minorities who were not wealthy. Further, they defined western communities as stable, coherent institutions, leading recent residents, especially, to bemoan the corrosive impact tourism had on them. The Wild West and alpine Europe drew skiers to resorts, but the vision of white leisure supported by an authentic community of locals created expectations that became increasingly difficult to fulfill.

Tourism and Skiing

Embracing tourism has become a common and problematic phenomenon in the American West, but it is hardly new.[4] Nor is its connection to winter sports. Denver boosters and their small-town counterparts seized on skiing's potential to draw visitors as soon as Scandinavian immigrants made their enthusiasm and the region's mountains known. Winter carnivals in places such as Hot Sulphur and Steamboat Springs beginning in the 1910s, the National Ski Association jumping championships held outside Denver in 1921 and 1927, national Alpine championships held at Aspen in 1941, and the international championships held there in 1950 all generated great hopes that skiing would bring people and their dollars to Colorado's Rockies.

After World War II, especially, Colorado residents, national media, and politicians identified winter tourists as promising generators of income. "The opening of the long-awaited chair lift," ski club member Leonard Woods declared in 1946, "is perhaps the first large and really tangible sign that Aspen has found a new, good, and profitable way of life."[5] *Collier's* noted that "for forty years the once bustling town of Aspen, Colorado was virtually abandoned. Then someone fitted it with skis and now everything's booming again."[6] At the state level, politicians worked to improve access to towns such as Aspen. In 1955, Governor Johnson appealed to the U.S. Senate to fund an interstate highway over the Continental Divide. By then, tourism was Colorado's second largest industry, he pointed out, and the state could not afford to see vacationers diverted away from its Rockies.[7]

This growth of tourism supported Colorado's ski industry, but it also fostered competition — between ski areas and other destination resorts, and among ski areas themselves. In this context, marketing and public relations departments became invaluable. Robert Parker, a former editor of *Skiing* magazine and a 10th Mountain veteran, became Vail's first director of marketing in 1961. Instead of relying on instructors or managers to talk up the area or produce the occasional ski film, as Aspen had in the 1940s, Vail hired Parker to focus on public relations full time.[8] Thanks to him, according to one author, "ski journalists and industry flacks everywhere were pounding the drums for Vail long before the first lift ticket was sold."[9] By the late 1960s, the *Skiing Area News* was publishing articles explaining how other ski areas could market themselves better and attract more business, winter and sum-mer. "This business is too competitive to allow you to overlook any possi-bilities which might build clientele," said one California manager. He hosted events such as beauty pageants, marathon runs, photo contests, straw skiing, and bicycle races to attract summer business and improve the area's visibil-ity.[10] Other articles explained how best to use radio and television in market-ing plans and even how to use methods that Disney's "imagineers" had developed to tackle the parking, crowd control, and lift line problems that threatened to keep customers from coming back.[11]

While individual ski areas did what they could to advertise on their own, they also teamed up with surrounding areas to attract tourist dollars. Colo-rado Ski Country USA kicked the marketing spree off in 1963, actively pro-moting its ski areas on radio and television and at regional ski shows. In the mid-1960s, Robert Parker started a campaign called "Ski the Rockies" with the support of ten major Rocky Mountain resorts. Their goal was to get easterners who had been skiing in Europe to come to the Rockies instead, and they achieved it by convincing tour operators and travel agents to promote the region.[12] Airline companies joined in and advertised vacation packages to the Rockies. United Airlines supported the campaign because, as a domestic carrier, it was interested in keeping tourists in America; later on, other air-lines ran similar ads. "Colorado's spectacular high country skiing is the best," one brochure exclaimed in 1976, "and, to save you money, Continental has a wide selection of special low-cost air fares. Nothing," it insisted, "can hold you back!"[13]

These powerful marketing strategies, all geared to bring skiers to Colorado mountain towns, identified destination ski resorts as engines of tourism as well as of the ski industry. The rising number of out-of-state skiers during the 1960s testified to the industry's success at integrating a winter sport into Ameri-cans' vacation plans. Drawing tourists to ski resorts fueled the ski industry's growth, and it had important repercussions for resort towns. Skiers came to the mountains to ski, and area managers crafted snowscapes designed for both safety and the opportunity for wild adventure. But tourists came to the moun-tains to tour, and that put them in a different position relative to resort land-scapes. They required more than the food, shelter, and gear necessary to ski down the mountain all day every day; they needed to experience a new and interesting place. Certainly ardent skiers could also be tourists, and when skiers put their tourist hats on (or when tourists went on ski vacations) they combined their kinetic love of mountain landscapes with an aesthetic appreciation for the region and town that housed the resort.

People on tour usually seek out new places, people, and cultures. They may enjoy recounting their adventures to friends, and saying "I've been there" confers a measure of status, but at the deepest level, they do it to learn more about themselves and their world.[14] At the very least, experiencing some cultural or geographical "other" provides a point of comparison. Escaping the city and finding a natural, rural, or historic place can give tourists a new perspective on their own home, heritage, or identity while also offering a diversion from routine life. Rural places and areas with access to impressive natural or wild landscapes offer visitors both mental and physical renewal. And sites with distinct regional or local histories give tourists a nostalgic taste of their past, along with a new perspective on present-day society. Ski towns offered visitors a powerful combination of scenic landscapes, rural communities, and western history to go with their outdoor fun.

Tourists have always wanted to see and ultimately be a part of something real or authentic, but what constitutes an authentically rural, wild, western, or otherwise historic community is hard to determine. Their expectations, moreover, have usually had little relationship to actual Rocky Mountain towns. Thus, if marketers wanted to attract visitors, they would have to design and package their towns for consumption, just as ski areas crafted mountain landscapes for a new population of skiers. Following this route could lead residents down a slippery slope and into the pit of "the tourist gaze," where tourists' visions could actually alter social realities. Architecture, landscape design, and marketing campaigns could transform a place's image to attract visitors, but organizing community events and local history for tourists' benefit could effectively rewrite the past and redefine the community itself.[15]

Alpine Europe and the Wild West

Local boosters and members of the ski industry worked hard to define resort towns as bits of Europe, living remnants of the Wild West, examples of lost Victorian culture, or some of each. They dressed up their respective towns and designed attractive marketing campaigns, but most importantly, they put these images in motion. By attaching such images to hotels, restaurants, stores, and the ski area itself, boosters made distant places accessible through the act of consumption. Skiers and tourists could literally buy their way into an alpine village or a western cow town, entering mythical landscapes as participants rather than observers. Skiing pushed this relationship further. As an ultimately physical act, sliding down a mountain made skiers move. Entwined with local history, it also gave visitors a way to join the community. Skiing invited them to interact with the surrounding landscape, to become a part of it in ways that brought the town's mythic images to life and transformed the skier into someone who belonged there. Local boosters, industry developers, and area marketers made all this happen on purpose. They created landscapes that let tourists enter the Alps or the Wild West through fairly straightforward acts of consumption and allowed them to forget the less glamorous social realities that created such places.

They began with the mountains. The Alps' magnificence and their famous resorts drew wealthy tourists to Europe, and linking Colorado's Rockies to the Alps made a lot of sense in some ways. Physical resemblances between the mountain ranges supported hope for Colorado tourism as early as the nineteenth century, and visitors have compared the two since then. In 1869, for instance, Samuel Bowles published an account of his summer vacation in Colorado under the title *The Switzerland of America*.[16] Many nineteenth-century tourists sought the Old World in the New. Calling the Rockies the Alps, according to one historian, "helped the traveler to transport himself in fancy to more famous scenes."[17] Colorado boosters encouraged the connection in 1913 when they described Hot Sulphur's conditions for winter sports as better than Switzerland, Norway, and Europe as a whole. Swiss mountaineer Andre Roch applied this idea again in 1936 when he wrote of Aspen's Mt. Hayden: "America could find here a resort that would in no way be inferior to anything in the Alps." Local residents clung to and repeated those words for over a decade.[18]

And in the 1960s, the state of Colorado built on this tradition with a campaign that advertised the Rockies as "the 'other Alps,'" featuring treeless "bowls" to ski in, gondolas, and ski villages, all reminiscent of Europe, to go with the state's distinctive powder snow and "genuine western camaraderie."[19] Vail's "Where Has Europe Gone?" ad would appear the following season. But calling Colorado towns European went beyond simply comparing mountain ranges or even their conditions for winter sports. It claimed a destination

*Colorado ski resorts played up a long tradition of comparing the
Rocky Mountains with the Alps. European landscapes and culture,
they argued, were closer and more affordable than consumers might
think. (Ski 32 [December 1967])*

resort setting and an atmosphere of elite leisure. This set of meanings influenced how resorts interpreted other historic connections they had to Europe:
working people.

Mining, ranching, and other forms of hard work connected Europe to
western towns and blended Colorado's ski history with its local history. Aspen
and its Pitkin County represented other Colorado mountain regions in their
immigrant diversity. Foreign-born residents made up over 20 percent of the
county's population from 1885 through 1930, a time span that encompassed
Aspen's silver mining boom years and its bust, as well as a period of regional
farming and ranching during "the quiet years" from 1910 to 1950.[20] From its
initial peak of about 9,000 residents in 1890 to its low point of just over 1,600
in 1950, Pitkin County was home to immigrants from Canada, Ireland, England, Germany, Sweden, Scotland, Austria, France, Italy, and Yugoslavia.
Immigrants from Scandinavia and other parts of Europe taught Colorado
residents to ski. They competed in contests, founded local clubs, and sparked
the advent of winter carnivals across the state. If they became known for their

skiing prowess, however, they held on to their day jobs — mining, farming, or, in the case of Carl Howelsen, stonemasonry. Europeans who came to the West in the 1930s to teach skiing at nascent resorts often used the sport to escape farm work or other labor at home and gain new identities as alpine experts. Such immigrants and their work connected Europe and Colorado, skiing history and local history.

The manual labor associated with it set early skiing apart from its postwar embodiment. The sweat, dirt, and physical exertion largely responsible for skiing's rise in Colorado disappeared in resort settings. Steamboat Springs cultivated the memory of Carl Howelsen, but he became an icon of sport and local community rather than of the West's working-class and immigrant roots. Towns embraced Alpine skiing's Europeanness over similar pasts. Architectural and cultural references to alpine villages sprouted up everywhere, from the Hotel St. Bernard, the Alpenhof, and the Edelweiss in Taos, New Mexico, to Vail's Austrian-style Lodge, its Gastof Grammshammer, and instructor Pepi Stiegler's self-titled restaurant in Jackson Hole, Wyoming. Such buildings, with low roofs and decorative cutouts on their shutters and porch railings, recalled visions of *Heidi* and the Matterhorn. Interior decorations and menu items welcomed guests more deeply into alpine culture. Aspen, for all its western mining town images, also boasted European restaurants, including Gretl's and the Wienerstube, as well as a spattering of Tyrolean-style buildings.[21] Privileging visions of skiing's alpine past over Colorado's history of immigrant labor helped reintroduce the model of elite resort skiing that the Highland Bavarian Lodge had aimed for in the 1930s. The romance of St. Moritz, St. Anton, and Sun Valley overshadowed local traditions of skiing associated with work, and it allowed skiing tourists to engage in a history that promoted their leisure.

Given the sport's historical context, such representations made some sense. In the 1930s, most good skiers learned in Europe, and afterward, many learned from Europeans who had immigrated to the States. Practical concerns also supported the appeal of European images: resorts at St. Moritz, St. Anton, Val d'Isere, and Garmisch Partenkirchen attracted skiers from all over the world; the most knowledgeable and experienced ski instructors came from Europe; Europeans consistently dominated international competitions; and European countries developed the newest technology in lifts and ski equipment. Images from Austria and Norway took on even more appeal in postwar America because popular culture romanticized those countries' wartime resistance movements. *The Sound of Music* (1965) made it easy, for example, for Americans to visualize Austrian ski instructors guiding the family Von Trapp across the Alps to freedom. Americans had years of practice associating world-class resorts, competitors, instructors, and equipment with Europe, and American resorts capitalized on this association by transporting Europe to the Rockies.

European references in Colorado resorts often had more to do with marketing than with the actual past. Because Vail grew out of an empty valley, and Vail Associates controlled both the town and the ski area's development, the company could choose "the look, the atmosphere, the layout [it] wanted."[22] Vail's managers cultivated European images designed to appeal to skier-tourists who wanted a cosmopolitan-feeling vacation without traveling across the Atlantic. Colorado Ski Country USA founder Steve Knowlton said that Vail's developers knew "they couldn't be another mining town, so the idea was to have a gondola, which most European resorts have, and to build the hotels and the main street . . . [like] another European resort."[23] In doing so, the area's founder referred directly not only to Alpine skiing's historical roots but also to an elite European resort culture. Vail's designers made this cultural reference self-consciously. Marketing director Bob Parker described the original reasons for building a gondola at Vail as "prestige, glamour, [and] promotional advantages against major European and domestic resorts." These same reasons, plus the unquestionable success of the first gondola, prompted Vail to build a second one in 1968.[24] This momentum carried into the 1980s, when Vail gave its high-speed quad chairlift European savoir faire by christening it the "Vista Bahn." In perhaps its most literal appropriation of the Alps, Vail actually imported a 400-pound piece of the Swiss Matterhorn and placed it in its Lions Head Plaza.[25] Vail's choice of lifts, architecture, businesses, and base area development in general created a distinct landscape in Colorado that encouraged visitors to associate Vail with glamour and elite European resorts. By the mid-1970s, Vail's combination of skiing terrain, resort development, and marketing success made it the first Colorado ski area with a million customers in a season, and it put more than $5 million worth of profits in Vail Associates' pockets.[26]

Mythically western images were more appropriate than alpine villages for resort towns that had a mining or ranching past, but they proved equally problematic, because few marketers believed that old industrial towns would appeal to tourists. Instead, boosters created images of the western past from select bits of local lore and colorful people. Early Aspen boosters proclaimed "its atmosphere of the old mining days" and the ranching legacy of children skijoring to school behind the milk truck as visions that would attract tourists and skiers alike.[27] Quaint images of children and amorphous concepts such as mining "atmosphere" gave marketers some help in crafting an optimistic and appealing vision of the town's history. Publicity with headlines such as "Aspen Booms Again" defined its present in terms of past prosperity and growth. Real-life residents from the mining days gave the town a character and charm, according to one resident, that set Aspen apart from other resorts.[28] Wizened ranchers, too, appealed to tourists and complemented mining references to fill out an image of the "Old West." Although most sold their land and moved on, a few of Aspen's ranchers took jobs in the ski industry selling tickets, operating lifts, and running bed-and-breakfasts. They connected the town's past with its present, serving tourists at the same time they represented the old days.

Historic buildings exercised similar symbolic power. Refurbished remnants of Aspen's Victorian heyday, including the Hotel Jerome, Wheeler Opera House, and mansions in the town's West End, recalled the romance, wealth, and leisure of the mining boom era without the mine tailings, labor disputes, and pollution that was familiar to nineteenth-century residents. Indeed, Victorian buildings in late-twentieth-century tourist towns painted a rosy picture of both the past and the present. Separated from their original economic context, they could emphasize a positive historic "atmosphere" that diverted attention away from current economic realities as well. Breckenridge restored its Victorian buildings and houses on Main Street, as did many other towns, to emphasize its historic roots.[29] Restaurants, shops, bars, and ice cream stands thus evoked images of nineteenth-century mining society rather than the tourist economy that supported them. Even local ranches could help redefine a town's past through new incarnations. The Starwood Ranch, which Art and Amelia Trentaz sold to Aspen developers in 1962, became an elite residential subdivision. Retaining the name honored the land's past identity, but "Starwood" also took on new meaning, as people including singer John Denver and Saudi Arabia's Prince Bandar moved in. Architectural restoration and real estate development

In 1968, Breckenridge business owners housed their shops in false-fronted buildings dating from the 1880s. Others inhabited Victorian houses. These architectural signs offered skiing tourists bits of the historic West along with their food, liquor, and ski gear. (Denver Public Library, Western History Collection, X-962, Dick Davis)

helped define Aspen and other towns as Victorian, historic, and quaint even as it brought them into a new tourist economy.

When combined with colorful individuals and selected images of the past emphasizing prosperity and leisure, old houses and ranches completed an effective set of tools for marketers to shape a town's past as stereotypically western. References to Victorian society stood in for mining in this scenario, and displaced ranchers represented a bygone era of cowboys instead of the family farms that dotted high mountain valleys. By 1979, Andre Roch proudly announced that "Aspen has become not only a winter resort, but a place of culture combining the saga of the Wild West, cowboys, and mining with all the modern day entertainments. Long live Aspen with its wild surroundings."[30] Focusing on such Victorian mining images, with a hint of ranching thrown in, was typical of many ski towns. Aspen, Breckenridge, and

Telluride marketed themselves in these terms most visibly. Other resort towns, notably Steamboat Springs, crafted a different sort of western image for themselves.

Developers at Steamboat Springs chose, as Aspen resort managers did, to play off the town's history. Steamboat Springs' roots as a ranching town and the legacy of community skiing that Carl Howelsen started in the 1910s gave them plenty of material. As early as 1946, proponents of Steamboat compared themselves with the "young and brash" Aspen by highlighting a historical "skiing tradition" and an unprecedented level of community involvement in the sport. These claims rang true. The town actually owned the local jumping and skiing area, Howelsen Hill, and its schools produced world-class athletes on an amazingly regular basis. "Juvenile delinquency is almost unknown," one reporter explained, "the kids keep busy, tired and happy skiing, and their interests are directed into sports rather than into mischief."[31] According to a *Collier's* article published in 1955, "Everybody Skis at Steamboat." Indeed, five of the sixteen U.S. ski team members in 1954 hailed from the town, population 2,000. Characterized as a "Ski Happy Town" and, more popularly, as "Ski Town, U.S.A.," Steamboat entered the public's consciousness as a fun, family, community resort.[32]

Although this wholesome image lingers and still attracts families to the resort, marketers also sought a way to characterize the town that would emit the kind of glamour that other resorts found in the Alps or Victorian high society. They saw an opportunity when Olympic racer Billy Kidd came to town. As a teammate and friend of the late Buddy Werner, Kidd reminded people of their lost local hero. Kidd's personality and his name — combined with his desire to earn some money in the ski business — provided the perfect opportunity for Steamboat to capitalize on its ranching past. By 1970, a downhill ski area at Mt. Werner (previously known as Storm Mountain) had taken shape and fallen into the hands of LTV, a corporation interested in marketing its product to skier-tourists across the country. LTV did not wait long, one ski writer noticed, "to besiege the nation with advertisements full of cowboys, stagecoaches, horses and a sheepishly grinning Bill Kidd."[33] Once he became a paid employee of the ski area, the Stetson-wearing Vermont native transformed into a Colorado cowboy and turned Ski Town USA into the Wild West. Billy (the) Kidd allowed Steamboat to publicize its ranching past and develop its image as a historic and wild cow town, thereby plugging

*Bill Kidd's fluid identity helped Steamboat market itself as quintessentially American and western. (*Colorful Colorado *[January/February 1971], courtesy Steamboat)*

the resort into a long tradition of Wild West iconography that tourists recognized and welcomed. His was a different version of the West than Aspen's elite Victorian references, one more focused on masculine action, but the Wild West proved such an elastic category that a variety of resorts could use it effectively.

And they took advantage of the mythic images wherever possible. Ski trail names supported romantic images of the West created by colorful individuals and local architecture. Just as Vail's gondolas and its Vista Bahn turned physical development of the mountains into signs of European savoir faire, other resorts used trail names and similar development to foster a western identity. Aspen Mountain's Tourtolette Park, Zaugg Dump, Last Dollar, and Silver Queen trails recalled real mining sites on the mountain, as well as a lost silver statue that bore the town's nickname. Telluride emphasized mining more generally with its Prospect Trail, Mine Shaft, Apex, and Silver Glade trails, not to mention its summit, Gold Hill. Steamboat Springs pushed its cow-town image when it named a midmountain lodge Rendezvous Saddle, lifts Rough Rider and Pony, and various ski trails Chute One, High Noon, Flintlock, Buckshot, and Quick Draw.[34] When the Aspen Skiing Corporation decided to build a gondola, it was named the "Silver Queen," and John Denver presided over the opening ceremonies. Nor did these names languish quietly on trail maps. Skier-tourists animated resort images when they made plans to meet friends on the mountain, described to one another where they had skied, and flaunted their athletic exploits later in the bar.

Adopting western and alpine images altered the physical landscape of resort towns from downtown areas to surrounding mountaintops. Manipulating categories such as the Wild West and alpine Europe created a local brand or home image for Vail, Aspen, and Steamboat Springs that celebrated well-established mythic visions of the West as well as local history. Town residents and ski area marketers simplified and sanitized the past for tourist consumption, but the ski industry and tourism actually had much more to do with western history than they let on. As they focused on images of elite European resorts and Victorian prosperity, they overlooked a tradition of extractive industry, with its accompanying boom-bust economy and transient populations, that ski town residents would recognize as familiar.[35] Tourism represented not a jump to an entirely new economy but a transition to an extractive industry dependent on snow and scenery rather than grass or minerals.

Although some of Colorado's destination resorts appeared virtually from nowhere, most moved to tourism after their mining, ranching, or railroad economies busted. Aspen, Breckenridge, Crested Butte, and Telluride all started originally as mining towns in the nineteenth century. Durango and Fraser, base towns for Purgatory and Winter Park, grew along with the railroads. Steamboat Springs and the areas around Vail and Snowmass all supported ranchers and farmers before skiers, though only Steamboat could boast its own town.[36] From the 1930s to the 1950s, most of these areas were experiencing something less than economic booms. About Aspen in the 1930s and 1940s, one local said, "it was all dead, dormant here."[37] Younger generations had fewer and fewer reasons to stay home. They left in search of education, better jobs, and more exciting times. One Telluride miner recalled that "people would go to high school here and go to college, they weren't going to return to go to a mine, so we had a population made up of babies up to eighteen-year-olds, and from that eighteen-year-old the next person was thirty-five or forty."[38] During the 1950s and 1960s, mountain valley farmers and ranchers worked to keep up with rising costs of land, labor, machinery, taxes, and federal grazing permits and to overcome the limitations of a high altitude and a short growing season. Indeed, some farm and ranch families even encouraged their sons and daughters to leave because, as one Roaring Fork Valley mother put it, ranching was "just a lot of hard work for not much in return."[39]

Their flight from the land during a period of economic difficulty mirrored the decision that many earlier townspeople had made when mining busted. Across Colorado, the productivity of silver and gold mines dropped radically between 1890 and 1920. A national economic panic and the demonetization of silver in 1893 caused silver prices to drop, mines to close, and populations to decline. A gold rush a few years later swelled Cripple Creek's ranks for a while, a demand for lead and zinc kept some mines open, and small groups of farmers and ranchers eked out a living in nearby valleys, but after World War I, all mining regions in Colorado lost money, hope, and people. Combined, the leading mining towns of Leadville, Aspen, Central City, Georgetown, and Cripple Creek had more than 30,000 residents in 1900; twenty years later, they were home to fewer than 10,000 "stubborn survivors."[40] That core of people who lasted through the depression and into the early ski industry days represented an authentic community for many. Colorado communities have always been rather difficult to pin down, however, tossed by waves of extractive industry and constantly fluctuating in size and shape. Movement and transience defined them, not stability. Even the souls who stayed on through one set of tough times often opted to leave later on.

Many farmers and ranchers across Colorado's Rockies reached the decision to sell their land and move at about the same time that resort developers began noticing the potential for skiing and tourism. Declining industry (including agriculture) and a perpetually weak service sector in rural areas meant that economies could no longer succeed through traditional means. High-paying urban jobs reduced the permanent rural population in the later twentieth century; improved access from cities increased the number of temporary, weekend residents; the rise of agribusiness threatened the family farm; and new corporate and individual landowners exercised closer control over rural landscapes.[41] For many rural communities in the American West — and around the globe — tourism offered a way to capitalize on the very characteristics that made farming and ranching so challenging. Isolation, limited economic development, and a small population all appealed to urban residents looking for scenic vacation spots.

Skiing thus represented another chance at the economic success that had proved so short-lived with mining and so elusive with farming and ranching. And skiing was not so different from these earlier mountain economic systems. They all depended on natural resources, be they mineral deposits, mountain grasses, fertile soil, or scenic landscapes covered with snow. Each faced bust cycles as a result of outside forces — in the ski industry's case, slowed growth due to years of little snowfall or national declines in leisure spending — and they all depended on the use of federal land for their success. Their use of the mountains made participants in each economic system increasingly dependent on technology and the government to develop their resources. Trail design, snowmaking, and special-use permits were the ski industry's equivalents to the mining techniques and laws, farm equipment and subsidized land-use practices, and range management and grazing permits that had supported previous fortunes. Changes in mountain landscapes brought about by destination resorts and their accompanying tourist economy, therefore, took on vaguely recognizable forms reminiscent of earlier times.

This new layer on the economic landscape incorporated some of the same people, too. Although many local residents sold their land to developers or remained skeptical of the growing ski industry, some joined in. Their experience in the mines or on farms and ranches, in fact, sometimes made them indispensable. One example from outside Colorado was a ski area in Minnesota that had earned a reputation for high-quality snow grooming. "If I had to pinpoint one thing [to explain our success]," one of the owners said, "it would have to be our farm background." As farmers, the area's two owners had approached the problem of snow grooming by adapting farm equipment to the task.[42] Their success speaks to a link between farming and skiing that was not limited to Minnesota. Some ranchers in Aspen's Roaring Fork Valley earned money in their winter off-seasons by running lifts. They did such a good job that *Skiing Area News* published an article commending Aspen's lift operators as key public relations figures for an industry that, ironically, had displaced many of them from their ranches.[43] A few local residents rose to higher positions within the ski industry. Red Rowland, the son of an Aspen miner, grew up working on local ranches and building diversion tunnels. He started working for the Aspen Skiing Corporation in 1946 as a private contractor and quickly rose to the status of assistant manager, a post from which he would retire thirty years later.[44]

People with mining backgrounds, too, helped ski areas with their technical knowledge and forged a bond between old and new economies. Telluride miner Keith Blackburn, who "knew tramways," started working at Purgatory building lifts before it opened and stayed on as a lift operator. Bill Mahoney used his mining expertise, local business connections, and familiarity with the mountains to help develop and manage Telluride's ski resort. Despite their reputation as crotchety critics, quite a few Aspen miners went to work for the Aspen Skiing Corporation as well.[45]

Although skiing and tourism shared important people and characteristics with their economic predecessors, what they proved most clearly was the utter malleability of the past. Pushing the comparison between mining and skiing could point to a series of rather disturbing similarities. Beyond using Rocky Mountain natural resources, technology, and the federal government, both industries demanded urban development; both produced pollution, overcrowding, and demographic turnover; and both depended on poorly paid workers. Tourists who were seeking history on vacation rarely wanted to see the ugly realities of the past repeated in front of their noses. Visions of the Alps and the Wild West invited skiing tourists to participate in a past that celebrated romance, leisure, and excitement, and these tourists did not question the environmental and economic implications of their vacation. European walking villages, Victorian architecture, and Wild West cowboys drew visitors into a history that separated them from the ugly extractive industry of the past (and present), as well as from their current workaday worlds. These images reaffirmed familiar views of the West and satisfied out-of-state skiers who were hungry for a landscape, community, and history different from their own. Cultivating mythic images and ignoring historical continuities made for popular resorts, but playing fast and loose with local history altered more than the identity of the town; it transformed people, too.

The Golden Stud

Ski area marketers needed individuals to back them up when they defined Colorado as home to the Alps, Victorian high society, and the Wild West. Whether they appeared in national ad campaigns (like Billy Kidd) or interacted with skiing tourists on a more intimate level as ski instructors, a wide range of people filled the role of resort spokesperson. As such, image mattered; these people had to support the broad conception of the town and its ski area, and they had to seem real. Town residency, skiing expertise, or some combination of both gave individuals a power within ski resorts as authentic locals or experts. At the same time, it reinforced the notion of an authentic local community and emphasized skiing's association with wealth and whiteness. The larger mythic images they supported, combined with their role in the resort, turned these people into icons.

The most ubiquitous and powerful spokespeople in the ski industry were the European ski instructors who imparted their knowledge of the sport (and displayed their good looks and foreign accents) to their pupils. Ski resorts made certain to hire as many European ski instructors as possible, and they publicized the Europeanness of their ski schools. Sun Valley was the first resort to capitalize on this image. Averell Harriman established his entirely Austrian ski school in 1936 and encouraged the instructors to wear native costumes — it seemed likely that at any moment they would start yodeling or burst into song. Through the 1960s, western resorts touted ski school directors and instructors from all over Europe, including Willy Schaeffler, Friedl Pfeifer, Fred and Elli Iselin, Alf Engen, Otto Lang, Pepi Grammshammer, Pepi

Stiegler, and Jean Mayer. "That was the big thing then," one Aspen instructor remembered. "People were very into all the foreign [instructors], the 'funny talkers.'"[46] Stein Eriksen, Olympic gold medalist and director of the Aspen Highlands ski school, returned to Norway regularly in the late 1950s and brought at least fifteen skiers from his homeland to instruct with him in Colorado.

Like others before him, Eriksen's expertise and success as a competitor, enhanced by his European heritage, helped him embark on a successful career as a professional skier and instructor in America. In the 1960s, Eriksen helped American skiers who sought his advice on technique by writing a number of articles and books encouraging them to "Come Ski with Me." Other European competitors-turned-professionals, including Fred Iselin and Jean-Claude Killy, took on similar roles and became noted spokesmen for their ski school programs or ski equipment.[47] European ski instructors may

Friedl Pfeifer lined up his ski school instructors here in Aspen's first years, where they displayed their outdoor expertise and gathered their pupils for the day. (Aspen Historical Society)

have emigrated before the war for economic or political reasons, but they continued to emigrate afterward because American ski culture created such a demand for their image that they were ensured employment, if not fame. Contemporaries tellingly described Pfeifer and Eriksen — and the image they gave their respective ski schools — as "glamorous."[48] Once in America, these instructors became icons of European expertise, which lent cachet to their home resorts and fueled their own fame as well. Guitarist Bob Gibson referred to "Stein Eriksen up on Ajax" in a song called "The Golden Stud."[49] Ski instructors became a commodity for ski resorts, which depended on them both as public relations people and as signs of Europeanness and glamour. Tourists in search of an authentic alpine resort experience found it when they signed up for a lesson.

Although coming directly from Europe remained optimal, American ski instructors could also serve as icons of authenticity if they had demonstrable ties to the international racing scene. Those ties grew after World War II, first with the 10th Mountain Division and later in international competition. In 1948, Gretchen Fraser took home America's first Olympic medals in skiing — a silver in Alpine combined and a gold in slalom. Andrea Mead Lawrence won two gold medals in 1952, earning national publicity for herself and drawing attention to future team members as well. It took a little longer for the men.

Steamboat Springs' Buddy Werner became a hero for winning races all over Europe; he was the first American to win the Hahnenkamm downhill at Kitzbuhel in Austria, and he did it twice. "As the most exciting personality in skiing today," *Ski* magazine stated in 1960, "he has become a symbol to young and old."[50] Americans alternately cheered and cried as Werner won more important races than any other American and reached for Olympic medals that thrice eluded him. He died in an avalanche in 1964 while skiing for a Willy Bogner film. His sister Skeeter made a name for herself as an international competitor, too, before returning to Steamboat Springs and heading the ski school there. In 1964, two American men finally won Olympic medals under coach Bob Beattie. Billy Kidd and Jimmie Huega took home silver and bronze medals, respectively, in the slalom. American successes on the international circuit gave them credibility as alpine experts and supported the transition that Skeeter Werner and others made from racing to ski schools. Billy Kidd and Steamboat Springs both capitalized on Kidd's Olympic medal when he moved there to represent the resort. Although his image was 100 percent American, Kidd's reputation as an expert was built on international competition. If resorts could not hire Europeans, Americans who competed in Europe offered similar cachet. European images conveyed class, expertise, and authenticity, but anyone could take on those characteristics if they skied well enough.

Ski areas depended on ski instructors, therefore, to do much more than teach skiing. They fueled resort town images, be it Vail's alpine village, Aspen's Victorian cosmopolitanism, or Steamboat's American West. This happened on the mountain as they taught class, in the bar as they lounged, and especially in ad campaigns as they posed with their colleagues. And it worked particularly well if they also happened to live in town. When Austrian racer Pepi Grammshammer came to Vail and opened a restaurant and hotel, he became a colorful and historically authentic local as well as an instructor — he became a spokesman for the resort and evidence of its Europeanness. The ability to claim important figures as residents helped resort towns shape their chosen identity, as well as establish an idealized community that tourists would want to visit.

It also changed the individuals' identity. Billy Kidd's Vermont past disappeared behind the aura of the Wild West. Others acquired an unexpected European flair. When the Vail Village Inn needed a chef, the owner hired Ed Kilby, a local construction crew cook with an Indian wife who specialized in chicken fried steak. But, eager to compete with the alpine-flavored lodge nearby, the owner announced that French chef "Pierre Kilbeaux" had arrived to preside over the kitchen.[51] New Englanders turned western and westerners turned French may sound confusing, but personal transformations such as these allowed ski resorts to reinforce their mythic identities with mythic people who seemed quite real. Sometimes that meant importing locals; other times it meant creatively publicizing actual residents.

Either way, such visible and iconic locals served important purposes for tourists at ski towns. Beyond supporting the town's image and creating a reputation for themselves, they gave visitors a peek into life behind the scenes. Tourists have historically wanted more than simply to observe a new landscape, regional past, or distinct culture; they want to participate and discover, to get involved and experience the "real life" lurking behind the public facade. Spokespeople like Billy Kidd, restaurateurs such as Pepi Grammshammer, and local ranchers–turned–lift operators gave tourists an entrée into that world every time they recommended a bar, answered a question, or even said hello. Just how authentic that world actually was is a difficult question.[52] Ski resort towns were carefully designed to please, and their populations grew even as older residents sold their land and moved away. The "real town" and the resort image grew indistinguishable from each other, but people's desire to see that real town only increased. Indeed, the whole concept of "local" became so important precisely because visitors needed it to separate the authentic community they were looking for from the glossy resort they inhabited. And the lines separating visitor from established resident clouded quickly. What exactly was a local? Who knew how long someone had to live in town before they became one? A season? A year? A generation? In claiming local status and directing tourists around their towns, resort spokespeople and even recent residents distinguished themselves from tourists and characterized themselves as insider, native, local.

Ski instructors, official spokespeople, and colorful old-timers made resort towns appealing by blurring the line between a resort's mythic image and the community of people that supported that resort. They encouraged visitors to buy into a European, Victorian, or western atmosphere and an authentic community that was based only partly on local history. This job created a particular public identity for the town as well as themselves, and it also had important repercussions for the sport of skiing. In their efforts to sell skiing to tourists across the country, industry marketers played up these few well-chosen images. And it worked: skiing had become widely popular among Americans during the 1950s and 1960s. During the 1960s and 1970s, marketers pushed resort images more aggressively, and they described skiing more narrowly as a sport for affluent white people.

Images of the Wild West, for instance, replete with ranchers, cowboys, soldiers, gunfighters, stagecoach drivers, golden-hearted prostitutes, and miscellaneous townspeople, characterized the West as white domain. Though the American West is historically the most diverse region of the nation, until very recently, the engines of culture that described it to the public focused their attention — and ours — on Anglo-Americans. Popular western films such as *Shane* and the works of John Ford, literature ranging from *The Virginian* to Louis L'Amour, histories celebrating Frederick Jackson Turner's frontier thesis, and the art of Frederic Remington, Charles Russell, and their successors all identified important actors in the West as white. When ski areas such as Steamboat Springs and Jackson Hole, Wyoming, employed these powerful images to sell their resorts, they bought into the racial assumptions behind them. They had to, one could argue, for their references to the Wild West to work. Even if Hispanic and Indian people were obviously present, as they were in Taos, New Mexico, Anglo tourism ultimately defined them as irrelevant. Visitors looking for quaint examples of the primitive West turned native peoples into sanitized objects for consumption.[53] As skiing tourists gazed into visions of the mythic West, they racialized the landscape to accommodate their expectations, and the landscape, in turn, racialized them.

Ski resorts that flaunted their mining pasts similarly characterized their history and their tourists as white. In order to escape the often ugly consequences of mining and focus on a happier if vague historic "atmosphere," public relations efforts referred to Victorian society rather than mining itself. The signs and symbols most easily associated with such society — Victorian mansions and gardens, women's fashions, horses and buggies — were exclusively white as well as upper class. Prostitutes fit in only if highly romanticized or upwardly mobile; immigrant workers and their rooming houses made no appearance, nor did the Chinese laborers who commonly faced violent discrimination. On walking tours, in ad campaigns, and through their landscapes, resort towns represented their historic selves as primarily white and elite. In doing so, they encouraged tourists of similar ilk — or aspirations — to come and visit.

References to alpine Europe reinforced destination ski resorts' associations with whiteness and wealth. European images were historically tied to class, because rich people had made famous the alpine resorts that Colorado areas mimicked. One employee explained the plethora of European instructors at Sun Valley by saying that the resort "had a lush clientele."[54] Vail, Aspen, and other areas made elite resort culture available — indeed, they sold it to as many tourists as possible — but its cachet depended on maintaining its elite status. In this, destination resorts differed from their smaller cousins. Rather than catering to local skiers making day trips, destination resorts worked to attract people for a week or two. Accordingly, they tended to target a wealthier clientele and to overlook those with more modest incomes. For this group, images of Europe and the Alps worked well.

Participation in this elite resort culture grew continually more expensive during the 1960s and 1970s as fashion, ski technology, and the hotel and

restaurant business grew along with ski resorts. The language of alpine whiteness thus became more explicitly the language of class as well. Advertisers
paired ski images that emphasized Europeanness — full of savoir faire and
glamour — with signifiers of wealth and status. They could become "discrimi-
nating skiers" by purchasing la Dolomite ski boots, an act that granted — or
reaffirmed — their access to brandy served on silver trays. Skiers who adorned
themselves with the latest and most expensive clothes and equipment advertised that they belonged at elite resorts. As they consumed products of the
ski industry and internalized the symbols surrounding those commodities,
skiers reinforced resort associations with whiteness and wealth.

Marketers used references to the West and the Alps to attract tourists to
their towns and their slopes, but not without consequence. Whereas skiing
had once been a fairly accessible activity for Americans at large, destination
resorts chose to define the sport as an act of upper-class leisure that required
a one- or two-week stay. Western and alpine themes, once applied to a ski
resort, generated enough energy to transform the town, its history, the people
who lived and worked there, and even the perception of skiing. Stein Eriksen's
looks, his complexion, and his fame as a ski instructor made him a Golden
Stud, and Colorado ski resorts were happy to be associated with him.

*Images of class and Europeanness
converged in advertisements that offered
style to those who spent their money on
the right things. (Ski 33 [Holiday 1968])*

Ski Bums and Old-Timers

The signs and symbols whirling around ski resorts fueled Eriksen's reputation as an international racer, a famous ski instructor, a spokesman for Aspen, and an authentic representative of elite resort culture. They overlooked, however, his role as a worker. The ski industry, with its commitment to tourism as well as sport, required a significant pool of paid help. Hotels, restaurants, retail stores, and other local businesses needed labor, and the ski area depended on service workers, lift operators, snowmaking engineers, salespeople, a maintenance staff, and ski patrollers, as well as a staff of instructors. This collection of people entered the mythic landscape of destination resorts and disappeared. By virtue of their commitment to skiing, claim to local status, upper-class identity, or some combination of all three, most resort workers defined themselves as part of resort culture rather than as outsiders looking in. This may sound strange in an industry that associated its product with money, glamour, and leisure. Ski resorts attached images of wealth to skiing, but they also celebrated skiing expertise and fostered the notion of an authentic local community for tourists to experience. Young men and women who took jobs in ski towns negotiated this terrain and dignified their labor through the unlikely concept of the ski bum.

In Colorado's big ski resorts, the people who held the lowest jobs managed to become icons of ski culture rather than its drudges. The name *ski bum* conjured romantic images of mobility, independence, and a life (or at least a season) dedicated to the pursuit of skiing. The term — coined in the late 1940s — referred to college-aged people who put their regular lives on hold, moved to resort towns, and took whatever jobs they could in order to ski. Charlie Paterson and a friend, for instance, took a bus from New York to Denver simply because they wanted to live near the Rockies. They took jobs at the Denver and Rio Grande Railroad "so we could stay alive" and spent every weekend skiing "all the different resorts around." Paterson heard about Aspen from a girl he met at Arapahoe Basin; the next week, he and his friend hitchhiked to town, slept wherever there was room, and earned lift tickets by volunteering to gatekeep for the race that day. Paterson eventually moved to town and opened the Boomerang Lodge.[55] Natalie Gignoux, too, began as an Aspen ski bum in 1949 and ended up owning her own business — a taxi service. Before that, she worked making hand-painted scarves for skiers, until she broke her leg and went home to recuperate. She returned that summer and worked at a series of service jobs. Her living arrangements were as flexible as her employment. "The first eighteen months I was in Aspen," she recalled, "I believe I moved eighteen times."[56] For Paterson and Gignoux — as for ski bums in general — simply living and playing in resort towns took precedence over the details of their housing and jobs. Most stayed for a winter, some for years; others started their own businesses and became permanent residents. Only some of them had money to spare; most who started their own businesses did so slowly and from the ground up. But in spite of their generally meager standard of living, ski bums occupied a powerful place within resort ski culture.

That ski bums accepted menial jobs in order to ski every day made them interesting rather than lower class. Writers recommended such a lifestyle, in fact, to people who would otherwise spend money on a ski vacation. One 1947 article, for instance, advised skiers to ask a hotel manager for a job that would allow them three hours during the day to ski. "Take a job as a waitress, a bellboy, a barboy, or waiter," the author said, "but beware of those executive positions" that take up too much time. The very worst sounding jobs, in this scenario, were the best. Making beds, for instance, ranked well above a management position, because it gave workers more time to ski. In response to the prospects of "getting your hands dirty" or "mingling with the masses," the author assured readers, "have no fear." "Your hands may get slightly soiled," he said, "but the people you meet on the job will be tops." In other words, "[you will meet] skiers like yourself who have flown the coop for the winter."[57] Sharing a love for skiing and the mountains put bellboys and paying guests on similar terms — both had invested in resort leisure, albeit one with their labor and the other with their vacation budget. As a result, upperclass young people could take menial jobs at no social cost. At one New Hampshire inn, for instance, "the employees form an inner circle to which the more socially minded guests hope someday to be admitted." "Every morning a charming young Boston debutante picked up the rooms and made the beds," the author observed, "and in the evening, before she set the table, she dropped into the bar for a cocktail with the guests."[58] It made sense to find elite young men and women posing as bums; ski resorts were attractive to the upper class, and being without cash did not prevent them from moving up the resort social ladder.

Those employees with less elite upbringings benefited from the reputations afforded them by their position in resort ski culture. Menial jobs and their ski bum identities connected them intimately to a culture characterized by status and wealth, images that could rub off. Ski bums got to live and ski at idyllic resorts that others could only visit briefly — they could claim a kind of ownership over magical mountain places even if they bused tables and lived in tiny apartments. "Have you ever noticed that the environs of most large ski areas harbor enough over-qualified milkmen, bricklayers, floor moppers, bartenders, salesmen, chambermaids and waitresses to staff a good sized university?" one author asked in 1967. "These are the people," she answered, "who got tired of being one of 'them' (the ski tourists) and decided to be-come one of 'us' (the ski community)."[59] They were, in a word, "in." Regard-less of their particular jobs, ski bums enjoyed status as local residents and committed skiers.

In resorts like Aspen, which had become by 1970 the mecca for young adventurers, skiers, and swinging travelers, ski bums became powerful icons. Usually college-aged, athletic, and focused on skiing and socializing, they seemed to be on vacation all the time, despite (and ironically because of) their menial jobs. The ski bum, explained one ski writer, "lived to ski, so to the squares who went home to work on Monday morning, he was a folk hero, the object of envy as much for his ski ability as for his lifestyle: drinking, dat-ing, and skiing."[60] Drawn by the town's reputation, young people who had money to spend and wanted to experience the inside of Aspen's social world moved there and defined themselves as ski bums. "They're Beautiful!" ex-claimed one *Ski* magazine article in 1970. "Not all of the ski bums of Aspen rent luxury condominiums, make $300 a week, have $200 Hart Javelins [skis], wear groovy clothes, have a great love life and eat deliciously at places like the Paragon," he wrote, "but enough of them do to make this the era of the Beautiful Bum in Aspen, which is likely to highlight the annals of bumming."[61] These characteristics exemplified resort culture's ideals: conspicuous con-sumption of food, lodging, clothes, and ski equipment; (relative) wealth; and "a great love life." Their jobs ranged from "nothing visible" to cashier, ski instructor, lift operator, wine steward, and bar owner. Living this life proved so popular that it did more than mark poor ski fanatics as hip. It attracted wealthy socialites to low-paying jobs in ski towns, where they practiced a kind of tourism that did not seem like tourism at all.

Ski bums internalized their cultural power — couched in terms of "beauty" or "unlimited access to the inner circles of the ski establishment," as another author put it — by defining skier-tourists as outsiders. Denigrated as mere "tourists," vacationing skiers were "virtually invisible to the beautifuls." "It's crazy to get involved with a tourist, even for a date," one ski bum explained. "What would you say to one? I have no idea."[62] That social differences separated service workers from skier-tourists was not surprising. That cashiers and lift operators could enjoy higher status than wealthy vacationers was. Resort ski culture had removed menial laborers from the scene and recast them as stylish, freewheeling icons of leisure that the ski industry advertised to tourists.[63]

Ski bumming could serve as an important entrée into Colorado's resort culture for people who loved to ski and were attracted to resort towns but had little money. They built their reputations by distinguishing themselves from the mere tourists who stayed for a short while and, as much as they may have wanted to, failed to penetrate the local scene too deeply. The problem was that tourists did not always stay tourists. Marketing experts demonstrated just how malleable resort town identities and those of their employees could be; "tourist" proved to be an equally flexible category. The pull of scenic landscapes and idyllic resort towns created a confusing mix of people even as powerful resort images emphasized the presence of a stable, coherent community. This backdrop of demographic change helped the growth of Colorado resorts. It illustrated at least initial local support of the ski industry, as well as the success of marketing campaigns. It also made it increasingly difficult — and therefore important — to discern tourists from residents.

Connected locals, newcomers with vision, and investors with cash combined their efforts to help skiing and its accompanying tourism take root in their towns.[64] Success for them, the industry, and the town depended on attracting business and tourists. In place of a mining economy's plethora of transient single men and the more permanent, family-centered economy typical of farming and ranching areas, skiing and tourism attracted waves of small businesspeople, second-home owners, workers, and vacationers who came and went with the seasons. Many of these temporary residents, moreover, enjoyed themselves so thoroughly that they decided to stay. As a result, the small group of longtime residents left over from mining or ranching days began to accumulate layers of recent residents eager to join the club.

From the start, visitors found themselves enamored with the landscape and the chance to be a part of a small community. Visiting places like Aspen, Vail, and Steamboat Springs not only offered a relaxing, scenic, and adventurous contrast to their everyday lives; it also tantalized them with the opportunity to make that world their own. The chance to get in on the ground floor of a burgeoning resort and call it home had attracted people to Colorado's mountain towns since the 1940s. A number of 10th Mountain veterans and other hopeful skiers moved to Aspen and other towns, opening up businesses ranging from ski schools and ski shops to restaurants, lodges, and architectural practices, incorporating themselves into the fabric of local life.

The sense of community in resort towns like Aspen — a result of their geographic isolation and their small, "colorful" populations of old-timers — drew city folk to the country for their vacations. Many of them bought second homes so they could participate in that community from the inside rather than as visitors. Walter and Elizabeth Paepcke encouraged their friends to come out to Aspen, telling them, "we love it and want to start something big and make it well known." They convinced photographer Ferenc Berko and Bauhaus designer Herbert Bayer to move there in the 1940s, when "it was a beautiful place but all the town was 300 miners."[65] June Hodges told her husband, who was a prominent Denver lawyer and president of the Arlberg Club, "we have just got to have a little place in Aspen — it is the most wonderful little town, beautiful mountains, and the locals all were wonderful." Friends of the Paepckes from Chicago, Arlberg Club members from Denver, and other upper-class urbanites invested in summer homes in Aspen that they used in the winter for skiing as well. As 10th Mountain veteran and ski instructor John Litchfield remembered it, "pretty soon [after Paepcke spread the word about Aspen] people came out of the woods and took the place over."[66]

Visitors who came to ski for a week or two also succumbed to the attractions of the town. "People just came and stayed all winter," Friedl Pfeifer remembered, "and the next thing you knew they were building a house!" Natalie Gignoux first came to Aspen because her aunt had asked her to make sure that her cousin went back to New York instead of staying in the West. "I came out and I made sure that she went back," Gignoux explained, "but I stayed."[67] Second-home owners, businesspeople, and ski bums thus joined local families and old-timers to make up Aspen's community in the 1950s.

These attractive young people called Aspen home in the late 1940s. They ran businesses such as this restaurant, the Red Onion; skied often; and enjoyed relaxing over drinks. The Wheeler Opera House in the background gave this little town a hint of Victorian class. (Denver Public Library, Western History Collection, X-6212)

Though separated by occupation and class, these people all wanted to call the town home and participate in it as locals, winter or summer. Vacationers, too, flocked to the area for summer culture and winter sports, adding yet another layer of less permanent Aspenites. "This influx of outsiders," a *Saturday Evening Post* reporter noted in 1950, "has imposed on the old mining community a heady, almost incredible mixture of diverse personalities, ideas and interests."[68] By the mid-1950s, one author's description of the Red Onion bar fit the town as a whole: "A mixed crowd is found here," she wrote, "as the old-timers sit in remote corners and watch society rallying around the bar."[69]

Aspen developed earliest in this regard; as other Colorado ski areas grew into destination resorts, they, too, acquired their own layers of locals. Vail's community, for instance, immediately reflected its development as a destination resort. The town of Vail was incorporated in 1966, four years after the ski area opened, and it was largely shaped by its parent organization, Vail Associates. By 1970, 484 residents lived within the town, and hundreds of others lived nearby. The resort's vacation-home owners, tourists, and businesspeople hailed from countries all over the world; its workforce came from all over America.[70] The ski resort united, at least physically, what Vail's pastor described as the town's diverse constituents: "skiers and non-skiers, old-timers and newcomers, hard-nosed businessmen who own expensive houses here and have-not local employees."[71] Nor has this demographic picture simplified over the years. Layers of residents continue to accrue in mountain towns, turning destination resort communities into a demographic spectrum of people where everyone is at once tourist and local to some degree.

One impact of this phenomenon was a boom in real estate. After the war, one man came to Aspen all the way from Florida, hoping to buy a small lodge or apartment building; another came from Texas looking for a dude ranch. By 1950, property that had been unsold at $10 a lot in 1945 was worth $250, and houses that once sold for $1,200 were hard to get for $12,000. Sixteen years later, the starting price for a good thirty-foot lot (two of which were necessary to build a house) had risen to $7,500, and one woman supposedly rejected a $90,000 offer for her "hillside shack" and homestead land, originally valued at $950.[72] New buildings and refurbished old ones rose on this land, right along with prices. Retail establishments in Aspen sprouted up, too; in the first four years after the lifts opened (from 1946 to 1950), about a dozen new bars opened for business. In 1961 alone, the town issued licenses to twenty-nine hotels with 1,139 beds, and the next year brought resort towns' most characteristic physical feature: condominiums. To accommodate such growth, the city authorized a new electric power system and decided to pave fourteen of its downtown blocks.[73] The "condominium craze," sparked by the prospect of affordable vacation homes, affected resorts across the country and did not slow for more than a decade. In 1969, *Skiing Area News* published an article discussing the relative appeal of condominiums and lodges. Either way, developers were eager to build.[74]

With the building of homes, lodges, and condominiums, real estate threatened to overtake skiing itself as a catalyst for growth. Ski corporations balanced their management and personnel accordingly, creating real estate divisions within their corporate structures and concerning themselves with growth off the mountain as well as on.[75] Such development supported the expansion of specific resorts, as well as the ski industry as a whole. Rising prices and sales demonstrated the success of resorts' marketing efforts, and they strengthened the association between destination resort skiing and wealth. They also thinned the ranks of longtime residents who gave towns a quaint, historic flavor. "Some small towns are changing," one Coloradan noted in 1970, "sacrificing their singularity to become plush look-alike playgrounds for urbanites."[76]

Old-timers and longtime local families who chose not to participate in the new economic landscape, or those who could not keep up with its snowballing momentum, found themselves pushed to the margins of their community. "The people who started [Aspen skiing] and who were enthusiastic in the beginning have mostly sold their homes and moved," Dick Durrance explained. "The new ones have come in and it's become a community of, well, you might say, outsiders."[77] This layering had political as well as social and economic meaning. "There can be no sense of community without a sense of power," explained New York Mayor John Lindsay, the keynote speaker at Vail's 1971 symposium. He was concerned with giving Vail's residents a voice in the town's development to counter the ubiquitous influence that Vail Associates initially exercised over its company town.[78] In Telluride, established residents wielded political power, not the ski company. Newcomers thus came into conflict with old-timers in their effort to shape local growth and define themselves as part of the established community. "The new finally took over the politics and they liked to make a big to-do about it," one old-timer noted. "They called themselves 'the slate' [and] they got rid of the old cronies in Telluride, guys like me." With the continuous movement of people to resort towns, however, "the slate" could not last. Once the newcomers had achieved political status as locals, they found themselves in the same position as those they had worked so hard to oust. Newer residents, in turn, threw them out of the political arena.[79]

Defining local and outsider status in this way often placed the newest (and wealthiest) at odds with the families and old-timers who had supported the resort's initial development. It also made "local" or "native" a constantly endangered and therefore increasingly valuable identity. Being under siege from the newest outsiders actually helped older outsiders define themselves as in. What all this ultimately proved was the power of a mythic community.

Struck by the quaintness of impoverished mountain towns, visiting skiers succumbed to the notion that these places represented some stable, coherent, and identifiable community.

Developed and enhanced by ski resort marketers, this idea took on a life of its own. Combined with powerful images of the Alps, Victorian society, and the Wild West, it helped draw tourists, ski bums, businesspeople, and second-home owners to ski towns throughout the Rockies. Once they were invested in it, these people worked hard to protect their local community from succeeding waves of tourists, businesspeople, and second-home owners. Western mountain towns are as transient and problematic as they have always been, but the advent of tourism has made that increasingly difficult to recognize. The act of skiing, opportunities for consumption, and icons of ski culture invited visitors into the mythic world of ski resort towns. They made the alpine, Wild West, and Victorian community of locals seem real, attractive, and worth fighting for. While destination resorts became increasingly wrapped up in mythic images turned real, real people turned mythic, and a range of people calling them home, their appeal continued to grow.

6

Shredding Aspen
Resort Culture and Its Critics

In 1976, reporters gave the American public a shocking look into destination resort living at Aspen, and it had little to do with skiing or mythic visions of the West. Instead, it was about celebrity, spectacle, and death. The *New York Times* reported on April 8, "Claudine Longet, a French singer and actress, was charged today with manslaughter in the shooting death of Vladimir [Spider] Sabich, twice the world professional ski racing champion."[1] He was killed in their Starwood home when the gun he was showing her how to use accidentally went off, according to Longet. The fame of the principals (plus Longet's ex-husband Andy Williams, who quickly appeared by her side), the mystery of what happened (ballistics data called Longet's story into question and raised the possibility of murder), and the location of the incident (an elite subdivision of by-then-famous Aspen), all drew attention to the incident. Thirteen Colorado news organizations fought to void a gag order barring press from the preliminary hearing, and the case quickly became national news.[2]

The press surrounding Sabich's death and Longet's trial publicized vivid images of decadence and intrigue and located them squarely in Aspen, Colorado. The town gained notoriety in this case not from its scenic landscape, mining past, western atmosphere, or colorful locals. It grew famous instead for its collection of celebrities and their extreme behavior. One *New York Times* article ostensibly about Longet's trial focused instead on Aspen's growing image as "a hedonistic place," noting that the federal Drug Enforcement Agency had labeled it "the cocaine capital" of the country and quoting a current

novel's description of the town as "a savage world of sensuous indulgence
. . . where the driving forces of power, money and sex culminate in violence
and murder."[3] Claudine Longet and Spider Sabich embodied this image.
Beautiful people living storied lives in an idyllic town, the lovers exposed
an ugly but equally fascinating side of Aspen's culture when Sabich's gun
went off.

And people paid attention. The story got picked up beyond print and television news coverage; it wound up on *Saturday Night Live*. The show aired a
skit during its first season in which Tom Tryman (Chevy Chase) and Jessica
Antlerdance (Jane Curtin) reported from the "Claudine Longet Invitational"
in "Vale," Colorado. Skiers competing in this men's freestyle event faced more
than a field of moguls. First out of the gate was Helmut Kingle, and he was
looking good until Tryman exclaimed, "Uh-oh! He seems to have been accidentally shot by Claudine Longet! Yes . . . and I'm afraid Helmut Kindle is
out of this race!" Next up was Jean-Paul Baptiste. He recovered twice from a
similar fate only to be "accidentally shot by Claudine Longet" for a third and
final time, just shy of the finish line. Later, Tryman and Antlerdance provided
commentary on a series of highlights showing the same falling skier, saying,
"here, she mistakenly dropped her gun and it went off." "Uh . . . here, she
was just showing the gun to a friend." "I think she was just cleaning her gun
here, wasn't she?" And "Here, I think she just put the gun down in the snow
and it went off by mistake."[4] Curtin and Chase expressed clear opinions about
Longet's innocence, but more generally they argued that skiing had become
inescapably intertwined with deranged famous people. They critiqued Aspen
(or "Vale") for its audacity, but they also promoted ski resorts as spectacle.

How did Aspen's identity move from downhill skiing mecca to home of
the rich, famous, and ill behaved? Surely the ski company and town residents
did not choose or even foresee this kind of image being attached to their resort. The Longet trial embodied for Aspen what many big ski resorts faced in
the 1970s and 1980s: the ramifications of alpine resort culture taken to the extreme. The failed Highland Bavarian Lodge had struggled mightily to bring
elite, cosmopolitan, and famous vacationers to the Rocky Mountains during
the 1930s. At that time, European ski instructors, film celebrities, and savvy
marketers created a fashionable and sexy "in crowd" at Sun Valley. Later, some
Colorado ski areas acquired a similar reputation when they embraced new
identities as destination resorts. They transposed a European resort culture

known for its wealth and consumption onto postwar Colorado landscapes once characterized by small, local ski clubs and tows — an act that affected the reputation and meaning of their towns as well as their skiing.

Aspenization

The term *aspenization* came to represent resort towns increasingly at odds with their surroundings, and it reflected a ski industry that had grown at once more popular and more problematic than ever before. It was not difficult for Chevy Chase and Jane Curtin to make fun of "Vale" on *Saturday Night Live*. By the 1970s and 1980s, destination ski resorts had grown practically into parodies of themselves. After postwar social and economic trends enabled small mountain towns to attract crowds of skiers and foster their own version of European resorts, Colorado skiing looked very different from its historical roots in the late nineteenth century. Resort marketers defined skiing as all about leisure and consumption rather than work or necessity; it was about wealth and whiteness instead of immigrant labor, and sex and celebrity overshadowed athleticism and sport. The growth of the ski industry set up a series of tensions and contradictions similar to those embodied in mountain landscapes and local ski communities, this time focused on an elite, white, and gendered consumer culture.

As members of the ski industry used the language of whiteness to attract customers, the historical memory of European skiing and emigration dwindled in importance and became detached from European ethnics and references. Owners and advertisers blithely made the conscious choice to "go Bavarian."[5] Vail marketers emphasized its chosen alpine identity over all else in their ad that tempted readers to discover Europe in Vail. Consumers, of course, did not expect to find all of Europe happily ensconced in Vail. They responded to the ad and embraced these aspects of European ski culture because they gave priority to the images associated with their purchases, not to the commodities' origins or practical uses. This is what happens when goods acquire meaning through advertising and marketing; they become cultural rather than functional goods, with symbolic meanings that grow separate from the reality of the commodity's production.

Referring to the Rockies as the American Alps allowed "European" westerners access to faraway places, and ski fashion let them look the part.

Clothes from Europe, like European ski equipment, transferred a sense of legitimacy and style to their owner. Klaus Obermeyer's clothes and German ski boots were popular in America, and he stressed their Bavarian roots in images as well as words by posing a St. Bernard dog next to his model in one ad. Norwegian sweaters approached the status of uniforms for any self-respecting skier, and Bogner's stretch pants revolutionized American ski fashion altogether. Bogner's pants did not *look* especially German, but they *were* German, and they were much sexier than the older "baggy look" fashions. For women who skied in the late 1950s and 1960s, they were almost mandatory. Ski slopes thus provided space to display feats of consumption as well as athleticism, infusing a skier's visibility with signs of class as well as white Europeanness and further incorporating consumer culture into the landscape.

Nor was this a solitary process. Ski culture celebrated whiteness and wealth within an explicitly social, heterosexual atmosphere. Emphasized in the European resorts of the 1920s and 1930s and visible even in nineteenth-century Colorado mountain communities, skiing's social aspects took on new importance when placed in Colorado's consumer- and leisure-oriented destination resorts. After World War II, socializing on and off the slopes offered valuable opportunities to share stories, show off new clothes, and consume symbols of ethnicity and class — not to mention get dates. When asked what she thought of the Rocky Mountain skiing boom in 1946, racer Barbara Kidder replied, "You mean social boom, don't you?"[6] Ski resorts' après-ski scene thus grew as an integral part of ski culture — especially at destination resorts, where visitors could go out every evening — and it joined images of class, gender, and sex.[7]

In many ways, this combination was not new. Sun Valley and earlier resorts in the Alps had earned reputations as places where the rich and famous consumed fashion, skiing, and members of the opposite sex all at once. Colorado's destination resorts acquired some of that sex appeal when they defined themselves as exotic alpine or mythically western places, welcoming visitors to escape their regular worlds and indulge themselves. Vacationers enjoyed a new identity as they played on the slopes and fraternized with locals, ski bums, and one another in town, and they relived some of that excitement every time they described where they had been and what they had done.

Representatives of the ski industry made sure to sell romantic adventure to every vacationer looking for some fun. One airline advertisement promised "après-skiing fun galore is yours for the asking." Park City (Utah) advertisers exclaimed, "Park City has 5 miles of lifts going up. Park City has 30 miles of runs going down. And Park City has a swinging time at the bottom." Nor did the adventure necessarily end when the bars closed. A boot-carrier ad, featuring a sultry blonde reclining in the background, stated with a wink and a nudge, "When boots are off . . . they're better off in a Boot-In."[8] Even *Business Week* noticed the trend and declared in 1964, "It's après-ski, or the business of making skiers happy from the end of the ski run to the wee hours — and its making Aspen and other ski spots happy, too."[9] Restaurants, bars, and retail stores flourished as they catered to skiers' and tourists' evening desires.

All this coincided with an increasingly public consumption of sex in America. After the birth control pill became available in 1960, the dating and mating habits of young people became a hot topic of conversation. Studies titled *Sex and the Single Girl* and *Sex and the College Girl* appeared in 1962 and 1964, respectively. Hit songs like "Will You Love Me Tomorrow" weighed the merits of premarital sex, and Chubby Checker's "The Twist" animated young people's bodies in new and somewhat startling ways. The counterculture of the early and mid-1960s moved sex further into the public realm with its emphasis on "free love," and the women's movement brought it into the courtroom as debates on abortion heated up.[10] What women could or should do with their bodies had become the focus of all kinds of attention by the 1970s, a phenomenon that freed them but also commodified them to a greater degree than ever before. Female bodies, sex, and sexuality were available for public consumption on the news, on television shows, in advertisements, and in feature films. Two James Bond movies, *On Her Majesty's Secret Service* (1969) and *The Spy Who Loved Me* (1977), connected sex and adventure directly to skiing in their opening chase scenes.[11]

It made perfect sense, in this cultural context, to use beautiful women and their bodies to sell all things ski-related. One skiwear ad — playing off stereotypically western images — showed photos of a man on horseback roping and leading away two smiling women. The text read: "Roffe captures what every skier wants."[12] The ski fashion industry typically emphasized sexual images more than anyone else. A *Ski* photo essay entitled "How the West Was (Re)Won" similarly incorporated western images and sex into its composition by picturing beautiful models in the Colorado ghost town of East Tincup. The text explained, "In the old days, it was the gunslingers, miners and wily

The accompanying text for this 1970 advertisement read, "Roffe Captures What Every Skier Wants." This ad described women skiers as targets, men as western frontier types, and the act of skiing as secondary to what might happen after. Buy these clothes now, Roffe promised, and you can take them off later. (Roffe, a division of Pacific Trail, Inc.)

sheriffs that conquered the West and pushed into the mountains. . . . This year," it went on, "SKI reports a re-conquest: pretty girls in gold and glamorous ski clothes invading the Rockies (and elsewhere) together with their handsome consorts."[13]

Beyond being mere objects, women skiers sought to act out their own sexual conquests. Their beauty and ability to spend, of course, determined the degree to which women could fulfill this dream. One female ski racer bemoaned the success that some "racer-chasers" had in luring male racers away from their female colleagues. "The racer-chaser always seems to be rich, blond, dressed in fantastic après-ski outfits, driving a hot sports car and offering to take the guys surfing in California after the last race," she said.[14] Real life seemed to bear out what the advertisers promised: dress right, look right, and spend money, and you can catch a man. Whether married or single, men and women seemed to transform into markedly sexual beings once they were in destination resorts. One writer described Aspen, for instance, as "a town where the waitresses exude sex appeal despite the fact their shoulder-length hair is windblown, they are wearing bulky, formless sweaters and skin-hugging ski pants, and they have peeling noses and complexions like tanned leather."[15] Men brought with them, perhaps, certain attitudes and goals that encouraged this kind of transformation. Too, the scenic, exotic, and après-ski atmosphere of resort towns, combined with strenuous outdoor activity all day, separated skiers from their workaday worlds and created magical landscapes suited for romance.

Linked with the sexy aura of resort consumer culture was the notion that people at such places somehow mattered more than most. As early as 1946, one skier emphasized, "skiing is rapidly becoming *the thing to do.*" "In Denver these days," she said, "you must learn to ski to be *in.*"[16] Indeed, skiing had signaled social status for decades already, distinguishing wealthy Americans who vacationed in the Alps in the 1920s, elite Ivy League college men during the 1930s, and prestigious 10th Mountain Division veterans in the 1940s and 1950s. Many of the industry's movers and shakers, for instance, held degrees from Yale — or membership in some such exclusive group — in common with their upper-class clientele.[17] When the ski industry opened the sport to people outside these groups in the 1960s, it still held up the elite as ski icons. Rich, influential people continued to frequent destination ski resorts. Famous skiers included, for instance, Norma Shearer; the shah of Iran; Leonard Bernstein; Leon Uris; Norman Mailer; Ernest Hemingway; members of the DuPont, Mellon, Ford, and Rockefeller families; Secretary of Defense Robert McNamara; Supreme Court Justice Byron White; and Sargent Shriver, his wife, "and a whole platoon of other Kennedys and Kennedy in-laws." Skiing was, in the words of one writer, "the sport of the establishment."[18] Although not everyone could achieve such wealth and power, skiers could get a taste of that world by visiting destination resorts. Taking a skiing vacation, then, became a sign of status. Developers, too, realized this and counted on the fact that "there's nothing quite as chic as dropping into the cocktail party conversation back in the city that you're going to spend Christmas at your condominium." "That's the kind of advertising," one crowed, "money can't buy."[19]

Beyond the elite of the "establishment," other sorts of famous people also helped put destination resorts on the map. International competitors and professional ski instructors used their skills on the mountain to attract serious skiers and students. Movie stars enhanced a resort's image merely through their presence as part-time residents or regular visitors, which was why Averell Harriman and his public relations guru convinced Gary Cooper, Claudette Colbert, Rosalind Russell, and others to move to Sun Valley. After World War II, many of Sun Valley's ski instructors, clientele, and famous residents moved to Aspen. Friedl Pfeifer, Gary and Rocky Cooper, and Claudette Colbert appeared in promotional films for the new resort, along with well-known skiers such as John Litchfield, Percy Rideout, Fred Iselin, and Dick Durrance, crafting Aspen as a mountain resort where celebrities and elite outdoors people could relax together.[20] During the 1940s and 1950s, Aspenites understood these stars as just classy neighbors or, as one resident put it, "part of the [town's] whole fabric."[21] When Aspen's population included such personalities as Walter and Elizabeth Paepcke, Herbert Bayer, Harold Ross (editor

Friedl Pfeifer, Gary Cooper, and his wife Rocky graced Aspen with their celebrity style both on and off the slopes, giving the town a reputation for glamour that resident and visiting movie stars continue to reinforce. (Aspen Historical Society)

of the *New Yorker*), Thornton Wilder, and a lot of other well-educated, well-traveled people from New York and Chicago, famous movie stars might seem colorful and interesting, but not so strange that they seemed foreign. In its "golden days" as the ultimate ski resort, many people in Aspen were famous and visible. Gary Cooper once jokingly complained, for instance, that "no one pays any attention to me up here!"[22] Later on, however, when resorts attracted a broader range of tourists and mass media turned celebrities' personal lives into matters of public consumption, famous residents and visitors became objects of tourism.[23]

People visited resort towns, in other words, partly to spectate — to watch upper-class and famous people enter and enhance glamorous and exotic resort landscapes. Sun Valley, Aspen, and, more recently, Telluride have acquired rich and famous residents (Bruce Willis, Don Johnson, and Oprah Winfrey among them), visible people who have helped create a glitzy atmosphere there. This atmosphere, foreign to most Americans' daily lives, appealed to tourists by offering tantalizing images of wealth and fame. Counting movie star sightings has become an affordable part of ski vacations for many. In this way, visitors can identify with wealth and fame the same way the rich and famous have linked themselves to western and alpine resort towns — through the consumption of images and iconic people. And just as celebrities advertise destination resorts, those landscapes in turn underscore the notoriety of its regulars. The national press probably would not have cared, for instance, if Claudine Longet had misfired a gun in Cleveland.

As images of class, sex, and celebrity converged within American ski culture, they eventually threatened to overpower the sport. Skiing, to some degree, became optional. A ski vacation could consist of relaxing on the mountain during the day and visiting local night spots later. This schedule maximized visible acts of consumption and minimized the need for physical effort — pretending to ski and looking the part was enough. One advertisement for (European) indoor footwear claimed that "some of the best skiing is done right here," reclining by a coffee table. The ad went on to explain that "half the fun of skiing is in the telling and half the fun of the telling is in the snug warmth of these Swiss-made after-ski boots."[24] Here, talking and wearing imported clothes rivaled the act of skiing in social importance. One historian observed this trend occurring in destination resorts as early as the 1930s and 1940s. "Since [the opening of Sun Valley in 1936]," he wrote, "visitors who come to the ski resorts simply to wear the latest in ski clothing from Abercrombie and Fitch, ride the chair tow, and recuperate from the trip over hot buttered rum or moose milk have sometimes exceeded the skiers."[25] Similarly, a Colorado racer noticed in 1946 that "the slopes are jammed with well-dressed people who ride the tows a couple of times and sit the afternoon out in the warming house."[26]

This trend has only increased in recent years. The Italian clothing line Fila appealed to such performances of consumption by stressing the significance of "stand[ing] in the lift line looking cool." One Aspen local noted, "we're getting an awful lot of people who come here for the nightlife and the shopping and to wear their fur coats around town and they never go up on the slopes."[27] In a world where seeing and being seen were the ultimate goals — on the slopes and around town — fashion could matter more than skiing. Buying images of sexiness and glamour in this way, or living vicariously through the celebrities who did, gave access to ski culture to those who were not prepared for the physical experience of skiing down a mountain.

Skiers and consumers became indistinguishable as the ski industry offered both the sport and symbols connected to it for sale. "Now," one industry veteran noted recently, "the perception of being a skier is really what matters."[28] One ski trade article accordingly reminded retailers to "Sell the Look First." Such an imperative often produced strange behavior. Even those who encouraged it could not help but notice. A store owner in Winnetka, Illinois, explained "How to Sell Expensive Fashions to the Nabob" in an article with the subheading: "Oh, the Rich People. They just love to buy strange things."[29] These wealthy people — and the people who came to watch and imitate them — flocked to destination resorts in the mood to recreate. Their behavior often matched their clothes in its distance from everyday norms. The Reverend Don Simonton noted of his parishioners at Vail: "Well, we have a lot of pure and simple gold-plated hedonists around here, a lot of people who are wholly dedicated to remaining young and good-looking."[30] Extreme behavior and brazen spending practices seemed normal at these places, and such decadent resort culture turned big resorts into caricatures of their earlier selves.

This situation endangered one of ski resorts' central icons: ski bums. Valued largely for their local status and skiing ability, these workers both scorned and could not afford the acts of consumption that came to characterize resort skiing. Young people who took jobs within the ski industry because they loved the sport, *Ski* magazine noted in 1967, often ran out of time to ski.[31] So they left, or they took on management positions, or they bought their own businesses and turned into legitimate businesspeople. As the ski industry grew more corporate in structure and management style, too, self-proclaimed ski bums appealed less to employers. Accessories of the 1960s youth culture — long hair, marijuana, and a lagging respect for elders — frightened many potential employers out of hiring them. If employed, ski bums could look forward to long hours, hard work, and bleak stretches of weather to go with their season of skiing, no matter what their job.[32] Bumhood proved difficult, from this perspective, to sustain.

Along with the conspicuously consumptive ski culture came a growth in resort and real estate development during the 1970s and a corresponding rise in the cost of living. Such a trend quickly excluded most young people from resort towns. Two ex-Aspen workers lamented in 1979, "it's just damn expensive being a ski bum these days." By their conservative figuring, a dishwasher or a maid in Aspen who skied would owe $141 a month on top of what they could earn.[33] Resort managers across the country supported the spirit of this claim. Sixty percent of major destination resorts surveyed in 1979 reported a definite drop in the number of applications for ski area jobs in the previous two or three years. The lack of reasonably priced housing near ski areas — a problem across the country, but especially acute in the West — posed a significant obstacle. Low wages and rising prices for housing, food, lift tickets, and incidentals prevented service workers from earning enough to support themselves and still ski.[34] Without the status of the ski bum persona and time off to ski, menial and service jobs were nothing but hard work for minimum wage. At the same time, continued growth of the ski industry and its accompanying culture created more service-oriented jobs than typical ski bums could fill. Destination resorts eventually sought workers who were not interested in skiing, and the ski bum disappeared into the muddy waters of low-wage labor.

The masses of skiers who led the industry's boom during the 1960s were among its casualties in later years. Middle-class skiers dropped by the wayside as the cost of lift tickets and the trappings of destination resort culture grew beyond their means. They chose instead to ski less frequently, at less-expensive, smaller ski areas, or both. Appropriate dress and behavior at places such as Aspen and Vail cost a lot to start with. Lift ticket prices had risen steadily since the beginning of the ski industry; big resorts that had to pay for major development and high insurance premiums led the way. Aspen Mountain and Vail charged, respectively, $6.50 and $5 for a full-day adult ticket during the 1962–63 season. They charged $9 during 1972–73, and by the 1982–83 season, their prices had skyrocketed to $22.[35] The annual household income of Aspen skiers jumped accordingly. During the 1973–74 season, 23 percent of those surveyed reported an income of over $50,000; ten years later, 27 percent said they earned over $100,000. Of all income brackets in the 1983–84 survey, more skiers fell into this top one by far.[36] By the mid-1990s, people were paying $50 for a one-day lift ticket at destination resorts, and the economic elitism of skiing had become a source of humor. Such jokes brought laughs precisely because readers understood the truth behind them. Wealth was fast becoming a requirement for visiting these areas, especially if one planned on staying for more than a day or two.

Ski Industry under Fire

Destination resorts and the industry that fueled their growth had become easy targets for attack by the 1970s, and not just from *Saturday Night Live* or the funny pages. People seeking an authentic wilderness or rural community experience at ski resorts grew frustrated, and so did many middle-class, female, and minority skiers. Tensions arose over the environmental impacts of development, obviously constructed landscapes, urban problems in resort

CAFE ANGST by Hans Bjordahl and Holley Irvine

Café Angst, 1996, reprinted with permission

[handwritten margin notes: Wanted to go back but w/out danger; Conflict; Women & Minorities vs. Elite White Men & Ski Ind.]

towns, and the exclusivity of skiing's consumer culture. Starting in the 1970s, different groups of people mounted critiques of the ski industry that spoke to these tensions. The environmental consequences of mountain development became an issue for the U.S. Forest Service, ski area companies, and local conservation groups. With new development, it grew more difficult to convince people that they were skiing in a pristine, natural, wild setting, and skiers expressed conflicting desires to be both more adventurous and protected from danger. Resort town residents began recognizing the urban and labor problems that accompanied their growth as tourist meccas. Ski culture itself became problematic as its whiteness, wealth, and sexiness felt increasingly exclusive.

The U.S. government opened the door for environmentalists to voice their concerns over ski resort development, and it altered the relationship between the U.S. Forest Service (USFS) and the ski industry from one of support to one of tight regulation. The Forest Service had always negotiated the tension between the public use of forest resources and their conservation, but during the 1960s the popular environmental movement took shape and policy swung toward conservation.[37] The clearest example of this was the National Environmental Policy Act (NEPA), which President Nixon signed on January 1, 1970. This law established the Environmental Protection Agency (EPA) and set the government to the task of "creat[ing] and maintain[ing] conditions under which man and nature can exist in productive harmony, and fulfill the social, economic, and other requirements of present and future generations of Americans." After this act took effect, every proposal for development on public lands had to include an examination of the environmental impact of that development, a consideration of alternative courses of action, and the opportunity for public involvement in the decision.[38] Through this now requisite environmental impact statement (EIS), NEPA forced the ski industry to examine the effects that its lifts, lodges, trails, and snowmaking had on the mountains, and document them for federal, state, local, and public appraisal.

This legislation increased the amount of red tape involved in ski area development exponentially, slowing expansion in the 1970s and making it extremely difficult for new areas to win USFS approval. Subsequent legislation — the Endangered Species Act of 1973, the Archaeological Resources Protection Act of 1979, and amendments to the Clean Water Act — added to the issues that resort developers had to face and increased the Forest Service's role as guardian of the national forests. Anticipating the environmental consequences of resort landscapes took the romance out of creating ski areas, to say the least. Future Silver Queens and Vista Bahns could no longer simply emerge and spirit skiers up mountains into a world of natural, scenic adventure. Instead, each would have its size, placement, design, and means of installment examined, questioned, and argued over — on paper and in public.

Vail's development of Beaver Creek became the focus of a herculean struggle over development. Begun in 1970, Vail Associates' planning and negotiations for Beaver Creek had cost $6 million by 1974, when the Forest Service filed its draft EIS. The resort had originally been planned for the 1976 Winter Olympics in Denver, but arguments over the necessary development and its costs had polarized Colorado residents, and in 1972, voters declined to host the games. Without the Olympics to help justify the project, Vail Associates entered a bureaucratic black hole. "The state's 13-agency review of the EIS was so critical," ranger Paul Hauk wrote, "that even development-oriented Governor John Vanderhoof requested the Forest Service to delay issuing a permit."[39] After a long debate between the USFS and Governor Lamm (who opposed the project and worked to reverse outgoing Governor Vanderhoof's last-minute approval of the area), the Sierra Club filed an appeal to block the development. Finally, after more studies, plans, and compromises, Vail Associates got its special-use permit for Beaver Creek in March 1976. Still, two more appeals from the Environmental Defense Fund and from

Calvin and Hobbes © 1993 by Watterson. Reprinted with permission of Universal Press Syndicate. All rights reserved.

an individual in Gunnison delayed groundbreaking ceremonies until July 1977. The resort finally opened in 1980.[40] Few ski corporations dared propose new resorts after that, lest they be subject to the same costly delays and controversies; no new ski area has been developed since.[41]

Even planning an expansion could lead to problems. Proposed expansions at Colorado destination resorts raised a variety of environmental issues that stirred up local communities, generated both regional and national press, and galvanized opposition from environmental groups. In the early 1990s, Snowmass planned to build ski lifts and trails on Burnt Mountain, thereby extending the resort to the edge of the Maroon Bells–Snowmass Wilderness Area and endangering local elk habitat. Plans for increased snowmaking, which would divert water from local streams during brown trout spawning season, prompted the Aspen Wilderness Workshop to bring the case before the Colorado Supreme Court. A *New York Times* reporter picked up the story (as had regional reporters) and introduced the environmental issues surrounding snowmaking to the national public.[42] The local population divided when it had to judge the relative importance of protecting the local elk herd, the integrity of the wilderness area, and brown trout spawning habitat against additional jobs and business for the town. These issues raised tempers across the state and placed the environmental consequences of resort development in the public forum.[43]

Telluride experienced similar controversy. In 1993, federal investigators accused ski area developers of violating the Clean Water Act when they built an eighteen-hole golf course, a parking lot, roads, ski runs, restaurants, and condominiums at the new Telluride Mountain Village. Between 1984 and 1990, the government declared, the company had filled in forty acres of wetlands. Useful as wildlife and waterfowl habitat, as filters for leaching toxins from groundwater, and as protection against floods, wetlands had recently been recognized as valuable natural resources. Telluride's corporation found itself in a sticky situation. Negotiations for a settlement with the EPA took years; delays boosted development costs by at least $2.5 million. Telluride executives agreed to pay a penalty, restore some wetlands at the resort, and construct new wetlands on land in the next county. Local public protest, however, criticizing the small size of the financial penalty and the fact that wetlands restoration would be outside the Telluride watershed, caused a U.S. district judge to reject the offer. The EPA later broadened the suit and claimed that the resort had actually destroyed sixty-two acres of wetlands.[44] As one of the largest such cases in Colorado, the Telluride wetlands case helped the EPA advertise a lesson that one executive learned early on: "Don't do anything to violate the Clean Water Act. Avoid it at all cost, like you avoid the IRS."[45]

The federal, regional, and local outcry that ski resort development prompted since the 1970s has drawn attention to the increased size of the ski industry as well as its environmental consequences. And while federal concerns over such issues have fluctuated with presidential administrations, environmental interest groups have mobilized to protect land and wildlife through the creation of land trusts, the purchase of development rights, and even violence. In October 1998, a group of environmental activists called the Earth Liberation Front (ELF) claimed responsibility for a fire that caused $12 million in damage to several of Vail Resort's buildings and chairlifts. The ELF issued a statement opposing Vail's new expansion onto a ridge overlooking a national forest, land that had been deemed appropriate for the reintroduction of lynx populations. The group stated that "putting profits ahead of Colorado's wildlife will not be tolerated" and justified the arson as being done "on behalf of the lynx."[46]

Another less extreme set of critiques also focused on the tension between built landscapes and nature, and it explained, in part, why Vail wanted to expand so close to "wild" land. In short, it helped make the development look natural. The growing public awareness of environmental issues in the 1970s made resort managers realize that skiers probably noticed the built environments that resort designers worked so hard to conceal. Ski area managers, at the urging of the USFS, proceeded to construct mountain landscapes more self-consciously than ever before. Area developers should "make the ski area look more like natural terrain." "Failing to produce this visual effect," one planner argued, "is the crux of much criticism of ski developments." Indeed, by the 1990s, the USFS was employing computer technology to assess the visual impact of expansion and stressing the need to paint lift towers an appropriate color.[47] Their efforts, though unconsciously appreciated by thousands of skiers, could not hide everything.

For skiers who loved serene mountain landscapes and the chance to feel alone in the wilderness, Colorado destination resorts had lost much of their appeal. Local communities and the federal government wrestled with constructed landscapes on legal and environmental terms, but skiers also struggled with them in more personal ways. Some gave up downhill skiing in the 1970s for a sport more akin to its nineteenth-century roots: cross-country skiing. Abandoning mechanized lifts renewed the possibility of skiing silently alone in the woods. The health and fitness craze of the 1970s, combined with Bill Koch's silver medal in the 1976 Olympics, drew Americans to cross-country skiing. A national survey in 1978 confirmed it. Thirteen percent of the country's active skiers, it found, skied cross-country exclusively; and 21 percent of downhill skiers participated in cross-country skiing as well. Most, moreover, were new to the sport.[48] A different survey that same year reiterated this point; more than half the respondents had just started cross-country skiing in the last year or two. This trend was a direct response, in part, to the increasing development of alpine resort areas. Of the almost 70 percent of cross-country skiers who were not also Alpine skiers, 40 percent had been Alpine skiers before and had quit or had "tried alpine skiing and did not like it." Almost 80 percent of respondents said that they liked cross-country skiing because it allowed them to "get into the country" — an impossible feat at destination resorts from most perspectives.[49]

Backcountry skiing and extreme skiing are more recent manifestations of this desire to get away from crowds and construction. Searching for an experience unmediated by lifts, lodges, and carefully designed trails, these skiers embark on trips between mountain huts or camping sites and climb rugged peaks for the thrill of skiing steep, narrow, rocky terrain on the way down. Both the wilderness and the extreme descents that these skiers seek, respectively, exist only where development and management do not. This fact poses both an attractive and a frightening situation, for where there are no crowds, lifts, or signs funneling skiers to the "easiest way down," there are also no signs to mark cliffs, no avalanche control, and no ski patrol. The unmitigated danger that has drawn skiers from resort areas to this scenic adventure called "the backcountry" has also brought them to the emergency room. In the seven years from the 1988–89 season to 1994–95, forty-one skiers died while skiing outside of ski areas.[50] Avalanches claimed these victims; exposure and frostbite left their marks on many others. Despite — and often because of — these real dangers, backcountry skiing and extreme skiing continue to attract people for whom ski resort landscapes feel too managed and developed.

While these skiers were reacting to resorts that they considered too designed and safe, others argued that ski areas were not offering enough protection from

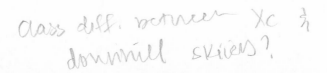

the wilderness and the dangers of skiing. Destination resort skiers made skiing part of an overall vacation experience, and they counted on resort amenities and après-ski activities to keep them busy. Skiers who took up the sport in the 1960s began, in the 1970s and later, to bring their children with them. They welcomed day-care facilities, special ski school classes, and conveniently designed lodges. Those just learning (and others, too) appreciated groomed snow, easy trails, and clear signs to lead them down safely. Ski areas knew this and advertised such amenities as reasons to visit their resorts. Most visitors took such development for granted. That skiers had come to expect such constructed resort landscapes, however unconsciously, also meant that they had a particular understanding of the area's legal responsibility to keep them safe. When that landscape fell short of their expectations they noticed, and then they went to court. Since the 1970s, then, ski resorts have had to cope increasingly with the legal repercussions of their developed landscapes — above and beyond what they faced from the EPA and members of the environmental movement. Skiers still assumed the normal risks of skiing when they bought a ticket, but their expectations for ski resort safety had grown.[51]

Dangers associated with weather, snow grooming, lift operation and safety, and trail maintenance, combined with potentially crowded conditions and people skiing out of control, could turn beautiful slopes into frightening places. In the seven years from 1988–89 to 1994–95, for instance, forty-one skiers died while inside ski area boundaries.[52] Skiers have sued resorts for all kinds of reasons; some won, some lost, and some settled out of court. Every suit filed, no matter what the outcome, expressed the notion that resort owners were not doing all they should to ensure the safety of their customers. A 1990 law seemed to uphold the established precedent by preventing skiers from suing for injuries resulting from the "inherent dangers and risks of skiing," including variations in steepness or terrain. The tables turned in 1995, however, when the Colorado Supreme Court ruled that not all dangers encountered on the ski slope were inherent to the sport. With this decision, one reporter noted, "the court refused to give Colorado ski-area operators blanket immunity from lawsuits by skiers injured on their slopes."[53] Legal battles over ski resort liability turn on a variety of factors, ranging from the specific facts of each case to the prevailing attitudes toward skiing, the ski industry, and personal responsibility in general. With skiers' increasing expectations of a constructed, managed, developed, and designed landscape came the assumption that those landscapes would be safe.

The tools and procedures that provided such a place, however, could also add to its danger. As a result, critiques of the resort landscape — in the form of lawsuits — grew more common.

Comments on skiing also took more creative forms. By the 1970s, Alpine skiing had become mainstream enough to generate a critique from young people who wanted to liven things up a bit. Rather than refine traditional technique or compete in Alpine racing events, these "hot doggers" did tricks and spins and jumps on their way down the mountain — turning skiing into a form of personal expression and using the landscape in new ways. According to one participant and ski writer, freestyle skiing "sprung up spontaneously among the young, exuberant skiers 'getting it on' by skiing on the back side of their mountains away from the stuck-in-a-rut ski school directors likely to criticize their unorthodox moves."[54] Such skiers translated countercultural trends of the late 1960s and early 1970s into action on the ski hill, setting themselves apart from the more conservative set through athletic feats that bordered on the subversive — jumping over things and flipping upside down, for instance. Sexy and colorful personalities such as Suzy Chaffee and Wayne Wong helped the sport gain in popularity, and competitions in ballet, moguls, and aerials drew crowds during the 1970s and after.[55]

Through the 1980s and 1990s, people drew attention not only to ski industry mountain landscapes but also to their resort towns. Critics of the industry bemoaned the growing tension between the authentic western, European, or rural community experience that tourists sought and the realities of resort town development. Popular resorts, with their real estate development and service economy, demanded both a workforce and a degree of urbanization that made many people uncomfortable. The mythic and white communities supported by images of the Wild West, Victorian culture, and the European Alps began to fray when their appealing ski bum laborers left town. Mexican Americans, Mexicans, eastern Europeans, and even some Africans began filling manual labor and service jobs, separating skiers from ski industry workers racially as well as economically. During the 1980s, Mexican immigrants and their families began coming to the Roaring Fork Valley because Aspen businesses recruited them as seasonal labor. As of 1994, there were at least 8,000 Hispanics living in the valley; at least 20 Africans ended up in Summit County, Colorado; and an estimated 7,000 undocumented workers could be found at different resorts between Leadville and Aspen. Some workers lived as far as sixty treacherous miles away from their work, cleaning hotel rooms and moonlighting at fast-food restaurants in an effort to make ends meet.[56]

Most ski industry workers — no matter their racial or ethnic identities — could not afford to live in or even near the resorts their work supports. Thirty-nine of Vail's forty-eight police officers and firefighters could not afford to live in town in 1995.[57] Ski resort workers resided in broken-down trailers, government-subsidized housing, cheap apartments two mountain passes away, tents on national forest land, and even vans parked in maintenance garages.[58] Housing problems — and other problems associated with a new, largely immigrant workforce — have made much of Colorado's ski country look like part of a developing country. Even the Catholic Church took notice. When Sister Annette Carrica of the Ohio-based Sisters of Charity sought to help Latin Americans, she went not to Central America but to the heart of Colorado's ski country. She joined Roman Catholic Archbishop J. Francis Stafford, who started the Villa Sierra Madre housing project in Silverthorne to help poor Hispanic workers on the Western Slope. Sisters Mary Jo Coyle and Mary Ellen Beyhan opened a similar low-income apartment complex in Glenwood Springs for the Denver archdiocese, which made plans for another in Carbondale and one near Winter Park.[59]

Revealing the problematic social relations that underlay Colorado's ski industry has been a matter of social justice for most, but it also reflects nostalgia for mythically white and quaint western communities. Tourists and western residents invested in an authentic local experience unmarred by the labor demands of industrialized leisure. Evidence of an impoverished and exploited workforce concerned them, as did other attendant problems that arose since the 1980s. Resort towns have come to resemble surprisingly urban places, for instance, despite their rural settings. Housing and child-care problems plague ski resort employees throughout the state. Though these workers support places characterized by whiteness and wealth with their labor, the surrounding communities they call home have more in common with urban slums than with the mythic West. In a reversal of typical urban geography, wealthy and white people live in the center — albeit an isolated mountain town center — while people of color and lower classes live outside. They commute out of necessity, spending wages on high-priced gasoline and time on dangerous roads in a ritual that only reinforces their economic situation. When placed in high mountain landscapes, moreover, urban problems such as traffic jams and pollution grow more deadly. The scenic winding road from Glenwood Springs to Aspen, for instance, which every worker must travel twice a day, is often covered with snow and ice, hidden in darkness, or both. Locals call it "Killer 82." Like their traffic, resort towns produce larger amounts of particulate emissions than mountain landscapes can handle. Well-used fireplaces in second homes and condominiums, cars, and the general activity of resort towns concentrate pollution in their high mountain valleys and box canyons, where it usually stays. These characteristics give new meaning to the saying, "It's a nice place to visit but I wouldn't want to live there."

Ski resorts thus struggled to retain their images as quaint, idyllic, and scenic at the same time that the realities of their tourist economies increasingly threatened that image. Maintaining this tension between the illusion of wilderness and the reality of development gave destination ski resorts their appeal, but that struggle had to remain behind the scenes — visitors did not want to see the unromantic framework supporting their vacation experiences. Since the 1970s, however, ski resort culture could no longer completely hide from view the environmental, physical, and social relationships on which it was based.

The whiteness, wealth, and sex that characterized skiing's consumer culture and resort landscapes glossed over similar complexities. A range of people voiced concerns about this during the 1970s and 1980s and tried to expand the social and cultural images attached to skiing. The National Brotherhood of Skiers (NBS) formed in 1973. An organization of black skiers, the NBS sought to eliminate the barriers that have kept minority children from the sport. Since its inception, the organization has helped children of color learn to ski and tried to place black skiers on U.S. Olympic teams. As of 2003, the group had more than eighty ski club affiliates in seventy-five cities across the country, with a total membership of over 20,000. Despite their numbers and the fact that members spent an estimated $36 million skiing during the 1993–94 season — a statistic that does not include the other estimated 100,000 black skiers in the country — advertisers and manufacturers have not supported either the organization in particular or black skiers in general. One spokesman noted that black skiers spent nearly $200 million a year on skiing. "If you look at the advertising here," he said, "you don't even see photos of blacks skiing in their brochures."[60] Through the NBS, African Americans questioned ski culture's overwhelming whiteness by drawing attention to their physical and economic presence on the slopes.

Through the 1970s, women expressed their discomfort with stereotypes that emphasized sexuality over athleticism and sport. The national movement for women's rights, Title IX's pledge for equal opportunity in sports and education across gender lines, and Billie Jean King's spectacular victory over Bobby Riggs all encouraged women to celebrate and expand their athletic abilities rather than shrink them to fit an outdated feminine ideal. Women had skied in significant numbers throughout the twentieth century, but during the 1970s, the tension between their athletic behavior and images that defined it as mainly sexual or social reached a breaking point. By this time, women who may have started skiing to get a date had children of their own. They continued to ski and took advantage of resort day-care facilities to do so, and they were not skiing to find men. As early as 1970, one female ski school director promoted a weekly Ladies' Day, which targeted local housewives. "Women seem to learn faster when their husbands aren't around," she said, "and since half the ski school staff is women, the local ladies are more comfortable taking lessons."[61] This approach worked because it treated women instructors and clients as skiers, separate from men and with their own strengths and weaknesses. Five years later, Elissa Slanger, an instructor at Squaw Valley, took these ideas further and designed a clinic specifically for women. Her Women's Way seminars took into account how skiers viewed themselves, how society viewed them, and each woman's sports history. Slanger treated her clients as female athletes with learning styles distinct from those of men, and she established a growing phenomenon in ski marketing.[62]

Gay and lesbian skiers, similarly, have critiqued resort culture's heterosexual assumptions by celebrating and emphasizing their own presence on the slopes. In Aspen, for instance, gay and lesbian skiers have organized an annual Gay Ski Week since 1977. In 1993, about 3,000 gay and lesbian skiers flocked to the town, and the numbers have continued to grow. They came on their own and with clubs from places including Kansas City, Florida, New York, New Jersey, Boston, and Los Angeles.[63] By reveling in Aspen's social atmosphere and redefining it, at least temporarily, for their group, gay and lesbian skiers drew attention to the heterosexual relationships on which the industry has depended. At the same time — during that week in Aspen — they spent millions of dollars on the ski industry.

Black, gay, and feminist skiers protested within the bounds of resort culture — they sought inclusion and used their power as consumers to get it.

Others protested by taking their dollars elsewhere. Cross-country, backcountry, and extreme skiers chose, at least initially, not to spend their money on lift tickets at all, while others gave up trips to big resorts for more affordable skiing at smaller areas. One of the most powerful critiques of the ski industry, however, came from outside that industry altogether. Snowboarders, a whole new set of mountain and gear consumers, launched a broad critique of the ski industry on all fronts. They were young and rebellious, and they spoke out against older and upper-class skiers who represented the "establishment."

Originating largely from surf and skateboard cultures in the 1970s, snowboarders attached their sport to a counterculture that set skiers' teeth on edge.[64] Like freestyle skiers, they used mountain landscapes in new ways, redefining them as part of an entirely different cultural scene. One California surfer, for instance, found himself living in Colorado's Rockies in 1985. He longed for "bikinis, convertibles, and Los Siete Burritos on Mission Beach." "But mostly," he wrote, "I wanted to surf."[65] He bought a snowboard and later became an instructor, teaching Californians and native Coloradans alike how to surf snowy mountain waves. More directly influential on snowboard culture, however, was the skateboarding world, which took surfing culture in the late 1960s and dropped it on city streets.[66]

Skateboarders kept the male countercultural feel of surfing but gave it a harder edge. If surfers rebelled by frequenting the beach, skateboarders did it by using urban and suburban landscapes for sport. They rode on city side-walks, on downtown streets, in empty swimming pools, and in civic gathering places. Public safety, to put it mildly, was not their concern. Snowboarders in turn subverted mountain landscapes, already barely clinging to their associations with the wilderness, by treating snow like pavement. In bringing skateboarding to the mountains, snowboarders redefined them as more urban than wild. And they sent this message in more ways than one. The skateboarders who originated freestyle and half-pipe snowboarding voiced an acutely urban and countercultural attitude. "Skaters hated everyone," skate and snowboarding magnate Tom Sims recalled. "'Everything Sucks' was the punk mantra that [skateboard magazine] *Thrasher* espoused and that was the modern skate culture in 1982." Skaters blended this punk attitude with references to black urban hip-hop culture in the early 1990s, which influenced boarding directly and described it as extremely male if not misogynistic.[67]

This half-pipe at Steamboat brings skateboarders' concrete world to the mountains, where snowboarders have redefined ski resorts and their culture. (Steamboat/Larry Pierce)

Snowboarders first appeared at ski areas in the early 1980s, and they immediately consumed resort landscapes in challenging ways. They hiked up trails to avoid the cost of a lift ticket. They became notorious for cutting off skiers. They traveled in packs. They "bonked," "jibbed," "tweaked," and rode "fakie" — acts that, among other things, included jumping over or actually riding something other than snow. They listened to the Beastie Boys. They wore baggy pants and neglected to respect their elders. Their adolescent maleness re-gendered mountain landscapes; their hip-hop style of clothes, music, and mannerisms declared black culture relevant (though few were black); and they treated mountains like urban skateboard parks, abandoning the image of nature and wilderness that others held sacred.

Snowboarders seemed to dismiss ski equipment, landscapes, clothing, coed social culture, and the older consumers who bought it all, and this riled people up. Their young, urban, in-your-face maleness threatened to overturn the basic tenets of the ski industry and its resort culture. In 1985, only 7 percent of U.S. ski resorts allowed snowboarding. Aspen and Keystone banned snowboarders from their slopes completely.[68] Animosity and even violence between skiers and boarders became expected. One running skier's joke went: "What's the difference between a boarder and a catfish? One is a bottom-dwelling, disgusting, rejected muck sucker and the other is a fish."

Although some of this conflict arose from skiers' low view of boarders, snowboarders also saw their actions as an explicit rejection of the ski industry. "Skiing was so elitist in the early '80s," said one of the founders of Avalanche Snowboards, "really cliquey, [and] exclusive." According to snowboarding historian Susanna Howe, the Avalanche crew "was formed by amazing skiers who wanted to break out of the scene." Jake Burton and his company in the East attracted ex–ski racers — "wildcards" of the sport, as Burton recalled.[69] Across the country, groups of people looking for something different turned to snowboarding.

Local environmental groups, gay and lesbian skiers, and snowboarders may seem to have little in common, but they all voiced serious critiques of the ski industry and its destination resorts. They noticed, as did Chevy Chase and Jane Curtin, that Colorado's large ski areas had grown more visible and popular, and they questioned the cost of that growth. Together these critics fueled a long-standing argument over what constituted an authentic skiing experience in the Rockies. Environmental groups and skiers who fled resorts questioned the legitimacy of skiing's "natural" landscapes; commentators on western tourist towns lamented the loss of rural communities; a variety of skiers spoke out against the exclusivity of ski resort culture; and snowboarders dismissed practically every aspect of the ski industry as tired and old — definitely in need of some new, real life. They all expressed a desire to make skiing a more authentic experience, but they disagreed on how best to accomplish that, and few had a clear idea of what that experience might be.

The Industry Lives

Given the range and seriousness of these critiques, it is a wonder that the ski industry has maintained forward momentum. The average annual increase in skier-visits to Colorado areas in the 1960s was an amazing 20 percent. Growth during the 1970s and 1980s remained significant, though it calmed down after the boom years of previous decades. During the 1970s, the average growth fell to 14 percent, and for the 1980s, it slowed to 3 percent.[70] These figures described an industry increasingly dominated by large destination resorts in competition with one another for business. Vail, Aspen's four areas, Breckenridge, Steamboat, Keystone, Winter Park, and Copper Mountain accounted for about 73 percent of the industry's market share through the 1980s — of which Vail alone made up about 14 percent. Skier-tourists dominated the consumer side of the equation. Out-of-state destination skier-visits grew from 55 percent of Colorado's total skier-visits in 1981–82 to 62 percent five years later. Millions of dollars of annual capital improvements became the norm as big resorts competed for business.[71] In 1982, Colorado ski areas and related facilities represented a $3.6 billion total capital investment. The industry had also created about 39,000 jobs statewide — including over half the total jobs in Summit, Eagle, Pitkin, and Grand Counties and more than 4,000 ski-related jobs in Denver.[72] Colorado's ski industry continued to grow during the early 1990s, albeit more slowly than in previous decades, and set records of 10.42 million skier-visits in 1991–92, 11.07 million visits for the 1992–93 season, and a peak of nearly 12 million visits during the 1997–98 season. Figures for the last few seasons hovered around the 11 million skier-visit mark.[73]

Although some smaller ski areas have fallen by the wayside, destination resorts and their ski culture have become larger and more powerful. Their ownership has reached gargantuan proportions as areas have changed hands to form ever-greater corporations. One merger added Keystone, Arapahoe Basin, and Breckenridge to the already substantial holdings of Vail Resorts, Inc. (owners of Vail, Beaver Creek, and Arrowhead), in 1996. These areas accounted for a total of 4.8 million skier-days. The Aspen Skiing Company, which operated Aspen Mountain, Buttermilk, Snowmass, and Aspen Highlands as of 1993, boasted 1.4 million skier-days.[74] In terms of size and capitalization, then, Colorado's destination resorts are alive and well to an amazing degree. How did the industry maintain such growth? It paid attention to its critics and generally embraced them. Colorado ski resorts incorporated voices of dissent into their landscapes, towns, and consumer culture.

They acknowledged environmental concerns and told skiers so. A 1994 survey found that skiers as a whole were more active and informed about environmental issues than the general public. Ski industry reporters told their readers: "If you have an environmental program, stick with it. If you don't, get one." Through these programs — focused largely on issues such as recycling and offering nature tours on skis — ski resorts marketed themselves as environmentally sensitive without spending too much money.[75] They took further advantage of this opportunity by celebrating one another's efforts. The industry created Eagle awards for environmental excellence in 1994, and those areas with the best programs or design in a range of categories get their names and awards published in national ski magazines.

Following environmental laws and competing for environmental awards, however, have not kept destination resorts from expanding. Vail, for instance, doubled its size to 3,787 acres in 1989 when it built two lifts and opened four bowls on the area's backside. The arson attributed to the ELF in 1998 was a direct response to another large expansion project at Vail. Developing a ski area has real environmental consequences, and skiers have become more aware of that reality than ever before. Resort managers addressed their customers' environmental concerns, but only superficially — a move that could not appease serious environmental groups but did improve the resorts' reputations with most skiers. To some extent, the ELF's alleged arson probably even helped Vail market its new Blue Sky Basin as a place of nature and adventure, by confirming the terrain's proximity to wild land and wild life.

This ability to claim both development and wilderness helped Colorado resorts woo back skiers who had abandoned their slopes in favor of less developed landscapes. The industry recognized the growing popularity of cross-country skiing and extreme skiing and managed, largely, to incorporate them both within expanded resort landscapes. As early as 1978, many ski areas offered organized touring centers with miles of maintained trails. And despite their desire to "get into the country," most cross-country skiers preferred to ski on a prepared track with guaranteed good-quality snow.[76] While rejecting downhill ski resort landscapes, these skiers came to accept similarly constructed ones that were often owned and operated by the very same developers.

The ski industry similarly co-opted the sport of extreme skiing. Once the province of mountaineer-alpinist daredevils, extreme skiing acquired a wide following in America during the 1980s. The sport grew to the point of having its own World Extreme Ski Championships in 1991. Rather than accepting the implicit criticism of resort landscapes that these thrill-seeking people acted out on the steeps, ski resorts welcomed them, too, into the fold. They reversed their 1960s decision to focus on intermediate terrain and opened steep, narrow chutes for people who wanted to test their skill and nerve. As of 1996, Breckenridge, Copper, Crested Butte, Telluride, Snowmass, Arapahoe Basin, and Loveland had all opened areas of difficult terrain and patrolled them, too. Plunging down steep, rocky chutes, it turned out, did not rule out lift service or resort safety measures; extreme skiers could have it all. [77] Destination resorts altered their landscapes for those disillusioned with the typical slopes, attracting them, ironically, to equally constructed spaces.

Real estate developers, too, rode along with the ski industry's growth and refined traditional ski resort images. Their landscapes — though crafted to be environmentally sensitive, more varied in terms of terrain, and frequented by minority and gay skiers as well as snowboarders — perpetuated resort culture's emphasis on whiteness, wealth, fame, and fashion. The luxurious Peaks Hotel in Telluride, for instance, which has hosted the likes of Donald Trump, Kevin Costner, Tom Cruise, Paula Abdul, and Sylvester Stallone, closed its doors in 1994 for a $3 million facelift. Its owners decided that it needed a sense of place and wanted to give it a "more rustic, traditional feel." "We'll go to leather-covered furniture, Indian prints and artwork that reflects its history and location," the president said.[78] In choosing to "go western," this developer recognized the importance of matching celebrity with a mythic landscape, as well as the need to include Native American references in his romantic version of the past.

Nor are western images the only option. In the 1990s, the ski industry still spoke the language of whiteness through European symbols. And the expanse of whiteness and wealth it has created — especially in the West — has approached the absurd. The Game Creek Club at Vail cost between $20,000 and $75,000 just to join and was designed to "create a warm atmosphere and a retreat for members reminiscent of some of the fine mountain restaurants found on the high slopes of the Alps — not unlike the Eagle Club in Gstaad or the Corviglia Club in St. Moritz." Another spokesman for Vail recognized the image the club presented but justified it anyway: "We don't want this to be an elitist thing," he said, "but there was a large specialized market for this service."[79]

Conspicuous consumption of whiteness and class created a need for places like the Peaks Hotel and the Game Creek Club. Finding people to staff such places has become more difficult. Lacking a sufficient source of ski bum labor, resort businesses came to depend on a multiethnic workforce to fill their many service jobs. These workers have yet to infuse ski culture with color, however. Outlandish housing prices, a high cost of living, and low wages have enabled ski resorts to accomplish physically what they had previously done culturally. When resort culture could no longer cloak relations of labor and class behind the idealized role of the ski bum, resort landscapes hid them in kitchens, on commuter busses, and in low-income housing developments miles away from the pristine slopes. Resort communities have struggled with the physical and environmental repercussions of this move, arguing about how best to ease traffic jams, reduce pollution, and house local professionals as well as service workers.

Although images of wealth and whiteness still sell, critics of the ski industry have had some impact. Managers within the ski industry have refined their perspectives on gender and sex. Gay and lesbian skiers are welcomed every year in Aspen and have been demonstrating their economic power as consumers. So, as a group, have women. Beginning in the 1980s, ski areas began to offer special workshops and ski school classes just for them. By 1988, at least seven major ski resorts offered three- to five-day camps, clinics, or seminars exclusively by and for women. Also in the 1980s, manufacturers began to design ski equipment specifically for women's bodies, and ski resorts promoted programs and facilities to accommodate children.[80] These changes treated women as more than dates or ornaments. Both developments suggest that women have become, in the eyes of the ski industry, economically and physically independent. They are valuable customers in their own right, as athletes rather than consumers of fashion or objects of consumption themselves.

Just as resorts and marketers have tried to attract women in new ways, so have they worked to attract young people on snowboards. Market analysts had warned the industry for years that skiers were getting older. Who to replace them with, especially given the huge amounts of capital now at stake, became a pressing question in the 1990s. The answer: snowboarders. During the 1980s, these creatures frightened and offended many. The very characteristics that made snowboarding annoying to skiers, however, turned out to make it cool, hip, and popular with young people. Shredding — physically and metaphorically tearing up the slope with aggressive boarding — came into its own. National contests in the early 1980s led to World

Championships in 1987 and a World Cup circuit the next year. ABC and MTV covered the 1987 Worlds at Breckenridge, and by 1988, even *Skiing* magazine included an article about the sport entitled "Shred Heads Go Mainstream." By then, two snowboarding magazines *(ISM* and *Transworld Snowboarding)* graced newsstands, and a wave of new riders pushed snowboard sales for the 1987–88 season to 80,000.[81]

Once snowboarders emerged as a significant market, the ski industry started to see them as a target rather than a problem. The editors of *Skiing* began to test and evaluate snowboards in their 1989 buyer's guide issue. Ski resorts went out of their way to attract this fast-growing segment of the market, hiring snowboarding instructors, playing alternative music on area loudspeakers, and placing snowboarding ambassadors on mountains to ease any residual acrimonious feelings. Entire sections of industry trade publications were dedicated to studying this economically significant group. Snowboard parks and half-pipes, which offer varied terrain for jumps and tricks and prohibit skiing, have become common at most areas. By 1995, over 97 percent of U.S. ski areas allowed snowboarding, and boarders accounted for 13 percent of all lift tickets sold.[82]

Snowboarding's critique of the ski industry quieted once boarding entrepreneurs and the ski industry expanded the sport's market. One result of this was that boarding became accessible to women. A group of young female pros began riding later in the 1980s, creating an image of women on snow that celebrated athleticism, skill, and ambition, and they attracted a following of girls to the sport. As inheritors of the changes wrought by the women's movement and Title IX, women boarders claimed their outdoor mobility and an active relationship to the mountains with more gusto than earlier generations of skiers could. Greta Gaines, the 1992 Women's Extreme Snowboard Champion, said, "We want to have fun, not the quilting circle style of fun, but the real kick-ass, exhilarating meet-your-maker kind of fun, we want to ride hard, we want to play damn it and stop cheerleading."[83] Pros such as Tina Basich, Michele Taggert, and Shannon Dunn rode hard and competed among men without abandoning their identity as women. Through this initially male critique of skiing, women snowboarders moved through mountain landscapes in new ways, defining a version of femininity that characterized them at once as strong, hip, and female. Some women have since moved into the industry, selling that femininity through their clothes and equipment and supporting ski resorts at the same time that they revise ski culture.

By the 1990s, Colorado resorts and the ski industry as a whole had responded to a wide variety of critiques, largely by incorporating their messages into their resort landscapes and consumer culture. Rather than dispel the tensions that led to these criticisms, however, the ski industry has heightened them. Skiers wanted a variety of experiences, and the industry realized it fairly early on. In 1974, the senior market research analyst for Colorado argued that it was "necessary to give the vacation skier much more today than in the past." He noted, "Not only is good skiing required, but also good food, good accommodations, good entertainment, good shopping, and good après ski activities are essential. Colorado ski areas," he concluded, "provide most of what today's vacation skiers want and have gained a competitive advantage by doing so."[84] Straddling the lines between adventure and safety, rural and urban, elite and hip allowed Colorado ski resorts to satisfy its increasingly diverse clientele. So luxury developments adjoin national wilderness areas, high-speed lifts offer access to extreme slopes, and immigrant workers support mythically white towns where all kinds of visitors hobnob with the rich and famous.

These contradictions surrounding ski resort landscapes, communities, and consumer culture made it difficult to define Colorado's ski industry and the experience it provided, but they proved to be a boon to the industry rather than a threat. They supplied a wide range of meanings and contexts for skiing often far removed from the sport's origins. But they also turned the environmental impacts of resort development, the local consequences of a tourist economy, and the social implications of elite consumer culture into issues of hot debate. These debates, in turn, suggested that there was some authentic experience or community or culture at stake. And by declaring nature, communities, or resort culture and its style under siege, these debates made them all the more attractive and all the more real.

Aspen Mountain finally opened its slopes to snowboarders during the 2000–2001 season. When they shredded Aspen that year, boarders deconstructed and criticized the establishment that the mountain and its resort represented. They also consumed it, however, and participated in the very culture they had opposed. In doing so, they redefined that culture to include snowboarders — as hip, cool, and real — and they recast themselves as skiers' kin rather than adversaries. With standardized gear, better manners, more women, and more money, snowboarders today look very different from the early rebels of the 1980s. There is now a large population of aging skiers who have taken up boarding, an act that makes familiar mountain slopes feel fresh and participants feel young. Today, when boarders shred Aspen, they are making a different kind of statement than Chevy Chase and Jane Curtin did in 1976. They are reviving Aspen and themselves through a subversive youth culture gone mainstream, giving and getting a sense of prestige, fashion, and style that has helped the entire ski industry.

In 1995, Disney entered the ski business. Its new Blizzard Beach in Orlando, Florida, sports its own peaks, a chairlift, snow, and even a warming hut. Clad only in bathing suits, visitors ride a chairlift up the 120-foot "mountain" at the center of this water park. Once at the top of Mount Gushmore, vacationers descend on toboggan slides, flumes, inner-tube chutes, or the Summit Plummet, a simulated ski jump on which sliding bathers can reach up to sixty miles an hour. Disney's imagineers "thought people would enjoy themselves in a ski resort atmosphere," so they built their own in Florida and brought downhill skiing to the beach.[1] And their instincts were right; Disney's unlikely winter wonderland, with its promises of water, fun, and sun, has attracted crowds of tourists since it opened.

Developments like this raised some eyebrows within the ski industry. Since the industry's growth after World War II, downhill skiers have enjoyed an almost exclusive relationship with mountain ski resort landscapes. Colorado became the center of a billion-dollar industry that encompassed ski areas, real estate development, restaurants, hotels, and retail stores, as well as the ski equipment and fashion industries. But at the heart of the ski industry — and Colorado's tourist economy — was the sport of skiing itself. Since the nineteenth century, skiers have described the experience as exhilarating and thrilling. They have also said that it creates an intimate bond between skier and mountain, beyond mere enjoyment of the scenery. Colorado's destination resorts pride themselves on their ability to provide this kind of experience to millions of skiers a year, and to do so in a compelling landscape that is at once safe and adventuresome, wild and comfortable, visually pristine and fully developed. Colorado's big ski areas consistently rank among the best and most popular ski resorts in North America because they walk this fine line so well.

Disney took the process one step farther. In humorous references to Colorado's mountains, the water park reminded visitors of "real" skiing and also referred to its own Disney location. Pikes Peak thus became Tike's Peak (with child-sized water rides), Steamboat Springs turned into Teamboat Springs (for five-passenger rafts), and Mother Nature's deadliest threat transformed into a cafeteria called Avalunch. Only with tongue in cheek could its posters encourage vacationers to "Ski Disney." Disney's water park customers respond to these skiing references precisely because they understand and accept the centrality of the Colorado Rockies to that sport. Colorado's ski landscapes are now commodities whose names and images prompt quick recognition and widespread copycatting. By mixing and merging the beach with the mountains, Blizzard Beach raises important questions about the nature of ski resorts as it reaffirms the relationship between skiing and the landscapes we have come to associate with it. The water park's premise works, in other words, because marketers know how much skiers love the Rockies, and because the ski industry has turned sport into a kind of brand-name experience. The connections among skiing, its practitioners, its promoters, and Colorado's mountains offer a view into the larger issues of how cultural meanings become inscribed on the landscape and how landscapes in turn influence culture.

The trip we have made from isolated Colorado mining towns to glitzy destination resorts, half-pipes, and Disney World may still seem a bit strange, but what it shows us is that the history of skiing in Colorado matters on many different levels. At its most basic, this book tells the history of a sport —skiing's growth throughout America and especially in Colorado, and its commercialization through the post–World War II ski industry. Economic, technological, and cultural changes all drove the process. Disney makes a logical ending to this story because it is an acclaimed master at commodifying leisure, and one from which the ski industry has learned quite a bit. By the end of the twentieth century, resorts in Colorado were selling skiing to millions of customers a year by embedding it within the context of a complete vacation, framing it with mythical images of the Alps and the Wild West, and making it accessible to skiers and nonskiers alike. Blizzard Beach took this process to extremes, offering a kind of ski vacation without any skiing at all.

Beyond a study of economic development and commercialization, however, this history also traces how the meaning of skiing changed over the twentieth century. Exactly who donned skis and why they did so hardly remained static; skiing mailmen and snowboarding girls have a few things in common, but not much. What is impressive about the ski industry is not that it attracted different kinds of people to its resorts by attaching new meanings to the sport, but that it did so while retaining its older clientele as well. Skiers today are more diverse in their race, ethnicity, gender, age, and sexuality, though chances are that they are collectively wealthier than fellow skiers from decades past. Local residents and cosmopolitan elites still ski, and so do swinging singles and serious athletes, environmentalists and slaves to fashion, families and celebrities, tourists and the occasional ski bum. These categories seem mutually exclusive or at least contradictory, but marketers learned that skiers often identified with both sides.

Offering multiple experiences and identities to their customers proved the way to succeed in late-twentieth-century commercialized leisure, and engines of the ski industry have made big money doing it. But this is not a simple story of corporate progress. Nor is it a tale of decline in which local communities, the environment, and skiers fall victim to an impersonal industrial machine. Rather, the history of skiing in Colorado illustrates how members of the ski industry, local boosters, and skiers came together to attach a wide range of meanings to the sport and create the destination resorts that define the Rocky Mountains.

They did all this within an important set of historical contexts that also affected what skiing meant to whom. Americans enjoyed recreational sports for different reasons in the 1920s, the 1950s, and the 1980s, and women's participation in them was colored by changing views of femininity and its proper relationship to athleticism. The rise of mass culture, especially visual media, brought ski resorts to the public consciousness, connected them to famous people, and offered them both up for popular consumption. That these resorts appeared to be natural and wild tapped into a long tradition of Americans seeking refuge in nature and, more recently, the practice of packaging bits of it for sale. Visiting such spots — as an expression of rugged masculinity or cosmopolitanism before World War II and of family solidarity afterward — connected Colorado's ski areas to larger trends in tourism and leisure. Young people, too, added new twists to skiing's meaning after World War II by associating it with the potentially subversive cultures of the ski bum, freestyle skier, and snowboarder. This set of larger historical contexts influenced and explained the way skiing, its resorts, and its industry looked at the end of the twentieth century.

Going on vacation and even skiing itself are acts of consumption, and in the end, skiing acquired the variety of meanings it did because the relationship between individual consumers and ski industry boosters demanded it. Complex and contradictory images surrounding ski resort landscapes, communities, and culture work because they offer what customers want. But it is the ski industry that makes these places and sells these images, the consequences of which make many cringe. So who has the most power in this relationship? In many ways, giant ski resorts and the ski industry have co-opted their critics. Environmentalists, minority skiers, and snowboarders (to name a few) seem to have gotten sucked in by a consumer culture that merely nods to their concerns while happily accepting their cash for lift tickets, gear, and the chance to hobnob with celebrities in real western communities. However, the product for sale has changed over the years as athletic women, minority skiers, and young people have become more visible. Seeing Oprah Winfrey and Michael Jordan ski on television may illustrate how wealth and celebrity status can erase color, but it may also mean that skiing has become less exclusively white. Similarly, the popularity of women's workshops and snowboarding could represent either success or failure for women and dissenting youth, depending on whose terms they won that popularity. Because they have all made their voices heard by consuming products and otherwise participating in the ski industry, it is a difficult call to make.

There is a similar dilemma in evaluating our increased awareness of environmental issues and the local consequences of development. National media coverage of the arson at Vail and the expensive housing, exploited labor, and dangerous pollution in mountain resort towns means that Americans know more about the problems attached to ski resort development than ever before. The strange thing is, that has not kept them from going to ski resorts. Industry growth has slowed since the 1980s, but millions continue to ski, and resorts still post profits — the industry itself is alive and well. Knowing about its problematic consequences may actually help business in some ways. Bemoaning the loss of untainted wilderness or a local community assumes that there was such a thing to begin with, and it implies that one can still get pretty close to those things by visiting the resort that is endangering them. If these places are so popular that they are expanding their terrain, supporting thousands of service workers, and too expensive for all but the wealthiest to live in, then they must be pretty good. What we wind up with, at the beginning of the twenty-first century, is a situation in which ski resorts' consumer culture and its critics both continue to gain ground. Today a place like Aspen can be simultaneously disgusting and appealing.

This may seem bizarre, but it has everything to do with America's post–World War II consumer culture and the commodification of outdoor recreation. The history of skiing in these pages recounts how skiing's boosters created appealing images for consumers to participate in — of nature and wilderness, of the Alps and the Wild West, of an elite, white, and fashionable identity — how it sanitized and homogenized mountain landscapes of leisure and separated these images from the less glamorous local history, labor relations, and environmental impact of ski areas' development. The ski industry is not the only leisure industry to separate its commodity from the realities of that commodity's production. Nor is it the only one to turn an activity — skiing down a mountain, in this case — into a more abstract identity or style.

Skiing transformed leisure in America after World War II, creating a now common situation in which people spend money to participate in some authentic activity or place that is actually a carefully crafted product — not really "real" at all. The ski industry linked a recreational and competitive sport with hip, sexy people wearing hi-tech gear, real old-timers with those who playact their roles in the present, and extreme wilderness with everyplace else via I-70 and a chairlift.

Ski resorts accomplished this by building exotic places where visitors could escape their everyday lives and enter an alpine village, a Victorian boomtown, the Wild West, or some mixture of each. Thematically coherent development kept people comfortable and let them play as cosmopolitan elites or rugged westerners, while the surrounding "wilderness" offered them adventure. Resort designers, local boosters, and industry marketers grafted this collection of images onto mountain towns replete with high-speed lifts, luxury spas, expensive restaurants, and endless retail establishments. They created enchanting landscapes of consumption — stages on which visitors could alter or enhance their own identities by dressing up and boogying down, sighting celebrities and getting to know locals, skiing the mountain and hanging around town. Recreational sports took on new cultural power in this context, as they allowed people to participate in mythic places not only through acts of consumption but also through real physical activity in real western landscapes.

As Colorado's big ski resorts sold mythic images, cultural references, local communities, and recreational landscapes disconnected from their pasts and the realities of their production, the act of skiing and the geography of its resorts grounded the ski industry in sport and in place. The rise of the ski industry has had a huge impact on the Rocky Mountain West, reorienting its economy, altering its physical and cultural landscape, and rewriting its past to include pristine landscapes and quaint rural communities. The West exists within the skiing world as both a place and an ideal, and skiers must ultimately come to terms with both the ski industry's images and the regional consequences of their sale.

The industry completely transformed the consumer culture surrounding skiing, but it altered the physical experience of the sport mainly through technological advancements that have made it easier than ever to experience the thrill of carving a turn. And that is also what skiing is about. No matter how fashionable or celebrity-ridden a resort town becomes, or how many different things a skier-tourist may want to experience on vacation, the act of sliding down a mountain remains central. Disney's Blizzard Beach resembles Colorado's destination ski resorts in many discomfiting ways, but no one will ever mistake it for a ski area. And though the ski industry has built a wild array of products and meanings attached to skiing and snowboarding, there is still room for people to wax poetic about the exhilaration, empowerment, and connection to the mountains that come with those sports. They are popular and important because the ski industry led far-reaching changes in American consumer culture and the sale of leisure, and also because they are fun. Skiing cannot be reduced to some essential physical experience because it has become inextricably tied to a powerful consumer culture, but we need not lament that Americans care only about image. In the end, it is the combination of the two that counts.

Portions of this book were published in earlier forms. Reprinted from "The Unbearable Whiteness of Skiing," *Pacific Historical Review* Vol. 65, No. 4, by permission of the University of California Press, © 1996 by the Pacific Coast Branch American Historical Association. Reprinted from "Call of the Mild: Colorado Ski Resorts and the Politics of Rural Tourism," in *The Countryside in the Age of the Modern State: Political Histories of Rural America,* edited by Catherine McNicol Stock and Robert D. Johnston. Copyright © 2001 by Cornell University and used by permission of the publisher, Cornell University Press. Reprinted from "From Snow Bunnies to Shred Betties: Gender, Consumption, and the Skiing Landscape" in *Knowing Nature through Gender,* edited by Virginia J. Scharff. Copyright © 2003 by the University Press of Kansas.

In citing manuscript collections, the following abbreviations are used:

AHS   Aspen Historical Society, Aspen, Colo.
BRL   Business Research Division Library, Graduate School of Business
            Administration, University of Colorado, Boulder, Colo.
BWML   Buddy Werner Memorial Library, Steamboat Springs, Colo.
CHS   Colorado Historical Society, Denver, Colo.
CUA   Archives, University of Colorado at Boulder Libraries, Norlin Library,
            Boulder, Colo.
DPL   Denver Public Library, Denver, Colo.
GCHA   Grand County Historical Association, Hot Sulphur Springs, Colo.
GLHS   Grand Lake Historical Society, Grand Lake, Colo.

SKIING ASPEN MOUNTAIN

1. Rolf W. Jackson, "A New Year's Day Ski Run," *Outing* 31 (January 1898), 395.
2. Theodore A. Johnsen, *The Winter Sport of Skeeing* (Portland, Me.: Theo. A. Johnsen Company, 1905; reprint, New Hartford, Conn.: International Skiing History Association, 1994), 6.
3. Janet Robertson, *The Magnificent Mountain Women: Adventures in the Colorado Rockies* (Lincoln: University of Nebraska Press, 1990), 43.
4. Giles D. Toll, interview by the author, February 2, 1996, Denver, Colo., tape recording and transcript, 5.
5. Mary V. McLucas, "Skiing for Pleasure," *Trail and Timberline* 230 (January 1938), 5.
6. Dolores LaChapelle, *Deep Powder Snow: 40 Years of Ecstatic Skiing, Avalanches, and Earth Wisdom* (Durango, Colo.: Kivaki Press, 1993), 101.

7. Elizabeth Oblock Sinclair, interview by the author, July 26, 1994, Aspen, Colo., tape recording and transcript, AHS, 2; Cherie Gerbaz Oates, interview by the author, July 17, 1994, Aspen, Colo., tape recording and transcript, AHS, 6.

8. Jay Laughlin, "Make Mine Ashcroft!" *Rocky Mountain Life* (February 1947), 39.

9. There is a range of scholarship on the history of skiing. The most prolific historian concerned with the topic is E. John B. Allen, who wrote *From Skisport to Skiing: One Hundred Years of an American Sport, 1840–1940* (Amherst: University of Massachusetts Press, 1993), as well as a number of articles. For a treatment of the more recent past, see Hal Clifford, *Downhill Slide: Why the Corporate Ski Industry Is Bad for Skiing, Ski Towns, and the Environment* (San Francisco: Sierra Club Books, 2002). Hal Rothman devotes three chapters to the history of skiing in his book *Devil's Bargains: Tourism in the 20th Century West* (Lawrence: University Press of Kansas, 1998), and Jack Benson has published a number of articles on nineteenth-century skiing, also with an emphasis on the American West. Other important ski history books include Abbot Fay's *Ski Tracks in the Rockies* (1984) and its revised edition entitled *A History of Skiing in Colorado* (Montrose, Colo.: Western Reflections, 1999), and Richard Needham, *Ski: Fifty Years in North America* (New York: Harry N. Abrams, 1987). Local histories of ski towns abound, and there are some very good biographies of people who were integral to the history of skiing and the ski industry in America. The International Skiing History Association publishes a newsletter, *Skiing Heritage;* maintains an excellent website (www.skiinghistory.org); and has the papers from its 2002 International Ski History Congress available.

10. Peirce F. Lewis, "Axioms for Reading the Landscape," in *The Interpretation of Ordinary Landscapes: Geographical Essays,* ed. Donald W. Meinig (New York: Oxford University Press, 1979), 12. See also D. W. Meinig, introduction to *The Making of the American Landscape,* ed. Michael P. Conzen (Boston: Unwin Hyman, 1990), and his introduction to *The Interpretation of Ordinary Landscapes;* John Brinkerhoff Jackson, *Discovering the Vernacular Landscape* (New Haven, Conn.: Yale University Press, 1984), *Landscapes: Selected Writings of J. B. Jackson,* ed. Ervin H. Zube (Amherst: University of Massachusetts Press, 1970), and *The Necessity for Ruins and Other Topics* (Amherst: University of Massachusetts Press, 1980); and John Stilgoe, *Common Landscapes of America, 1580–1845* (New Haven, Conn.: Yale University Press, 1982).

11. For a discussion of landscape as a historical agent, a normative force, or "discourse materialized," see Richard H. Schein, "Normative Dimensions of Landscape," in *Everyday America: Cultural Landscape Studies after J. B. Jackson,* ed. Chris Wilson and Paul Groth (Berkeley: University of California Press, 2003), 202–3, and "The Place of Landscape: A Conceptual Framework for Interpreting an American Scene," *Annals of the Association of American Geographers* 87, no. 4 (1997), 660–64; and Sharon Zukin, *Landscapes of Power: From Detroit to Disney World* (Berkeley: University of California Press, 1991), 16–20.

12. On the disappearance of labor, see Don Mitchell, *The Lie of the Land: Migrant Workers and the California Landscape* (Minneapolis: University of Minnesota Press, 1996). On defining spaces as natural, see Roderick Nash, *Wilderness and the American Mind,* 3rd ed. (New Haven, Conn.: Yale University Press, 1982).

13. On the history of western tourism, see Rothman, *Devil's Bargains;* David M. Wrobel and Patrick T. Long, eds., *Seeing and Being Seen: Tourism in the American West* (Lawrence: University Press of Kansas, 2001); Marguerite S. Shaffer, *See America First: Tourism and National Identity, 1880–1940* (Washington, D.C.: Smithsonian Institution Press, 2001); and the classic by Earl S. Pomeroy, *In Search of the Golden West: The Tourist in Western America* (New York: Alfred A. Knopf, 1957; reprint, Lincoln: University of Nebraska Press, 1990). Works relevant to my analysis from outside the field of history include Dean MacCannell, *The Tourist: A New Theory of the Leisure Class* (New York: Schocken Books, 1976, 1989); John Urry, *The Tourist Gaze* (New York: Sage Books, 1990), and *Consuming Places* (New York: Routledge, 1995).

14. For an examination of this process in detail, see Bonnie Christensen, *Red Lodge and the Mythic West: From Coal Miners to Cowboys* (Lawrence: University Press of Kansas, 2002).

15. For analyses of women and sports, see Susan Kathleen Cahn, *Coming on Strong: Gender and Sexuality in Twentieth-Century Sport* (New York: Free Press, 1994; reprint, Cambridge: Harvard University Press, 1995); Helen Lenskyj, *Out of Bounds: Women, Sport and Sexuality* (Toronto: Women's Press, 1986); J. A. Mangan and Roberta J. Park, *From "Fair Sex" to Feminism: Sport and the Socialization of Women in the Industrial and Post-Industrial Eras* (London: Frank Cass, 1987); and Allen Guttmann, *Women's Sports: A History* (New York: Columbia University Press, 1991). On gender and mobility, see Steven A. Reiss, "Sport and the Redefinition of American Middle-Class Masculinity," *International Journal of the History of Sport* 8 (1991), 5–27; Kathy Peiss, *Cheap Amusements: Working Women and Leisure in Turn-of-the-Century New York* (Philadelphia: Temple University Press, 1986); Virginia Scharff, *Taking the Wheel: Women and the Coming of the Motor Age* (New York: Free Press, 1991; reprint, Albuquerque: University of New Mexico Press, 1992), and *Twenty Thousand Roads: Women, Movement, and the West* (Berkeley: University of California Press, 2003).

16. See Elliott J. Gorn and Warren Goldstein, *A Brief History of American Sports* (New York: Hill and Wang, 1993), 188–97; Joshua Gamson, "The Assembly Line of Greatness: Celebrity in Twentieth-Century America," *Critical Studies in Mass Communication* 9 (1992), 1–24; and Charles L. Ponce de Leon, *Self-Exposure: Human Interest Journalism and the Emergence of Celebrity in America, 1890–1940* (Chapel Hill: University of North Carolina Press, 2002).

17. See Karl B. Raitz, ed., *The Theater of Sport* (Baltimore: Johns Hopkins University Press, 1995); James M. Mayo, *The American Country Club: Its Origins and Development* (New Brunswick, N.J.: Rutgers University Press, 1998); and Richard J. Moss, *Golf and the American Country Club* (Urbana: University of Illinois Press, 2001).

18. See Cahn, *Coming on Strong,* for an excellent twentieth-century history of American women and sports. Gretchen Fraser was the first American to win an Olympic gold medal in the winter games when she brought home gold in slalom and silver in combined from the 1948 Olympics; Andrea Mead Lawrence followed up with two golds in 1952 in slalom and giant slalom. Title IX and Billie Jean King's victory over Bobby Riggs represent two important intersections of sports and the women's movement in the early 1970s.

19. See Nash, *Wilderness and the American Mind;* Leo Marx, *The Machine in the Garden: Technology and the Pastoral Ideal in America* (New York: Oxford University Press, 1964); and Peter J. Schmitt, *Back to Nature: The Arcadian Myth in Urban America* (New York: Oxford University Press, 1969).

20. On nature tourism, see Richard Butler, C. Michael Hall, and John Jenkins, eds., *Tourism and Recreation in Rural Areas* (New York: John Wiley and Sons, 1998). For a history of commodified nature, see Jennifer Price, *Flight Maps: Adventures with Nature in Modern America* (New York: Basic Books, 1999).

21. See Jane Tompkins, *West of Everything: The Inner Life of the Western* (New York: Oxford University Press, 1992); Elliott West, "Selling the Myth: Western Images in Advertising," in *Wanted Dead or Alive: The American West in Popular Culture,* ed. Richard Aquila (Urbana: University of Illinois Press, 1996), 269–91; and Liza Nicholas, "1-800-SUNDANCE: Identity, Nature, and Play in the West," in *Imagining the Big Open: Nature, Identity, and Play in the New West,* ed. Liza Nicholas, Elaine M. Bapis, and Thomas J. Harvey (Salt Lake City: University of Utah Press, 2003), 259–71.

22. Hal Rothman refers to this phenomenon as "bagging experience," and it underlines the connections among consumption, landscape, and identity.

23. John M. Findlay makes an argument for the westernness of Disneyland, Stanford Industrial Park, Sun City, and the Seattle World's Fair in his *Magic Lands: Western Cityscapes and American Culture after 1940* (Berkeley: University of California Press, 1992). On skateboarding, see Michael Brooke, *The Concrete Wave: The History of Skateboarding* (Los Angeles: Warwick Publishing, 1999), and Judith A. Davidson, "Sport and Modern Technology: The Rise of Skateboarding, 1963–1978," *Journal of Popular Culture* 18, no. 4 (Spring 1985), 145–57. On rap, see Nelson George, *Hip Hop America* (New York: Viking Press, 1998), and Elizabeth Grant, "Gangsta Rap, the War on Drugs and the Location of African-American Identity in Los Angeles, 1988–92," *European Journal of American Culture* 21 (Fall 2001), 4–15.

24. See Douglas Booth, "From Bikinis to Boardshorts: *Wahines* and the Paradoxes of Surfing Culture," *Journal of Sport History* 28, no. 1 (Spring 2001), 3–22.

1. SNOWSHOE ITINERANTS AND FLYING NORSEMEN

1. John L. Dyer, *The Snow-Shoe Itinerant: An Autobiography of the Rev. John L. Dyer* (Cincinnati: Cranston and Stowe, 1890), 170.

2. Ibid., 164. Dyer was assigned to the Blue River Mission in Summit County, Colorado, in the spring of 1862 and then to South Park in 1863, when he accepted the mail contract covering Buckskin Joe, Mosquito, Cache Creek, and California Gulch for a winter. He continued his preaching in Colorado until 1865 and resumed it in 1879, when he was appointed to the Breckenridge circuit.

3. E. John B. Allen, "Skiing Mailmen of Mountain America: U.S. Winter Postal Service in the Nineteenth Century," *Journal of the West* 29 (April 1990), 78; Abbott Fay, *Ski Tracks in the Rockies: A Century of Colorado Skiing* (Evergreen, Colo.: Cordillera Press, 1984), 3.

4. See Duane A. Smith, *Rocky Mountain West: Colorado, Wyoming, and Montana, 1859–1915* (Albuquerque: University of New Mexico Press, 1992).

5. See Walter Nugent, "Frontiers and Empires in the Late Nineteenth Century," in *Trails: Toward a New Western History*, ed. Patricia Nelson Limerick, Clyde A. Milner II, and Charles E. Rankin (Lawrence: University Press of Kansas, 1991), 161–81.

6. Charles M. Dudley, *Sixty Centuries of Skiing* (Brattleboro, Vt.: Stephen Daye Press, 1935), 22; Dolfe Rajtmajer, "The Slovenian Origins of European Skiing," *International Journal of the History of Sport* 11 (April 1994), 97–101; see also Stein Eriksen, *Come Ski with Me* (New York: W. W. Norton, 1966), and Leif Hovelsen, *The Flying Norseman* (Ishpeming, Mich.: National Ski Hall of Fame Press, 1983).

7. E. John B. Allen, *From Skisport to Skiing: One Hundred Years of an American Sport, 1840–1940* (Amherst: University of Massachusetts Press, 1993), 11, 49; E. John B. Allen, "The Modernization of Skisport: Ishpeming's Contribution to American Skiing," *Michigan Historical Review* 16 (1990), 1–20.

8. Eriksen, *Come Ski with Me*, 20; Hovelsen, *Flying Norseman*, 8; Kenneth Bjork, "'Snowshoe' Thompson: Fact and Legend," *Norwegian-American Studies and Record* 19 (1956), 70, 78; Eriksen, *Come Ski with Me*, 20, 21.

9. *Sacramento Union*, October 13, 1862; *Sacramento Union*, August 28, 1863, as quoted in Bjork, "Snowshoe Thompson," 69.

10. *Marysville Herald* in *Sacramento Daily Union*, January 29, 1853, as quoted in Allen, *Skisport to Skiing*, 14. The first documented use of snowshoes in Colorado occurred in 1857 during the Mormon War. Lost in a storm, Jim Baker, who was leading the Marcy expedition, crafted a pair of skis and used them to find Cochopeta Pass, east of what is now Gunnison. Fay, *Ski Tracks in the Rockies*, 3.

11. Dyer, *Snow-Shoe Itinerant*, 144; Warner Root, in Frank L. Wentworth, *Aspen on the Roaring Fork* (Denver, 1950), 21; Warner Root, "Aspen," *Aspen Times*, first issue, n.d., reprinted in *Aspen Times*, January 4, 1979; also cited in Jack A. Benson, "Before Skiing Was Fun," *Western Historical Quarterly* 8 (October 1977), 432, and Allen, *From Skisport to Skiing*, 34, 184.

12. "Pioneering Near Steamboat Springs, 1885–1886, as Shown in Letters of Alice Denison," *Colorado Magazine* 28 (April 1951), 89.

13. Frank S. Beyers, "The History of Berthoud Pass," clipping (January–February 1923), 13, Berthoud Pass file, CHS.

14. Allen, *Skisport to Skiing*, 16; Allen, "Skiing Mailmen," 76–77; Bjork, "Snowshoe Thompson," 62–88; Hovelsen, *Flying Norseman*, 8–9.

15. Elder, "From Hunters Pass," *Aspen Daily Times*, February 4, 1899, 5, as cited in Benson, "Before Skiing Was Fun," 437.

16. Janet Robertson, *The Magnificent Mountain Women: Adventures in the Colorado Rockies* (Lincoln: University of Nebraska Press, 1990), 75. Anderson arrived in Fraser in 1907, two years after the town grew up along the railroad tracks on the west side of Rollins Pass.

17. Jean Wren, *Steamboat Springs and the "Treacherous and Speedy Skee": An Album* (Steamboat Springs, Colo.: Steamboat Pilot, 1972), 4.

18. Jim Wier, "The Beginning of Skiing in Grand County," *Grand County Historical Association Journal* 4 (January 1984; reprint, March 1988), 9 (page numbers refer to reprint edition).

19. "Pioneering Near Steamboat Springs 1885–1886," 89.

20. Wier, "Beginning of Skiing in Grand County," 12.

21. Jack A. Benson, "Before Aspen and Vail: The Story of Recreational Skiing in Frontier Colorado," *Journal of the West* 22 (January 1983), 52, 57; Wier, "Beginning of Skiing in Grand County," 12.

22. Benson, "Before Aspen and Vail," 57; photographs in Fay, *Ski Tracks in the Rockies*, 2, 5, 6; Wren, *Steamboat Springs*, 6.

23. Victorian constructions of womanhood consigned women to the home, where they were to care for the moral, educational, and emotional well-being of their husbands and children. Contemporary medical understandings of women argued that excessive physical, intellectual, or emotional activity would deplete their nonrenewable "vital force," thereby threatening women's ability to reproduce as well as their general health. Women in mining towns, however, even those few among the middle and upper classes, were faced with much greater physical demands in caring for their families. Such women necessarily subscribed to a femininity that incorporated a higher degree of physical labor and activity than that of their urban sisters. See Helen Lenskyj, *Out of Bounds: Women, Sport, and Sexuality* (Toronto: Women's Press, 1986), 23, and Patricia Vertinsky, "Feminist Charlotte Perkins Gilman's Pursuit of Health and Physical Fitness as a Strategy for Emancipation," *Journal of Sport History* 16 (Spring 1989), 13.

24. E. John B. Allen, "Sierra Ladies on Skis in Gold Rush California," *Journal of Sport History* 17 (Winter 1990), 347; Wier, "Beginning of Skiing in Grand County," 12.

25. Fay, *Ski Tracks in the Rockies*, 2, 5, 6; Wren, *Steamboat Springs*, 6.

26. Typical of nineteenth-century mining communities, this type of ski racing began in the California Sierras during the 1860s and appeared in Colorado in the 1880s. For more on early California ski racing, see Allen, *Skisport to Skiing*, 21–28.

27. Jim Voorheis was one of Silverton's best skiers. See Benson, "Before Aspen and Vail," 57.

28. Benson, "Before Aspen and Vail," 52.

29. E. R. Warren, "Snow-shoeing in the Rocky Mountains," *Outing* 9 (January 1887), 350–53; Benson, "Before Aspen and Vail," 53–55.

30. Benson, "Before Aspen and Vail," 54.

31. Fay, *Ski Tracks in the Rockies*, 6; Benson, "Before Aspen and Vail," 57; Elder, "From Hunters Pass," 5, as cited in Benson, "Before Skiing Was Fun," 437.

32. Smith, *Rocky Mountain West*, 84.

33. Ibid., 157.

34. Hovelsen, *Flying Norseman*, 2–5; Dudley, *Sixty Centuries of Skiing*, 36; Eriksen, *Come Ski with Me*, 18–20.

35. T. W. Schreiner, "Norway's National Sport," *Outing* 37 (March 1901), 711–15; W. S. Harwood, "Ski Running," *Outing* 21 (February 1893), 339–46.

36. Hovelsen, *Flying Norseman*, 6, 4–5.

37. Paul P. Bernard, *Rush to the Alps: The Evolution of Vacationing in Switzerland* (Boulder, Colo.: East European Quarterly, 1978; distributed by Columbia University Press), 151, 147. See also Alice Crossette Hall, "Winter Sport in Switzerland," *Outing* 33 (March 1899), 391–95.

38. Schreiner, "Norway's National Sport," 711.

39. Hovelsen, *Flying Norseman*, 7–8; Eriksen, *Come Ski with Me*, 20; Dudley, *Sixty Centuries of Skiing*, 37–42; Johannes Hroff Wisby, "Carrying the Mail over the Andes on Skis," *Outing* 37 (March 1901), 672–75.

40. More than 390,000 came in the next ten years, and 488,000 between 1900 and 1909. N. Carpenter, "Immigrants and Their Children," *U.S. Bureau of the Census Monograph*, No. 7 (Washington, D.C., 1927), 324–25, as cited in Alan M. Kraut, *The Huddled Masses: The Immigrant in American Society, 1880–1920* (Arlington Heights, Ill.: Harlan Davidson, 1982), 20–21. Between 1875 and 1895, some 263,000 of those came from Norway. Hovelsen, *Flying Norseman*, 10.

41. Allen, *Skisport to Skiing*, 50–53. Some Italians and Irish participated in midwestern ski clubs. Allen notes that because the Scandinavian population was much smaller in the West, western ski clubs did not practice ethnic exclusivity. See also Allen, "Modernization of Skisport."

42. Eriksen, *Come Ski with Me*, 22; Hovelsen, *Flying Norseman*, 11–12; Allen, *Skisport to Skiing*, 47–50.

43. John Muir, "The Wild Parks and Forest Reservations of the West," *Atlantic Monthly* 81 (1898), 15, as cited in Roderick Nash, *Wilderness and the American Mind*, 3rd ed. (New Haven, Conn.: Yale University Press, 1982), 140; Nash, 143.

44. Earl S. Pomeroy, *In Search of the Golden West: The Tourist in Western America* (New York: Alfred A. Knopf, 1957; reprint, Lincoln: University of Nebraska Press, 1990), 141, 143–44 (page numbers refer to reprint edition). Antecedents to the Appalachian Mountain Club, which was formed in 1876, were the British Alpine Club, formed in 1857, and a similar club formed by the Swiss in 1863.

45. Nash, *Wilderness and the American Mind,* 132. The Oregon Alpine Club was established earlier than the Sierra Club, in 1887. Pomeroy, *In Search of the Golden West,* 144.

46. See Enos A. Mills, *The Spell of the Rockies* (New York: Houghton Mifflin, 1911).

47. Hugh E. Kingery and Elinor Eppich Kingery, *The Colorado Mountain Club: The First Seventy-five Years of a Highly Individual Corporation, 1912–1987* (Evergreen, Colo.: Cordillera Press, 1988), 23, 11.

48. Allen, *Skisport to Skiing,* 75–79; Dudley, *Sixty Centuries of Skiing,* 56–58.

49. Evelyn Runnette, "Skiing with the C.M.C.," *Ski Bulletin,* March 19, 1937, 6–7.

50. See Hovelsen, *Flying Norseman,* 13–64, for Carl Howelsen's biography.

51. Barnum and Bailey Circus ad copy, from Hovelsen, *Flying Norseman,* 29; see also Wren, *Steamboat Springs,* 9–12.

52. "Sulphur Springs Successful Winter Sports," *Denver Post,* January 7, 1912, clipping, General Ski Collection, GCHA.

53. Hovelsen, *Flying Norseman,* 36–40; Jim Wier, "Skiing at Hot Sulphur Springs," *Grand County Historical Association Journal* 4 (January 1984; reprint, March 1988), 13–14 (page numbers refer to reprint edition).

54. Hovelsen, *Flying Norseman,* 39.

55. *Rocky Mountain News,* January 29, 1912, as cited in ibid., 39.

56. *Denver Post,* January 19, 1913, and *Daily News,* January 31, 1913, as cited in Hovelsen, *Flying Norseman,* 41.

57. "Ski Jumping Added to Denver Winter Sport Schedule," *Denver Post,* December 2, 1913, clipping, GCHA; Hovelsen, *Flying Norseman,* 47; Rachel Zeiner, "The Jump at Genesee," *Denver Post,* November 15, 1981, 37, clipping, recreation-skiing file, CHS.

58. *Rocky Mountain News,* January 19, 1914, as cited in Hovelsen, *Flying Norseman,* 45.

59. Hovelsen,, *Flying Norseman,* 76–77; "Denver Will Cinch Fame," clipping, February 18, 1923, General Ski Collection, GCHA.

60. "Denver Will Have Week of Winter Carnival Sports in February," clipping, 1927, General Ski Collection, GCHA; "National Ski Meet Is Coming to World's Playground in Rockies," clipping, *Denver Post,* 1927, ibid.

61. Hovelsen, *Flying Norseman,* 46.

62. Wren, *Steamboat Springs,* 14–21.

63. Sureva Towler, *The History of Skiing at Steamboat Springs* (Denver: Frederic Printing, 1987), 52.

64. Wier, "Skiing at Hot Sulphur Springs," 13. The next year, junior jumpers had their own contests as well. Children participated in local skiing communities more often and to a higher degree than did most adults.

65. Wier, "Skiing at Hot Sulphur Springs," 14–15; Wren, *Steamboat Springs,* 17. Only two women competed in the free-for-all race in 1914. Towler, *History of Skiing at Steamboat Springs,* 68.

66. Wren, *Steamboat Springs,* 21–22.

67. Towler, *History of Skiing at Steamboat Springs*, 85; "Winter Sports Club Active in Steamboat," *Steamboat Pilot*, May 16, 1930, 2; Towler, 84.

68. These annual events fell short of the classic Bakhtinian carnival, in which class, gender, and racial identities became inverted. See Michael Holquist, *Diologism: Bakhtin and His World* (New York: Routledge, 1990), 89–90; and Mikhail Bakhtin, *Rabelais and His World*, trans. Helene Iswolsky (Bloomington: Indiana University Press, 1984).

69. Runnette, "Skiing with the C.M.C.," 6–7. The CMC's programs proved so popular that affiliate clubs popped up in Colorado Springs, Boulder, and Estes Park by the early 1920s. See Kingery and Kingery, *Colorado Mountain Club*.

70. Colorado Winter Season Program, January 1 to April 1, 1925, Rocky Mountain National Park Ski Club, Groswold Ski Collection, GCHA.

71. Program, Annual Amateur Ski Tournament of the Denver Rocky Mountain Ski Club, January 28–29, 1922, General Ski Collection, GCHA.

72. Program, Denver Rocky Mountain Ski Club Annual Amateur Tournament, January 28–29, 1922, General Ski Collection, GCHA; see also General Ski Collection and Groswold Ski Collection, GCHA. For more on women's sports in the 1920s, see Susan Kathleen Cahn, *Coming on Strong: Gender and Sexuality in Twentieth-Century Women's Sport* (New York: Free Press, 1994; reprint, Cambridge: Harvard University Press, 1995), ch. 2.

2. THE ROMANCE OF DOWNHILL

1. Otto Lang, *A Bird of Passage: The Story of My Life* (Helena, Mont.: Skyhouse Publishers, an imprint of Falcon Press, 1994), 167; see also Friedl Pfeifer and Morten Lund, *Nice Goin': My Life on Skis* (Missoula, Mont.: Pictorial Histories Publishing Company, 1993), 76–77.

2. John Allen, in *From Skisport to Skiing* (Amherst: University of Massachusetts Press, 1993), focuses on the transition from Nordic to Alpine skiing and argues that the utilitarian and nationalistic aspects of Scandinavian skiing gave way to Alpine skiing in the 1920s and 1930s because the new form of skiing better reflected modern society. This is especially true, given the ways Alpine skiing became incorporated into America's consumer-oriented culture during these decades.

3. Pfeifer and Lund, *Nice Goin'*, 6. See also Lang, *Bird of Passage*, 54–61.

4. Pfeifer and Lund, *Nice Goin'*, 14. Filmmaker Arnold Fanck made a number of films about mountaineering and skiing during the 1920s, many featuring Hannes Schneider, which greatly increased the popularity of the sport. See Richard W. Moulton, "Film's Role in Popularizing Alpine Skiing in America," in *Collected Papers of the International Ski History Congress*, ed. E. John B. Allen (New Hartford, Conn.: International Skiing History Association, 2002), 190–94; and "The Films of Hannes Schneider," *Skiing Heritage* 5 (Spring 1993), 8–10.

5. Charles M. Dudley, *Sixty Centuries of Skiing* (Brattleboro, Vt.: Stephen Daye Press, 1935), 86.

6. For a more extensive discussion of Lunn's development of slalom racing and how it spread to the eastern United States, see Allen, *Skisport to Skiing,* 98–103.

7. Many of the resorts that first held Alpine events in the early 1930s are still famous for their races and continue to attract tourists and ski racers from all over the world. They include, among others, Davos and St. Moritz in Switzerland, Megeve and Chamonix in France, Germany's Garmisch, and the Austrian areas Kitzbuehel and Innsbruck. Alpine skiing gained the ultimate recognition when downhill and slalom events became part of the annual Federation Internationale de Ski (FIS) championship competition in 1931.

8. Pfeifer and Lund, *Nice Goin',* 30; Lang, *Bird of Passage,* 50.

9. Pfeifer and Lund, *Nice Goin',* 30.

10. Carl Blaurock, "A Ski Trip on the Breithorn, Switzerland," *Trail and Timberline* 160 (February 1932), 21, 25.

11. I have no evidence of women guiding. Some women may have worked as ski instructors at alpine resorts, but they were likely in charge of teaching children rather than adults.

12. Pfeifer and Lund, *Nice Goin',* 36. Austrian ski schools in general, and Schneider's in particular, were much more regimented and formal than ski schools today. Students attended the same class with the same instructor daily for their entire stay and had to pass rigid standards of qualification to advance into the next-level class.

13. Dick Tompkins, "'Much Ado about Nothing,'" *Trail and Timberline* 230 (January 1938), 3.

14. John L. Frisbee, "Why Do We Ski?" *Ski* (November 1953), 19, 36–37.

15. Pfeifer and Lund, *Nice Goin',* 23.

16. Elizabeth D. Woolsey, *Off the Beaten Track* (Wilson, Wyo.: Wilson Bench Press, 1984), 99.

17. Lang, *Bird of Passage,* 41; see also Paul P. Bernard, *Rush to the Alps: The Evolution of Vacationing in Switzerland* (Boulder, Colo.: East European Quarterly, 1978; distributed by Columbia University Press).

18. Pfeifer and Lund, *Nice Goin',* 33. Lang came to St. Anton in the winter of 1929–30 as a government-licensed ski instructor and mountain guide. From Salzburg and fluent in French and English, Lang was, according to Pfeifer, "exactly the kind of instructor Hannes needed for his growing international clientele." Pfeifer and Lund, 32; Lang, *Bird of Passage,* 49.

19. Pfeifer and Lund, *Nice Goin',* 36.

20. Stephen H. Hart, "Skiing at St. Moritz," *Trail and Timberline* 158 (December 1931), 189.

21. John L. Jerome Hart, "Skiing in Switzerland and Norway," *Trail and Timberline* 95 (August 1926), 1–3.

22. Pfeifer and Lund, *Nice Goin',* 24–25.

23. Lang, *Bird of Passage,* 62.

24. Pfeifer and Lund, *Nice Goin',* 27.

25. Allen, *Skisport to Skiing,* 100–103.

26. Ibid., 103; John Litchfield, interview by the author, September 29, 1994, Denver, Colo.

27. Lang, *Bird of Passage,* 80, 99–101; Pfeifer and Lund, *Nice Goin',* 49; Litchfield interview.

28. Sigi Engl and Hannes Schroll, from near Salzburg, started a ski school at Yosemite Valley; Otto Tschol probably instructed somewhere, as Pfeifer saw him at the 1938 Boston and New York ski shows. Lang, *Bird of Passage,* 107–8; Pfeifer and Lund, *Nice Goin',* 52, 66.

29. Woolsey, *Off the Beaten Track,* 105.

30. Pfeifer and Lund, *Nice Goin',* 53–60.

31. Lang, *Bird of Passage,* 180.

32. Woolsey, *Off the Beaten Track,* 105.

33. Lang, *Bird of Passage,* 180–83; Pfeifer and Lund, *Nice Goin',* 73–74.

34. Lang, *Bird of Passage,* 95–99.

35. Ibid., 124–27; Pfeifer and Lund, *Nice Goin',* 51–52.

36. David J. Bradley, "Heil, Otto!" *American Ski Annual* (1936–37), 63–64.

37. Ibid., 65; Carl E. Shumway, "America's First Ski School," *Trail and Timberline* 173 (March 1933), 32, 38–39.

38. Editors of *Ski* Magazine, *America's Ski Book* (New York: Scribner, 1973), 42.

39. David Bradley, "Invasion of the Swiss," *Ski Bulletin,* March 26, 1937, 5. See also David J. Bradley, "S.A.S.," *American Ski Annual* (1937–38), 115–19.

40. Henry Buchtel, "Skiing B.E.P.," *Trail and Timberline* 241 (January 1939), 5–6; J. C. Blickensderfer, "Reminiscences of Skiing in Colorado, 1922–1968," Ski Collection, CHS.

41. "Climax Ski Area Has Had a Lively, Exciting History," *Summit County Journal,* March 11, 1960, 4, Agnes Wright Spring Collection, CUA.

42. See Frank Willoughby, "History of Aspen's Course and Jump," *Aspen Times,* n.d., clipping, Ski Collection, AHS; Fred Willoughby, "Andre Roch Brought Racing, a Dream," *Aspen Times,* January 31, 1980, 5A, Andre Roch biography file, AHS. See also Anne Gilbert, "Re-Creation through Recreation: Aspen Skiing from 1870 to 1970" (manuscript, April 1995), 14–35, Ski Collection, AHS. Chapter 3 discusses the formation of Colorado resorts and the results of Roch's recommendations in more detail.

43. "Definite Advantages," *Ski Bulletin,* March 26, 1937, 15.

44. Mary Eshbaugh Hayes, "The Town Got Excited about Skiing," *Aspen Times,* March 2, 1978, Skiing 1938–45 file, AHS; Hildur Anderson, interview by Ramona Markalunas, January 18, 1979, Aspen, Colo., tape recording, AHS.

45. "Miner and Ski Pioneer Fred Willoughby Dies," *Aspen Times,* January 27, 1983, 8A, clipping in Willoughby biography file, AHS; Frank Willoughby, "Aspen Skiing:

An Account by Frank Willoughby" (manuscript, n.d.), Early Skiing file, AHS; Kathleen Daily and Gaylord T. Guenin, *Aspen: The Quiet Years* (Aspen, Colo.: Red Ink, 1994), 220, 468.

46. Abbott Fay, *Ski Tracks in the Rockies: A Century of Colorado Skiing* (Evergreen, Colo.: Cordillera Press, 1984), 25.

47. The road over Berthoud Pass was not regularly kept open until 1933, and until 1928, trains had to travel over the often snowed in Corona Pass. Blickensderfer, "Reminiscences," 2. See also Steve Patterson and Kenton Forrest, *Rio Grande Ski Train* (Denver: Tramway Press, 1984).

48. Grand County Historical Association, *Winter Park: Colorado's Favorite for Fifty Years, 1940–1990* (Winter Park Recreation Association, 1989), 17–18. One original member of the Arlberg Club was a Denver native, graduate of Williams College, and head of the Merrill Lynch offices in Denver. Another graduated from Yale, practiced law with the Hughes and Dorsey firm, and enjoyed tennis and polo before taking up skiing. This member was known to show up at the clubhouse in a chauffeured Packard. *Winter Park,* 18, 19.

49. Bill Engdail, "Mountain Club Making State Skiing Center," clipping, n.d., General Ski Collection, GCHA.

50. "Rocky Mountain Notes," *Ski Bulletin,* March 26, 1937, 14.

51. "Ski Instruction Classes," *Trail and Timberline* 182 (December 1933), 178; David Rosendale, "Skiing in the Colorado Mountain Club," *Trail and Timberline* 208 (February 1936), 11.

52. "Grand Lake Will Hold Winter Sports Week," *Denver Post,* December 25, 1931, clipping, ski scrapbook, GLHS.

53. "New Style Ski Race in Grand Lake Meet," *Denver Post,* January 20, 1933; Dave Lehman, "Leading Skiers in Meet," *Rocky Mountain News,* January 20, 1933, clipping, GLHS.

54. Program, Twenty-third Annual Winter Sports Carnival, Hot Sulphur Springs, Colo., January 29, 1933, General Ski Collection, GCHA.

55. Giles D. Toll, interview by the author, February 2, 1996, Denver, Colo.

56. Willoughby, "Andre Roch Brought Racing, a Dream."

57. The first National Downhill and Slalom Championships were held at Mt. Rainier. For a description of the 1938 and 1939 regional championships and their results, see "Ski Heil to Aspen," *Trail and Timberline* 232 (March 1938), 31–33; "Aspen Antics," *Trail and Timberline* 244 (April 1939), 43–44.

58. Robert Balch, "Steamboat Springs," *Ski Bulletin,* March 19, 1937, 8.

59. *Western Colorado and Eastern Utah* (January 1939), Ski Town file, Routt County Collection, BWML; *Ski-Hi Stampede,* 1939, Oversize Pamphlet file, CUA.

60. Ellen Wiley Todd, "Art, the 'New Woman,' and Consumer Culture: Kenneth Hayes Miller and Reginald Marsh on Fourteenth Street, 1920–40," in *Gender and American History since 1890,* ed. Barbara Melosh (New York: Routledge, 1993), 130–32. See also Carroll Smith-Rosenberg, "The New Woman as Androgyne: Social

Disorder and Gender Crises, 1870–1936," in her *Disorderly Conduct: Visions of Gender in Victorian America* (New York: Oxford University Press, 1985).

61. Bradley, "S.A.S.," 115.

62. Tompkins, "Much Ado about Nothing," 3.

63. Helen Lenskyj, *Out of Bounds: Women, Sport, and Sexuality* (Toronto: Women's Press, 1986), 73–74; see also Todd, "Art, the 'New Woman,' and Consumer Culture," 130–31.

64. Frisbee, "Why Do We Ski?" 19, 36.

65. Eileen O'Connor, "Genesee Mountain Ski Tournament Proves to Be Winter Fashion Display," clipping, February 19, 1923, General Ski Collection, GCHA.

66. Feminist historians might argue whether this made women more or less powerful. As consumers, women in the 1920s and 1930s made important decisions that affected their own lives and influenced consumer culture generally. Helen Lenskyj notes that by conforming to male-defined standards of beauty and heterosexual attractiveness, however, women competed with other women for the attraction and protection of men, thereby accepting a subordinate role in society. Lenskyj, *Out of Bounds*, 56.

67. Neale Howard, "Junior Skiing for Girls," *American Ski Annual* (1939–40), 93.

68. Susan Kathleen Cahn, *Coming on Strong: Gender and Sexuality in Twentieth-Century Women's Sport* (New York: Free Press, 1994; reprint, Cambridge: Harvard University Press, 1995), 57; see also Lenskyj, *Out of Bounds*, 71.

69. Neither wealthy Americans familiar with European resort culture nor residents of small mountain towns in Colorado were affected by the depression in ways that prevented them from skiing. One group had enough money to keep skiing despite the depression; the other needed so little to ski that they just kept on doing it.

70. Bradley, "Heil, Otto!" 65; "Ski Trips, 1932–33 Season," *Trail and Timberline* 170 (December 1932), 174; "Skiing Instruction Classes," *Trail and Timberline* 182 (December 1933), 178.

71. Willoughby, "History of Aspen's Course and Jump"; "New Members for 1937," *Trail and Timberline* 229 (December 1937), 135.

72. Program, Twenty-sixth Annual Winter Sports Carnival of the Hot Sulphur Springs Ski Club, February 6–7, 1937, General Ski Collection, GCHA.

73. "C.M.C. Members Place in Berthoud Ski Races," *Trail and Timberline* 229 (December 1937), 136; "Aspen Antics," *Trail and Timberline* 244 (April 1939), 43, 44; "Ashley Wins Downhill at Berthoud," "Ashley Wins Downhill Race," and "Frank Ashley Wins Slalom at Berthoud," clippings, General Ski Collection, GCHA.

74. "C.M.C. Members Place," 136; Ashley clippings, GCHA.

75. Lang, *Bird of Passage*, 157. Lang and Pfeifer refer to her by her later married name, Kaier.

76. Pfeifer and Lund, *Nice Goin'*, 49. They trained there every winter from the fall of 1934 until the Anschluss in 1938, hiring Friedl Pfeifer as coach and competing in

races, including the annual FIS Championships, Arlberg-Kandahar, and the 1936 Olympics. Three American women finished in the top ten of the 1937 Arlberg-Kandahar, and Clarita Heath finished fourth in the world championships — the highest ever for an American. The next year, Betty Woolsey tied the record by finishing fourth in the 1938 world championships. See Pfeifer and Lund, 53, 73; Woolsey, *Off the Beaten Track*, 56–104.

77. Woolsey, *Off the Beaten Track*, 54.

78. Mary V. McLucas, "Skiing for Pleasure," *Train and Timberline* 230 (January 1938), 5.

79. Woolsey, *Off the Beaten Track*, 56, 59, 63.

80. Woolsey, *Off the Beaten Track*, 65, 100; Pfeifer and Lund, *Nice Goin'*, 68. Brewer escaped paralysis but did not return to competitive skiing.

81. Helen Boughton-Leigh, "Racing for Women," *American Ski Annual* (1936–37), 41–45. The editors of the *Ski Annual* disagreed with Boughton-Leigh, but apparently at least one husband agreed with her. He made his wife — a French racer who had a chance of winning the 1948 Olympic downhill — diet so that she would be thinner and prettier, and as a result, she grew weak and fell in the race. One may wonder why he let her race at all. James Laughlin, "Inside Report," *Ski* 13, no. 1 (November 1948), 9. For a broader discussion of this debate, see Cahn, *Coming on Strong*, 81, and Lenskyj, *Out of Bounds*, 78.

82. Eugene F. Pilz, "Barbara Kidder — Queen of the Slopes," *Rocky Mountain Life* (December 1946), 46.

83. Luanne Pfeifer, *Gretchen's Gold: The Story of Gretchen Fraser* (Missoula, Mont.: Pictorial Histories Publishing Company, 1996), 82, 108, 101.

84. Dick Durrance and John Jerome, *The Man on the Medal: The Life and Times of America's First Great Ski Racer* (Aspen, Colo.: Durrance Enterprises, 1995), 59.

85. "Echoes from Sun Valley," *Trail and Timberline* 232 (March 1938), 28.

86. Pfeifer and Lund, *Nice Goin'*, 68.

87. Ibid., 70.

88. Woolsey, *Off the Beaten Track*, 109.

89. Harriette Aull, "Smith College 'Shees,'" *American Ski Annual* (1939–40), 72.

3. A SHACK AND A ROPE TOW

1. Andre Roch, "A Once and Future Resort: A Winter in the Rocky Mountains of Colorado" (trans. Ernest H. Blake), *Colorado Heritage* 4 (1985), 19, 23; originally published in French as "Un Hiver aux Montagnes Rocheuses du Colorado," *Der Schnee Hase* (1937), the Swiss Academic Ski Club yearbook.

2. Andre Roch, interview by George Madsen, February 16, 1967, tape recording #C55, AHS. For a more detailed account of Aspen's early ski history, see Anne Gilbert, "Re-Creation through Recreation: Aspen Skiing from 1870 to 1970" (manuscript, April 1995), AHS.

3. For the most extensive history of the resort, see Wendolyn Spence Holland, *Sun Valley: An Extraordinary History* (San Francisco: Palace Press International, 1998).

Hal Rothman's *Devil's Bargains: Tourism in the 20th Century* (Lawrence: University Press of Kansas, 1998), discusses Sun Valley within the larger context of western tourism. For more on the American St. Moritz, see Holland, 161, 206.

4. Averell Harriman, as quoted in Holland, *Sun Valley*, 183.

5. Holland, *Sun Valley*, 197–99, 211.

6. Harriman subsidized, for instance, the expenses of the Swiss, Austrian, and Chilean teams for the first Harriman Cup. Ibid., 289.

7. Hannagan, as quoted in ibid., 209.

8. Holland, *Sun Valley*, 206–13.

9. See Richard W. Moulton, "Film's Role in Popularizing Alpine Skiing in America," and Margaret Supplee Smith, "The Image of Skiing in American Popular Culture," in *Collected Papers of the International Ski History Congress*, ed. E. John B. Allen (New Hartford, Conn.: International Skiing History Association, 2002), 190–94; 141–45.

10. T. J. Flynn, "Highland Bavarian Lodge, Highland, Colorado," Highland Bavarian Corporation file, AHS.

11. Robert Benchley, "How to Aspen," pamphlet, Skiing: Aspen, History file, AHS; "Aspen Ski Films Shown at Chicago Travel Exposition," *Aspen Times,* June 10, 1937, 1; Delphine Carter, "I'm Aspen You," *Ski Bulletin*, February 5, 1937, 5; Evelyn Runnette, "Skiing with the C.M.C.," *Ski Bulletin*, March 19, 1937, 7; "Rocky Mountain Notes," *Ski Bulletin*, March 26, 1937, 15; Kathleen Daily and Gaylord T. Guenin, *Aspen: The Quiet Years* (Aspen, Colo.: Red Ink, 1994), 235.

12. Theodore S. Ryan, interview by George Madsen Jr., March 23, 26, and 30, 1965, transcript of three "Commentary" programs recorded and broadcast over WSNO, Aspen, Colo., manuscript, Highland Bavarian Corporation file, AHS; T. J. Flynn, "History of Winter Sports Developments at Aspen," *Aspen Times,* n.d., clipping, Skiing 1938–45 file, AHS; unidentified manuscript, 171–75, Highland Bavarian Corporation file, AHS; Roch, "A Once and Future Resort," 17–23; "Highland Bavarian Winter Sport Club Dedicated Sunday," *Glenwood Post,* December 24, 1936, clipping, Highland Bavarian Corporation file, AHS; T. J. Flynn, "Mount Hayden to Date," *Ski Bulletin,* December 8, 1939, 6. For a more detailed history of the Highland Bavarian Corporation, see Gilbert, "Re-Creation through Recreation," 14–35.

13. Clippings, February 18, 1923, and n.d., 1927, General Ski Collections, GCHA.

14. "Towns in Colorado Active in Support of Winter Sports," unidentified clipping, General Ski Collection, GCHA.

15. Duane A. Smith, *Rocky Mountain Boom Town: A History of Durango, Colorado* (Niwot: University Press of Colorado, 1980), 112.

16. "Grand Lake Will Hold Winter Sports Week," clipping, General Ski Collection, GCHA.

17. Henry Buchtel, "Steamboat Springs," *Trail and Timberline* 254 (February 1940), 28.

18. *Steamboat Pilot,* May 30, 1940, Routt County Collection, BWML.

19. *Aspen Times,* November 26, 1936, clipping, Skiing 1938–45 file, AHS.

20. Russ Holmes, in Mary Eshbaugh Hayes, "The Town Got Excited about Skiing," *Aspen Times,* March 2, 1978, C1.

21. *Western Colorado and Eastern Utah,* January 1939, 10, Ski Town file, Routt County Collection, BWML.

22. When Gordon Wren was growing up in Steamboat Springs, "every kid had a jumping hill in their backyard." They all had names, such as Webber's Hill, Wither's Hill, Studer's Hill, and, more creatively, the Suicide Six, the Man Killer, the Baby Amateur. "We'd just take a shovel, build a jump, and jump." Gordon Wren, interview by the author, August 25, 1995, Steamboat Springs, Colo., tape recording and transcript, 10, 1.

23. Hayes, "The Town Got Excited," C1.

24. For an excellent historical geography of Colorado, see William Wyckoff, *Creating Colorado: The Making of a Western American Landscape, 1860–1940* (New Haven, Conn.: Yale University Press, 1999).

25. Steve Patterson and Kenton Forrest, *Rio Grande Ski Train* (Denver: Tramway Press, 1984), 11. Other sources say that Berthoud Pass was not open in the winter until 1933; still others recall that it was 1935. Snowstorms and slides probably closed it temporarily throughout this period.

26. Colorado Department of Highways, *Paths of Progress* (manuscript, n.d.), 12, Pamphlet file, CUA; Patterson and Forrest, *Rio Grande Ski Train,* 11; Continental Oil Co., Official Road Map of Colorado, c. 1928, CUA; Texaco Touring Map of Colorado, 1939, map case 9, CUA; for more on the impact of the automobile and tourism on Colorado during the 1920s, see Carl Ubbelohde, Maxine Benson, and Duane A. Smith, *A Colorado History,* 6th ed. (Boulder, Colo.: Pruett Publishing Company, 1988), 327–29.

27. Graeme McGowan, "A Rocky Mountain Prophecy," *Ski Bulletin,* March 19, 1937, 5.

28. "Paved Roads in Colorado, 1940," in Thomas J. Noel, Paul F. Mahoney, and Richard E. Stevens, *Historical Atlas of Colorado* (Norman: University of Oklahoma Press, 1994), map 31.

29. "The C.M.C. Ski-Bus," *Trail and Timberline* 207 (January 1936), 153.

30. David Rosendale, "Skiing in the Colorado Mountain Club," *Trail and Timberline* 208 (February 1936), 12.

31. A. Ridgeway, *A History of Transportation in Colorado* (manuscript, 1926), 78, CUA; Patterson and Forrest, *Rio Grande Ski Train,* 14; Ubbelohde, Benson, and Smith, *Colorado History,* 253.

32. Patterson and Forrest, *Rio Grande Ski Train,* 14.

33. Ibid., 14–15.

34. Grand County Historical Association, *Winter Park: Colorado's Favorite for Fifty Years, 1940–1990* (Winter Park Recreation Association, 1989), 17.

35. Runnette, "Skiing with the C.M.C.," 7; Rosendale, "Skiing in the Colorado Mountain Club," 13.

36. *Denver Rocky Mountain News,* January 24, 1936, as cited in Patterson and Forrest, *Rio Grande Ski Train,* 18.

37. Patterson and Forrest, *Rio Grande Ski Train,* 19.

38. The Boston and Maine Railroad carried almost 200 skiers to the mountains of New Hampshire on its first ski train, January 11, 1931. The New York, New Haven and Hartford Railroad first experimented with its own ski train in 1935. The Snowball Express brought skiers from San Francisco to Truckee starting in 1932, and the University Book Store in Seattle sponsored a ski train to the Cascades in 1935. See E. John B. Allen, *From Skisport to Skiing: One Hundred Years of an American Sport, 1840–1940* (Amherst: University of Massachusetts Press, 1993), 104–9.

39. Berthoud Pass, Pikes Peak, and Rocky Mountain National Park were also listed as "Western Winter Playgrounds," but no trains serviced those particular areas. Burlington Route, "Winter Sports," pamphlet, Recreational Skiing file, CHS. The Denver and Rio Grande Railroad offered service to Aspen from Denver, Pueblo, or Colorado Springs. Patterson and Forrest, *Rio Grande Ski Train,* 21, 22.

40. Rope tows were essentially a constantly moving loop of rope, anchored at the top and bottom of the hill and powered by a motor. Skiers stepped up to the rope on their skis, grabbed hold of it with their hands, and hung on as the rope pulled them up the hill. During the 1930s, rope tows were the most prevalent ski tow in the country, although some areas experimented with new technology. For a good synopsis of ski tow technology in the 1930s, see Allen, *Skisport to Skiing,* 109–14.

41. Robert S. Monahan, "Skiing in the National Forests," *American Ski Annual* (1938), 125, CHS.

42. Ibid.

43. See Graeme McGowan, "Future Skiing in the National Forests," *Trail and Timberline* 218 (December 1936), 145–46, reprinted in *Ski Bulletin,* January 1, 1937, 4–5; Graeme McGowan, "Ganchos de Nieve," *American Ski Annual* (1937–38), 87–95, CHS. The National Park Service also promoted skiing and winter recreation at this time. Rocky Mountain National Park officials kept Trail Ridge Road open to timberline to provide access to ski trails. The Park Service developed ski trails and built shelters at Hidden Valley, a ski area within the park, but did not install tows. It promoted skiing most actively in Yosemite National Park, where facilities in the 1930s could not accommodate the 25,000 skiers who came to Badger Pass in the winter. Here the Park Service built a huge new lodge from which skiers could see the lift and the bottom of three downhill runs, and it expanded the trail system after skiers continued to crowd the area during the 1935–36 season. "Ski Trip," *Trail and Timberline* 219 (January 1937), 9; "Skiing Comes of Age in California," *American Ski Annual* (1936–37), 159–60, CHS; Fanning Hearon, "Skiing in the National Parks," *American Ski Annual* (1941–42), 69–86, CHS.

44. The luxurious Timberline Lodge, built by the CCC on Mt. Hood, Oregon, at the cost of $650,000, represents the largest and most visible single federal investment

in skiing. More important were the many smaller investments made across the West. One could argue that early support from the CCC and the PWA enabled communities to develop local ski areas — many of which became destination resorts after the war — that they otherwise would not have been able to develop. For a discussion of the New Deal and America's recreational landscape, see Phoebe Cutler, *The Public Landscape of the New Deal* (New Haven, Conn.: Yale University Press, 1985).

45. Reynolds Morse, "The High Trails of Winter," *Trail and Timberline* 194 (December 1934), 163; Rosendale, "Skiing in the Colorado Mountain Club," 12.

46. J. C. Blickensderfer, "Reminiscences of Skiing in Colorado, 1922–1968" (manuscript, n.d.), 2, Ski Collection, CHS; Frank Ashley, "Colorado Skiing," *American Ski Annual* (1936–37), 110, CHS.

47. Jack Kendrick, "Winter Sports Development," *Trail and Timberline* 238 (September–October 1938), 104; Blickensderfer, "Reminiscences," 3; letter from L. R. Kendrick to J. R. Pechman, August 22, 1938, Colorado Ski Clubs and Associations Collection, CHS; "Thrilling Winter Sport in Colorado, Top of the Nation," pamphlet, 1941, CUA.

48. Barrion Hughes, an original Arlberg Club member who worked as a lawyer in Denver, donated $3,000 to build a lodge for the club. GCHA, *Winter Park*, 17–19; on the CMC, see "Ski Cabin," *Trail and Timberline* 210 (December 1938), 126, 127.

49. Morse, "High Trails of Winter," 163; "The Ski Races," *Trail and Timberline* 198 (April 1935), 45.

50. Ashley, "Colorado Skiing," 112; letter from Kendrick to Pechman, August 22, 1938, Colorado Ski Clubs and Associations Collection, CHS.

51. GCHA, *Winter Park*, 24.

52. Kendrick, "Winter Sports Development," 105. Kendrick was chairman of the Winter Sports Committee.

53. Ibid.; letters from Jack Kendrick to J. R. Pechman, August 22 and 30, 1938, Colorado Ski Clubs and Associations Collection, CHS; "Ski Tows," *Trail and Timberline* 240 (December 1938), 125.

54. GCHA, *Winter Park*, 28–35; "Thrilling Winter Sports in Colorado, Top of the Nation," CUA; Patterson and Forrest, *Rio Grande Ski Train*, 25.

55. Blickensderfer, "Reminiscences," 4–5.

56. Ibid., 4–5, 8–9; J. C. Blickensderfer, "One Day Skiing Trips from Denver," *Trail and Timberline* 253 (January 1939), 10–11; "Colorado's National Forests," *Ski Bulletin*, March 26, 1937, 16.

57. "Glenwood Springs," *Western Colorado and Eastern Utah* (January 1939), 10, Ski Town file, Routt County Collection, BWML.

58. Ski club workers crafted Pioneer's chairlift out of old mine towers and hoists from a mine above Tin Cup in 1939. Abbott Fay, *Ski Tracks in the Rockies: A Century of Colorado Skiing* (Evergreen, Colo.: Cordillera Press, 1984), 25. Bill Mahoney, interview by the author, June 6, 1994, Telluride, Colo., tape record-

ing; David Lavender, *The Telluride Story* (Ridgeway, Colo.: Wayfinder Press, 1987), 60, 62.

59. The club and the Forest Service were waiting in 1941 for Highway 550 to be relocated before they planned a larger ski area on forest land. C. R. Towne, "Durango Skiing Area," *Rocky Mountain Winter Sports News,* January 16, 1941, 2; Smith, *Rocky Mountain Boom Town,* 125.

60. "Ouray," *Western Colorado and Eastern Utah* (January 1939), 10, Ski Town file, Routt County Collection, BWML; "Thrilling Winter Sports in Colorado," CUA; Southern Rocky Mountain Ski Association member clubs, 1941–42, McLaren Collection, GCHA.

61. C. Minot Dole, *Adventures in Skiing* (New York: Franklin Watts, 1965), 90–91. The National Ski Patrol was an organization of volunteers that worked to ensure the safety of skiers at ski areas across the country. See chapter 4 for a more detailed treatment of the NSP. See also Gretchen Besser's book, *The National Ski Patrol: Samaritans of the Snow* (Woodstock, Vt.: Countryman Press, 1983).

62. See Dole, *Adventures in Skiing,* 90–125; Fred H. McNeil, "Skiing and the National Defense," *American Ski Annual* (1941–42), 5–21, CHS; Charles McLane, "Of Mules and Skis," *American Ski Annual* (1942–43), 21–34, CHS. There are dozens of books about the 10th Mountain Division. See Dole, *Adventures in Skiing;* and Hal Burton, *The Ski Troops* (New York: Simon and Schuster, 1971) for excellent overviews and for how the 10th fit into developments in skiing. For a complete bibliography, see "The 10th's Books," *Skiing Heritage: Journal of the International Skiing History Association* 7, no. 2 (Fall 1995), 33. The most recent books on the 10th include Tom Wolf's *Ice Crusaders: A Memoir of Cold War and Cold Sport* (Boulder, Colo.: Roberts Rinehart Publishers, 1999); Harris Dusenbery, *North Apennines and Beyond with the 10th Mountain Division* (Portland Ore.: Binford and Mort Publishing, 2001); and McKay Jenkings, *The Last Ridge: The Epic Story of the U.S. Army's 10th Mountain Division and the Assault on Hitler's Europe* (New York: Random House, 2003). Documentary films on the 10th include *Soldiers of the Summit* (Council for Public TV, Channel Six, Inc., 1987) and *Fire on the Mountain* (1995) by Beth and George Gage. The 10th Mountain Division Resource Center is located at the Denver Public Library.

63. Charles M. Dole, "Mountain Forces to Be Enlarged, Bulletin 10C," *American Ski Annual* (1942–43), 108, CHS. For examples of letters of recommendation, see Jack Pechman re: Frank Bulkley II, January 27, 1942, and Pechman re: Muldrow Garrison, March 22, 1942, Colorado Ski Clubs and Associations Collection, CHS. H. Benjamin Duke Jr., "Skiing Soldiers to Skiing Entrepreneurs: Development of the Western Ski Industry" (paper presented at the 1989 Western Historical Association conference), 4, DPL. The War Department also experimented for a time with ski paratroops. James Laughlin IV, "Ski Parachute Troops," *American Ski Annual* (1942–43), 94–96, CHS; Dick and Margaret (Miggs) Durrance, interview by Jeanette Darnauer, August 18, 1993, video and transcript, 8, AHS.

64. McLane, "Of Mules and Skis," 24–27; McNeil, "Skiing and the National Defense," 18–20. For short biographies of Walter Prager and Torger Tokle, including their role in the 10th Mountain Division, see Kenneth S. Templeton, ed., *10th Mountain Division: America's Ski Troops* (Chicago: privately published, 1945), 172, 174.

65. Dole, *Adventures in Skiing,* 109.

66. Letter from Peter Wick to Robert Woody, December 29, 1981, in John Imbrie and Hugh W. Evans, eds., *Good Times and Bad Times: A History of C Company 85th Mountain Infantry Regiment 10th Mountain Division* (Queechee, Vt.: Vermont Heritage Press, 1995), 188.

67. Lt. Charles C. Bradley, "A Mountain Soldier Sings," *American Ski Annual* (1944–1945), 38–39.

68. Duke, "Skiing Soldiers," 5; Jack A. Benson, "Skiing at Camp Hale: Mountain Troops during World War II," *Western Historical Quarterly* 15 (April 1984), 164; Dole, *Adventures in Skiing,* 117.

69. Dole, *Adventures in Skiing,* 118.

70. Duke, "Skiing Soldiers," 5; Burton, *Ski Troops,* 143; Benson, "Skiing at Camp Hale," 173. One source said that the majority of volunteers came from the universities of Dartmouth, Vermont, Maine, Williams, Harvard, Yale, Princeton, Cornell, Michigan, Wisconsin, Minnesota, Montana, and Washington. During the winter of 1944, about 60 percent of the 10th Mountain Division were college students, about 20 percent had been born and raised in the Rockies, and the rest were foreign-born Americans. Templeton, *10th Mountain Division,* 15–18.

71. Wren interview, 3–4.

72. David Brower and Morely Nelson, as quoted in the Gages' film *Fire on the Mountain* (1995); Dole, *Adventures in Skiing,* 116; Benson, "Skiing at Camp Hale," 166–67; Dusenbery, *North Apennines,* 9.

73. Steve Knowlton, interview by the author, October 19, 1994, Denver, Colo., tape recording and transcript, 1, AHS.

74. Fay, *Ski Tracks in the Rockies,* 29; Friedl Pfeifer and Morten Lund, *Nice Goin': My Life on Skis* (Missoula, Mont.: Pictorial Histories Publishing Company, 1993), 116. When Torger Tokle, a ski jumping champion from Norway, joined the 87th Regiment, he said to friends, "I will do everything for my adopted land to help it remain the champion of the small and downtrodden nations of Europe." Templeton, *10th Mountain Division,* 172. It is also possible that the U.S. government made some Austrians and Germans choose between signing up for the military and returning home.

75. Practically every 10th Mountain Division veteran testifies to their common love of the outdoors and the mountains. See, for example, *Fire on the Mountain;* John Litchfield, interview by the author, September 29, 1994, Denver, Colo., tape recording and transcript, 3, AHS; Knowlton interview, 1. Harris Dusenbery considered himself "a passable skier and loved the mountains." He joined up in part because he thought that he would be safer fighting in the mountains than any-

where else. "Alpine terrain is familiar and comforting," he wrote, " I feel at home there, but war offers only the terrible unknown conjured up in vivid imagination." Dusenbery, *North Apennines*, 10.

76. Wren interview; Robert Woody, in Imbrie and Evans, *Good Times and Bad Times,* 129; Dole, *Adventures in Skiing*, 122–23; Benson, "Skiing at Camp Hale," 166.

77. Imbrie and Evans, *Good Times and Bad Times,* 31.

78. Dole, *Adventures in Skiing,* 124; see Benson, "Skiing at Camp Hale," for a thorough critique of the 10th at Camp Hale; Litchfield interview, 3.

79. Imbrie and Evans, *Good Times and Bad Times,* 6; *Fire on the Mountain.* See also Hugh Evans's recollections of D-Series in Imbrie and Evans, 198; Dusenbery, *North Apennines,* 13.

80. Dusenbery, *North Apennines,* 150, 157.

81. S/Sgt. Edwin C. Gibson, "On Cooper Hill," *American Ski Annual* (1944–45), 60–61, CHS.

82. Dusenbery, *North Apennines,* 109, 28, 74.

82. Friedl Pfeifer, interview by the author, July 21, 1994, Aspen, Colo., tape recording and transcript, 2, AHS.

84. Most spouses lived in Glenwood Springs, Buena Vista, or Denver; a few lived in Aspen and Leadville. Litchfield interview, 3; Knowlton interview, 1–2.

85. Knowlton interview, 1; Wren interview, 4.

86. "Climax Ski Area Has Had a Lively, Exciting History," *Summit County Journal,* March 11, 1960, 4, Pamphlet file, CUA; Wren interview, 4; Knowlton interview, 1–2. The GIs from Camp Hale won. Barney McLean, interview by Ruth Whyte, October 15, 1986, tape recording #C89, AHS.

87. Elizabeth Oblock Sinclair, interview by the author, July 26, 1994, Aspen, Colo., tape recording and transcript, 3, AHS.

88. Percy Rideout, Jack O'Brien, and Steve Knowlton, interview by Ruth Whyte, March 24, 1991, Aspen, Colo., tape recording, AHS; Rideout interview.

89. There are considerable primary and secondary sources recounting the military actions of the 10th Mountain Division. This narrative pulls from first- and secondhand accounts in Dole, *Adventures in Skiing;* Imbrie and Evans, *Good Times and Bad Times;* Templeton, *10th Mountain Division;* the films *Soldiers on the Summit* and *Fire on the Mountain;* and accounts from veterans Duke, Pfeifer, Litchfield, and Knowlton.

90. See Wolf, *Ice Crusaders,* for a thoughtful range of views on the 10th Mountain Division. Documents in Templeton, *10th Mountain Division,* and Imbrie and Evans, *Good Times and Bad Times,* illustrate high praise for the 10th's performance from people such as the commanding general of the 5th Army and commanding general of the XIV Panzer Corps, which opposed the 10th in the Po Valley. At a 1959 reunion of the 10th, Dave Fowler, division historian and combat commander of the 87th, remarked that its veterans "have the firm conviction that the Tenth Mountain Division was the finest combat division our Army ever had." Dole, *Adventures in Skiing,* 151.

91. Letter from William C. Douglas to Kent Clow, March 28, 1945, in Templeton, *10th Mountain Division*, 109.
92. Bill Bowerman, from *Fire on the Mountain*.
93. Pfeifer and Lund, *Nice Goin'*, 111; Benedict, in *Fire on the Mountain*.
94. Duke, "Skiing Soldiers," 8; *Fire on the Mountain*.

4. CALL OF THE MILD

1. Elizabeth Paepcke, "Memories of Aspen" (manuscript, n.d.), 7, Elizabeth Paepcke biography file, AHS.
2. Mary Bird Young, from Richard W. Moulton, *Legends of American Skiing, 1840–1940* (*Skiing* magazine, 1986), videocassette.
2. For accounts of Aspen's opening ceremonies, see Dick Smith, "Once Again Aspen Is a Boom Town," *Rocky Mountain News*, January 11, 1947; Leonard Wood, "Aspen Ski Club to Celebrate Opening of Longest Chair Lift," *Aspen Times*, December 12, 1946, 1; and Friedl Pfeifer and Morten Lund, *Nice Goin': My Life on Skis* (Missoula, Mont.: Pictorial Histories Publishing Company, 1993), 145–150.
4. Leonard Woods, "Aspen, Now," *American Ski Annual* (1946–47), 158, CHS. See also Leonard Woods, "Memorandum," to Directors of the Aspen Skiing Corporation, October 15, 1946, AHS.
5. Fred H. McNeil, "Skiing and the War," *American Skiing Annual* (1942–43), 99–101, CHS.
6. Paepcke was never really interested in skiing; he got involved mainly to control the growth of the sport in Aspen. For more on Paepcke and his cultural goals, see James Sloan Allen, *The Romance of Commerce and Culture: Capitalism, Modernism, and the Chicago-Aspen Crusade for Cultural Reform* (Chicago: University of Chicago Press, 1983).
7. Pfeifer and Lund, *Nice Goin'*, 136–42; Dutch Hodges, "The Beginning of the Dream" (manuscript, n.d.), AHS; Smith, "Once Again Aspen Is a Boom Town"; Woods, "Memorandum"; Paul Hauk, "Aspen Mountain Ski Area Chronology" in *Ski Area Chronology: Chronologies of the Ski Areas on and Adjacent to the White River National Forest, Colorado* (Glenwood Springs, Colo.: U.S. Department of Agriculture, Forest Service, White River National Forest, 1979), 2; "Schedule B," Aspen Skiing Corporation Balance Sheet, May 31, 1947, Aspen Skiing Corporation Collection, AHS.
8. Seibert would go on to develop Vail. See Peter W. Seibert, *Vail: Triumph of a Dream* (Boulder, Colo.: Mountain Sport Press, 2000). Seibert's future public relations guru Bob Parker also joined the ski patrol in Aspen, and veterans Dick Wright and Andy Ransom joined the ski school. Steve Knowlton and John Litchfield also became Aspen businessmen, owning and operating the Golden Horn and the Red Onion nightspots, respectively.
9. Some agreed to sell or lease the surface rights to their mines on Aspen Mountain so the ASC could build ski trails and run the lift over them; others helped with the construction of the lift. A few locals would enter into the ASC's employ. See

Anne Gilbert, "Re-Creation through Recreation: Aspen Skiing from 1870 to 1970" (manuscript, April 1995), AHS.

10. Paul Hauk, "A-Basin Ski Area Chronology," in *Ski Area Chronology*, 2; "Colorado Ski Areas," *Rocky Mountain Life* (December 1947), 51; Giles D. Toll, interview by the author, February 2, 1996, Denver, Colo., tape recording and transcript, 6.

11. Bill Fetcher, "A History of the Emerald Mountain Ski Lift" (manuscript, April 19, 1992), Emerald Mountain Ski Lift file, BWML. Steamboat's "world's longest single-span lift" was longer (at 8,850 feet) than Aspen's Lift No. 1 (at 8,480 feet), but Aspen included its Lift No. 2 in its claim to fame by characterizing the lifts as one, albeit in two sections. See also Maurice Leckenby, "Skiing Steamboat," *Rocky Mountain Life* (October 1947), 23.

12. Steve Patterson and Kenton Forrest, *Rio Grande Ski Train* (Denver: Tramway Press, 1984), 25. See also Betty Hosburgh, "Colorado's Newest Ski Developments," *Rocky Mountain Life* (March 1946), 8–9; "Heavy Snows Open Colorado Ski Areas," *Rocky Mountain Skiing*, December 1, 1948, 1; Grand County Historical Association, *Winter Park: Colorado's Favorite for Fifty Years, 1940–1990* (Winter Park Recreation Association, 1989), 47–67.

13. Hauk, "A-Basin Ski Area Chronology," 1–5; Abbott Fay, *Ski Tracks in the Rockies: A Century of Colorado Skiing* (Evergreen, Colo.: Cordillera Press, 1984), 41–42; Larry Jump, "Arapahoe Basin — The Promised Land," *Rocky Mountain Life* (January 1947), 38–39, 42.

14. One skier-visit consists of one skier spending one day at any given area. Skier-visits at Arapahoe Basin grew from 33,000 during the 1956–57 season to almost 90,000 in 1965–66; at Aspen Mountain, they jumped from 83,000 to 143,000 over the same period; and at Winter Park, they more than tripled from 70,000 to 213,000. J. B. Kline, "Western Mountain Region Study" (Business Research Division, Graduate School of Business Administration, University of Colorado, 1967), 32. Statewide, skier-visits rose equally dramatically, increasing anywhere from 8.7 percent to 37.6 percent each year between 1963–64 and 1974–75;, total skier-visits grew from 801,000 in 1963–64 to over 5,194,000 eleven years later. Page Dabney, "An Impact Study — The Colorado Ski Industry: A Study of the Influence of the Industry upon the Economies of Selected Mountain Counties and Communities," Colorado Ski Country USA, 1974, updated 1976, 17, BRL.

15. "Ski Areas in Colorado, Wyoming, and New Mexico," *Rocky Mountain Life* (November 1946), 48–50; "Colorado Ski Areas," *Rocky Mountain Life* (December 1947), 51–53; "Colorado Ski Directory," *Rocky Mountain Life* (December 1948), 52, 54; "Skiing Centers of Colorado," *Colorado Wonderland* (December 1950), 21; *The Manual of Colorado Skiing at the Top of the Nation* (Denver: Colorado Ski Information Center, 1954); L. J. Crampon and Ronald D. Lemon, "Skiing in the Southern Rocky Mountain Region" (manuscript, Business Research Division, Graduate School of Business Administration, University of Colorado at Boulder, 1957), BRL; *1961–62 Colorado Ski and Winter Sports Manual* (Denver:

Colorado Visitors Bureau, Winter Sports Committee, 1961); *1966–67 Colorado Skiing: Resorts, Lodges, Services, Transportation* (Denver: Colorado Visitors Bureau, 1966); *Colorful Colorado* 1 (Winter 1966), 69–83; *1968–69 Colorado Skiing: Resorts, Lodges, Services, Transportation* (Denver: Colorado Visitors Bureau, 1968). See also Tommy Neal, "Purgatory — An Exciting New Word in Skiing" and other articles in the *Durango-Cortez Herald,* November 27, 1966, for information on the development of ski areas in the southwestern part of the state. See Hauk, *Ski Area Chronology,* for the development of ski areas within the White River National Forest.

16. Those areas were Aspen, Berthoud Pass, Grand Mesa, Hidden Valley, Pikes Peak, Winter Park, and Wolf Creek.

17. Of the state's skiers in 1957, 69.1 percent came from Colorado, with another 3.5 percent from other mountain states. Most out-of-state skiers came from the central states, contributing 19.7 percent of Colorado's business. Illinois, Texas, Minnesota, and Kansas sent the most skiers to Colorado. Crampon and Lemon, "Skiing in Southern Rocky Mountain Region," 4–5. For out-of-state spending statistics, see Gerald L. Allen, "Colorado Ski and Winter Recreation Statistics" (manuscript, Business Research Division, Graduate School of Business Administration, University of Colorado at Boulder, 1969), 35, BRL. See also Morten Lund, "The Texans Are Coming!" *Ski* 32, no. 5 (December 1967), 90.

18. Cal Queal, "Skiing's Still Fun for Fred," *Empire Magazine,* November 1968, clipping, Fred Iselin biography file, AHS.

19. Paul S. Boyer et al., *The Enduring Vision,* vol. 2 (Lexington, Mass.: DC Heath, 1990), 1017, 1018, 1022. By 1950, daily, weekend, and vacation leisure hours constituted a third of Americans' waking lives, and in 1959, each working American took more than one week of paid vacation. Marion Clawson and Jack L. Knetsch, *Economics of Outdoor Recreation* (Baltimore: Johns Hopkins Press, 1966), 16–17.

20. Automobile trips accounted for 94 percent of all outdoor recreation trips in 1953. John A. Jakle, *The Tourist: Travel in Twentieth-Century North America* (Lincoln: University of Nebraska Press, 1985), 186. Crampon and Lemon, "Skiing in Southern Rocky Mountain Region," 32.

21. Colorado Department of Highways, *Paths of Progress,* 14, Pamphlet file, CUA; State Highway Map of Colorado, Colorado Department of Highways, 1952, CUA.

22. Editors of *Ski* Magazine, *America's Ski Book* (New York: Scribner, 1973), 46, 50.

23. Stan Cohen, *A Pictorial History of Downhill Skiing* (Missoula, Mont.: Pictorial Histories Publishing Company, 1985), 89–106.

24. One Forest Service poll taken in 1947 established that "most skiers would willingly trade two rope tow tickets for a ticket on a chair lift or T-bar tow." "Forest Service Surveys 1947–48 Season," *Rocky Mountain Skiing,* December 1, 1948, 2.

25. Only eight of the state's thirty ski areas had an hourly capacity of less than 1,000 skiers. "Colorado Ski Areas," *Colorful Colorado* 1, no. 3 (Winter 1966), 69.

26. Nils Ericksen, "If You Build It, They Will Come," *Ski Area Management* 35, no. 1 (January 1996), 52.

27. Jump, "Arapahoe Basin — The Promised Land," 38.

28. U.S. Forest Service, U.S. Department of Agriculture, and the National Ski Areas Association, *Planning Considerations for Winter Sports Resort Development* (1973), 15.

29. Jim Snobble, interview by the author, July 11, 1994, Aspen, Colo., tape recording and transcript, 2, AHS.

30. Toll interview, 9.

31. H. Peter Wingle, *Planning Considerations for Winter Sports Resort Development* (U.S. Department of Agriculture, Forest Service, Rocky Mountain Region, 1994), 77.

32. Tod Martin, foreword to *Skiing Colorado* by Curtis W. Casewit (Old Greenwich, Conn.: Chatham Press, 1975).

33. *Aspen Times,* October 14, 1948, 1.

34. John Litchfield, interview by the author, September 29, 1994, Denver, Colo., tape recording and transcript, 4, AHS.

35. Dick and Margaret (Miggs) Durrance, interview by Jeanette Darnauer, August 18, 1993, Aspen, Colo., videotape, AHS.

36. Steve Knowlton, interview by the author, October 19, 1994, Denver, Colo., tape recording and transcript, 3, AHS.

37. Paul Nitze, interview by the author, July 20, 1994, Aspen, Colo., tape recording and transcript, 4, AHS.

38. Snobble interview, 3; Litchfield interview, 5; Stephen Bradley, "What's the Ideal Ski Hill?" *Skiing Area News* 2 (April 1967), 36–38.

39. Few designers understood the degree to which they affected the mountain landscape or the impact on plant and animal populations. Chet Anderson, interview with the author, June 7, 1994, Durango, Colo. After 1971, developers used helicopters, rather than building roads and using heavy equipment, to install lift towers in fragile mountain environments over 11,000 feet.

40. Pfeifer and Lund, *Nice Goin',* 140.

41. U.S. Forest Service, *Planning Considerations* (1973), 19.

42. Cal Queal, "Colorado Skiing 1968," *Empire,* November 1968, clipping, Skiing 1968 file, AHS.

43. Anderson interview.

44. Peter Miller, "Make Love to the Mountain," *Ski* (November 1979), 157. Jean Mayer, a former French junior national ski champion, directed the Taos Ski Valley ski school.

45. Steve Knowlton, from the 1995 documentary *Fire on the Mountain;* Charles Paterson, interview by the author, June 28, 1994, Aspen, Colo., tape recording and transcript, 10, AHS.

46. C. Minot Dole, "Whither American Skiing?" *Ski* 12 (January 1948), 15.

47. Fay, *Ski Tracks in the Rockies,* 43; GCHA, *Winter Park,* 72.

48. Gordon Wren, interview by the author, August 25, 1995, Steamboat Springs, Colo., tape recording and transcript, 5.

49. For an excellent cultural history of snow, see Bernard Mergen, *Snow in America* (Washington, D.C.: Smithsonian Institution, 1997).

50. "Minutes," Rocky Mountain Ski Area Operators' Association meeting, February 13, 1963, Aspen, Colo., Aspen Skiing Collection, AHS.

51. Letter from Walter Orr Roberts to Steve Knowlton, March 11, 1963, Aspen Skiing Collection, AHS.

52. "New Future," *Ski* 22, no. 3 (December 1957), 68–72.

53. "Ski Areas," *Historic Georgetown Centennial Gazette 1868/1968*, 23, Colorado Tourism file, Routt County Collection, BWML.

54. Eddie Box and his group performed a rain dance in Vail on December 9, 1963, and agreed to let it be called a snow dance. A blizzard hit a week later. Three years later, on December 4, Box and his dancers traveled to Purgatory. Before they finished dancing, snowflakes the size of quarters were coming down. It snowed for three days. June Simonton, *Vail: Story of a Colorado Mountain Valley* (Denver: Vail Chronicles Inc., 1987), 84; Charlie Langdon, *Durango Ski: People and Seasons at Purgatory* (Durango, Colo.: Purgatory Press, 1989), 43.

55. Dolores LaChapelle, *Deep Powder Snow: 40 Years of Ecstatic Skiing, Avalanches, and Earth Wisdom* (Durango, Colo.: Kivaki Press, 1993), 46.

56. Paepcke, "Memories of Aspen."

57. This was as much an argument for skiing's widespread appeal to postwar Americans as it was to those in the 1930s. C. Minot Dole, *Adventures in Skiing* (New York: Franklin Watts, 1965), 36.

58. J. C. Blickensderfer, "Reminiscences of Skiing in Colorado, 1922–1968" (manuscript, n.d.), 11–12, CHS. "Beartrap" bindings were about the only kind available in the 1930s and 1940s; they tied the skier's foot securely to the ski and did not release.

59. Dole, *Adventures in Skiing,* 50–52.

60. Ibid., 53.

61. Ibid., 54.

62. Colorado's first fatality occurred on Loveland Pass on May 21, 1939. Fay, *Ski Tracks in the Rockies,* 21. Graeme McGowan, "Ski Landscaping and Improvements," *Ski Bulletin,* January 29, 1937, 7.

63. Schussing means skiing straight down without turning. Graeme McGowan, "Future Skiing in the National Forests in the Rocky Mountains," *Ski Bulletin,* January 1, 1937, 5.

64. McGowan, "Ski Landscaping," 7.

65. Roland Palmedo, "Ski Patrols," *Ski Bulletin,* January 8, 1937, 5.

66. Dole, "Whither American Skiing?" 15. Dole's implication was that novices skied down trails that were too advanced for them, not that they skied outside the ski area's boundaries.

67. Robert S. Monahan, "Skiing in the National Forests," *American Ski Annual* (1938), 129, CHS.

68. See Dole, *Adventures in Skiing,* for the founder's account of how the NSPS developed.

69. Leonard Woods, "Annual Report of the Aspen Ski Patrol, 1947–48 Season" (manuscript), 2, Skiing–Ski Patrol file, AHS. The Aspen Skiing Corporation soon divided up these duties between the ski patrol and a trail packing crew.

70. Woods, "Annual Report, 1947–48," 2, 5. Seventy-one of the skiers who got rides down the mountain had only minor injuries, mainly sprained ankles.

71. "12,000 Skiing Injuries Predicted in U.S. This Year," *Denver Post,* January 22, 1967, 24, clipping, Skiing file, AHS.

72. Fred H. McNeil, "The Skier and Uncle Sam," *American Ski Annual* (1946–47), 114, CHS.

73. Monahan, "Skiing in the National Forests," 126.

74. Ibid. See also Henry I. Baldwin, "Forestry and Ski Trails," *Ski Bulletin,* January 29, 1937, 5.

75. Hauk, "A-Basin Ski Area Chronology," 3.

76. William C. Kamp, "Administration of Skiing Areas — By Whom? How Much?" *American Skiing Annual* (1944–45), 93–96, CHS.

77. McNeil, "The Skier and Uncle Sam," 111.

78. Slim Davis, "U.S. Forest Service Develops Skiing," *Rocky Mountain Skiing,* November 10, 1948, 5, General Ski Collection, GCHA.

79. Ibid., 6.

80. Pfeifer and Lund, *Nice Goin',* 136; Hauk, "Aspen Mountain Ski Area Chronology," 2.

81. Durrance interview (1993); D. R. C. Brown, interview by Jeanette Darnauer, April 10, 1979, Aspen, Colo., tape recording #C10, AHS. Aspen Mountain's permit was amended, however, to cover Lift No. 3 in 1954, and again in 1957 to increase the annual use fee.

82. Wren interview, 7.

83. It did not hurt that Anderson himself had worked for the USFS as a wildlife biologist and snow ranger, or that he applied his graduate degree in forest ecology to his ski area planning. Mike Elliott, interview by the author, June 7, 1994, Purgatory, Colo.

84. Paul Hauk scouted the White River National Forest for potential ski area sites and accompanied developers who were interested in a particular area. Chet Anderson and his colleagues did so for the San Juan National Forest after working as snow rangers at areas such as Loveland Basin, Winter Park, and Arapahoe Basin. See Hauk, *Ski Area Chronology;* Langdon, *Durango Ski,* 11.

85. Hauk, "A-Basin Ski Area Chronology," 2.

86. Whip Jones, interview by the author, July 12, 1994, Aspen, Colo.

87. "Forests Draw Ski Boom Plan," *Denver Post,* October 4, 1959, 7E, clipping, Skiing 1956–60 file, AHS.

88. Ibid.

89. Paul Hauk, "Buttermilk Ski Area Chronology," in *Ski Area Chronology*, 1, 2.

90. Hauk, "Aspen Mountain Ski Area Chronology," 3–4; "Interview: DRC Brown," *Aspen* (February–March 1976), 20, DRC Brown biography file, AHS. It is not clear how much of the $278,277 went toward Aspen Mountain's permit fees. Organizations such as the National Forest Recreation Association sprouted up in the early 1960s and spent hours of their annual meetings discussing and negotiating permit fees. "Summary of National Forest Recreation Association Winter Sports Section Meeting," May 10, 1963, Reno, Nev., Aspen Skiing Collection, AHS.

91. Steve Knowlton, "Proposal by Rocky Mountain Ski Area Operators' Association — Ski Country USA," letter to Darcy Brown, March 14, 1963, Aspen Skiing Collection, AHS; Knowlton interview, 6.

92. "Inside NSAA," *Ski Area News* 7 (Spring 1972), 28.

93. The Multiple-Use Sustained-Yield Act of 1960 redefined the policy of highest use by declaring "the National Forests are established and shall be administered for outdoor recreation, range, timber, watershed, and wildlife and fish purposes." Forest Service policy, therefore, had to let all these interest groups share forest resources and manage the forests "so they are utilized in the combination that will best meet the needs of the American people." The Wilderness Act of 1964 established the means to set up "wilderness areas" within the national forests and prohibited any kind of construction or use of machinery in them.

94. GCHA, *Winter Park,* 125.

95. Ibid., 134–38.

96. Elliott interview.

97. Wren interview.

98. Jerry Hulse, "The Idea Is to Keep Them Captive after the Snow Melts . . . ," *Los Angeles Times,* October 26, 1975, clipping, Routt County Collection, Ski Town file, BWML. For a thorough discussion of the corporate ski industry and its problems, see Hal Clifford, *Downhill Slide: Why the Corporate Ski Industry Is Bad for Skiing, Ski Towns, and the Environment* (San Francisco: Sierra Club Books, 2002).

99. Paul Hauk, "Breckenridge Chronology," in *Ski Area Chronology,* 7; Nitze interview.

100. Carol Kocivar, "The Lawsuit Tide: Ebb or Flood?" *Skiing Area News* 7 (Winter 1972), 30.

101. George Gillett, in William Oscar Johnson, "A Vision Fulfilled," *Sports Illustrated,* January 30, 1989, 82.

102. For an early discussion of resort planning, see Franziska Porges, "On Planning Ski Resorts," *American Ski Annual* (1946–47), 131–34, CHS.

103. Alex Katz, "Skiing," *Colorful Colorado* 1, no. 3 (Winter 1966), 67.

104. "Snowmass-at-Aspen — Exciting New Shangri-la of Skiing," *Denver Post,* November 12, 1967, 19, clipping, Snowmass file, AHS; watch also for Margaret

Supplee Smith's forthcoming work on ski resort architecture and design. "All you add is people . . . ," clipping, n.d., Snowmass file, AHS. See also Gilbert, "Re-Creation through Recreation," for a more complete history of Snowmass.

5. THE WHITE WEST

1. Vail advertisement, *Skiing* 21 (October 1968), 41.
2. See June Simonton, *Vail: Story of a Colorado Mountain Valley* (Denver: Vail Chronicles, 1987).
3. This is a process that cultural geographers have described in a variety of places. See Don Mitchell, *The Lie of the Land: Migrant Workers and the California Land-scape* (Minneapolis: University of Minnesota Press, 1996), and Sharon Zukin, *Landscapes of Power: From Detroit to Disney World* (Berkeley: University of California Press, 1991).
4. See Hal Rothman, *Devil's Bargains: Tourism in the 20th Century West* (Lawrence: University Press of Kansas, 1998); David M. Wrobel and Patrick T. Long, eds., *Seeing and Being Seen: Tourism in the American West* (Lawrence: University Press of Kansas, 2001); Bonnie Christensen, *Red Lodge and the Mythic West: From Coal Miners to Cowboys* (Lawrence: University Press of Kansas, 2002); and Earl S. Pomeroy, *In Search of the Golden West: The Tourist in Western America* (New York: Alfred A. Knopf, 1957; reprint, Lincoln: University of Nebraska Press, 1990).
5. Leonard Woods, "Aspen Ski Club to Celebrate Opening of Longest Chair Lift," *Aspen Times*, December 12, 1946, 1.
6. Patricia Coffin, "Aspen," *Look* 8 (November 1949), 59–67; Evan Wylie, "Ghost Town on Skis," *Colliers*, February 7, 1948.
7. "Big Ed Makes Plea for East-West Link," *Denver Post*, April 13, 1955, 1, as cited in Thomas Alexis Thomas, "Colorado and the Interstate Highways: A Study in the Continuity of Western Tradition" (master's thesis, University of Colorado, 1991), 17.
8. John Litchfield, interview by the author, September 29, 1994, Denver, Colo., tape recording and transcript, 5, AHS; Friedl Pfeifer and Morten Lund, *Nice Goin': My Life on Skis* (Missoula, Mont.: Pictorial Histories Publishing Company, 1993), 134; Dick and Margaret (Miggs) Durrance, interview by Jeanette Darnauer, August 18, 1993, Aspen, Colo., videotape and transcript, 14, AHS.
9. William Oscar Johnson, "A Vision Fulfilled," *Sports Illustrated*, January 30, 1989, 77.
10. Burt Sims, "For Summer Profits, Try a Little Imagination," *Skiing Area News* 2 (April 1967), 30.
11. Martin Padley, "Are Radio & TV Good for You?" *Skiing Area News* 4 (Spring 1969), 50; Ron Taylor, "Add One Large Crowd," *Skiing Area News* 5 (Spring 1970), 24.
12. Member areas included Aspen Highlands and Aspen Skiing Corporation areas, Breckenridge, Winter Park, Steamboat Springs, and Vail, as well as Taos Ski Valley, Sun Valley, Park City, and Jackson Hole outside of Colorado. As destination

resorts with similar characteristics but different strengths, member areas complemented one another and offered tourists from the East and even Europe a variety
of skiing experiences. Johnson, "Vision Fulfilled," 77; Mike Korologos, "Bringing
Our Skiers Back Home," *Skiing Area News* 6 (Fall 1971), 34.

13. "Ski Colorado," Continental Airlines brochure (1976–77), pamphlet, 3, Recreational Skiing file, CHS.

14. John Jakle, *The Tourist: Travel in Twentieth-Century North America* (Lincoln:
University of Nebraska Press, 1985), xi, 22; Dean MacCannell, *The Tourist: A New
Theory of the Leisure Class* (New York: Schocken Books, 1989), 5, 13; Wrobel and
Long, *Seeing and Being Seen*, 15–18. See also Marguerite S. Shaffer, *See America First:
Tourism and National Identity, 1880–1940* (Washington, D.C.: Smithsonian Insti-
tution Press, 2001), and Rothman, *Devil's Bargains.*

15. See John Urry, *The Tourist Gaze* (New York: Sage Books, 1990). Scholars have discussed the local implications of tourism at length. See Wrobel and Long, *Seeing
and Being Seen,* and Rothman, *Devil's Bargains,* for historical perspectives. For
discussions that deal explicitly with images of place and rurality, see John Urry,
Consuming Places (New York: Routledge, 1995); Richard Butler, C. Michael Hall,
and John Jenkins, eds., *Tourism and Recreation in Rural Areas* (New York: John
Wiley and Sons, 1998); and Colin Mitchell Hall, *Tourism and Politics: Policy, Power
and Place* (New York: John Wiley and Sons, 1994), 178.

16. Samuel Bowles, *The Switzerland of America: A Summer Vacation in the Parks and
Mountains of Colorado* (Springfield, Mass.: Samuel Bowles and Co., 1869). See also
William Wyckoff, *Creating Colorado: The Making of a Western American Land-
scape, 1860–1940* (New Haven, Conn.: Yale University Press, 1999), 78–88.

17. Pomeroy, *In Search of the Golden West,* 33. See also Shaffer, *See America First.*

18. Andre Roch, "A Once and Future Resort: A Winter in the Rocky Mountains of
Colorado" (trans. Ernest Blake), *Colorado Heritage* 4 (1985), 17–23; originally published as "Un hiver aux Montagnes Rocheuses du Colorado," *Der Schnee-Hase*
(1937).

19. *Ski* 32 (December 1967), 89.

20. Anne M. Gilbert, "Rural People with Connections: Farm and Ranch Families in
the Roaring Fork Valley, Colorado" (master's thesis, University of Colorado, 1992),
83, 84. See also Annie Gilbert Coleman, "'A Hell of a Time All the Time': Farmers, Ranchers, and the Roaring Fork Valley during 'the Quiet Years,'" *Montana:
The Magazine of Western History* (Spring 1997), 32–45.

21. Elizabeth Paepcke noticed such houses and restaurants throughout town and
characterized them as "bastard Tyrolean." Elizabeth Paepcke, "Memories of
Aspen" (manuscript, n.d.), 13, Elizabeth Paepcke biography file, AHS. For a smart
analysis of how buildings take on cultural meaning, especially with regard to race,
see Kirk Savage, *Standing Soldiers, Kneeling Slaves: Race, War, and Monument in
Nineteenth-Century America* (Princeton, N.J.: Princeton University Press, 1997).

22. John Henry Auran, "'Vail-Type Operation' — A Dissection," *Skiing Area News*

1 (April 1966), 38. Vail founder Pete Seibert had attended hotel school in Switzerland after his stint in the 10th Mountain Division, on the assumption that he would someday develop his own ski area; he used his experience and expertise to shape Vail. See Peter W. Seibert, *Vail: Triumph of a Dream* (Boulder, Colo.: Mountain Sports Press, 2000), and William Peter Philpott, "Visions of a Changing Vail: Fast-Growth Fallout in a Colorado Resort Town" (master's thesis, University of Wisconsin, 1994).

23. Steve Knowlton, interview by the author, November 14, 1995, Denver, Colo., tape recording and transcript, 9.

24. An eye toward real estate further convinced them; the new Lion's Head gondola would raise property values at its base area to the same level as those in the original Vail Village. Bill Tanler, "Vail's Case for the Second Gondola," *Skiing Area News* 4 (Fall 1969), 35–36. See also Donald Mrozek, "The Image of the West in American Sport," *Journal of the American West* 17 (July 1978), 9.

25. Duane Thompson, "Vail Preparing for 'Big' Winter Carnival," *Rocky Mountain News,* January 10, 1985, 21, clipping, CHS.

26. Paul Hauk, "Vail Chronology," in *Ski Area Chronology: Chronologies of the Ski Areas on and Adjacent to the White River National Forest, Colorado* (Glenwood Springs, Colo.: U.S. Department of Agriculture, Forest Service, White River National Forest, 1979), 7–8.

27. Leonard Woods, "Aspen, Now," *American Ski Annual* (1946–47), 159, CHS.

28. Bill Marolt, interview by the author, August 11, 1994, Boulder, Colo., tape recording and transcript, 1, AHS.

29. See Michael Carlton, "Breckenridge," *Denver Post,* October 18, 1987, T1. Breckenridge and other ski towns were not the only communities to engage in this process. See Christensen's *Red Lodge and the Mythic West* for an excellent discussion of how this played out in a Montana mining town.

30. Andre Roch, letter or speech, December 10, 1979, Geneva, Switzerland, Andre Roch biography file, AHS.

31. Francis Smith, "Ski Town — Ski Padre," *Rocky Mountain Life* (December 1946), 50; Bob Collins, "Steamboat's Unique Plan Produces Ski Champs," *Rocky Mountain News,* February 14, 1954, 36.

32. Lucile Maxfield Bogue, "Everybody Skis at Steamboat," *Collier's* 4 (February 1955), clipping, Ski Town file, BWML; "Ski Happy Town," *Denver Post Empire Magazine,* November 2, 1958, 9, clipping, Ski Town file, BWML.

33. Jeff Frees, "The Steamboat Aura," *Steamboat Magazine* (Winter 1974–75), 7, clipping, Ski Town file, BWML. See also Jerry Hulse, "On the Go: The Cow Town that Kowtows to Skiers," *Los Angeles Times,* October 26, 1975, X1, clipping, Ski Town file, BWML.

34. Vail exercised a self-conscious sense of humor in this naming process — its famous Riva Ridge trail, named after a ridge the 10th Mountain Division captured from the Germans in Italy, connected to a trail called Tourist Trap.

35. See Anne F. Hyde, "Round Pegs in Square Holes: The Rocky Mountains and Extractive Industry," in *Many Wests: Place, Culture, and Regional Identity,* ed. David M. Wrobel and Michael C. Steiner (Lawrence: University Press of Kansas, 1997), 93–113.

36. For local histories of these areas, see Richard L. Fetter and Suzanne Fetter, *Telluride: From Pick to Powder* (Caldwell, Idaho: Caxton Printers, 1990); David Lavender, *The Telluride Story* (Ridgway, Colo.: Wayfinder Press, 1987); Carl Ubbelohde, Maxine Benson, and Duane A. Smith, *A Colorado History,* 6th ed. (Boulder, Colo.: Pruett Publishing Co., 1972); Duane A. Smith, *Rocky Mountain Boom Town: A History of Durango, Colorado* (Niwot, Colo.: University Press of Colorado, 1980); Simonton, *Vail;* John Rolfe Burroughs, *Steamboat in the Rockies* (Fort Collins, Colo.: Old Army Press, 1974); Jean Wren, *Steamboat Springs and the "Treacherous and Speedy Skee": An Album* (Steamboat Springs, Colo.: Steamboat Pilot, 1972); Mark Fiester, *Blasted Beloved Breckenridge* (Boulder, Colo.: Pruett Publishing Co., 1973); Duane A. Smith, *When Coal Was King: A History of Crested Butte, Colorado, 1880–1952* (Golden, Colo.: Colorado School of Mines Press, 1984); and Malcolm J. Rohrbough, *Aspen: The History of a Silver Mining Town, 1879–1893* (New York: Oxford University Press, 1986).

37. Red Rowland, interview by Elli Fox, February 12, 1987, Aspen, Colo., tape recording #C57, AHS.

38. Bill Mahoney, interview by the author, June 6, 1994, Telluride, Colo., tape recording and transcript, 5.

39. Art and Amelia Trentaz, interview by the author, March 26, 1992, Aspen, Colo., tape recording, AHS.

40. Wyckoff, *Creating Colorado,* 75.

41. Mark Drabenstott and Tim R. Smith, "Finding Rural Success: The New Rural Economic Landscape and Its Implications," in *The Changing American Countryside: Rural People and Places,* ed. Emery N. Castle (Lawrence: University Press of Kansas, 1995), 180–82.

42. Dick Dillman, "Snow Grooming: A Harrowing Experience," *Ski Area News* 1 (January 1966), 22–24.

43. John Henry Auran, "Lift Attendant: No. 1 P.R. Man," *Skiing Area News* 2 (October 1967), 58–59.

44. Sam and Elizabeth Stapleton, interview by the author, March 24, 1992, Aspen, Colo., tape recording, AHS; Trentaz interview; Cherie Gerbaz Oates, interview by the author, July 13, 1994, Aspen, Colo., tape recording and transcript, 12, AHS; Joy Caudill, interview by the author, July 26, 1994, Aspen, Colo., tape recording and transcript, 4, AHS; Mary Eshbaugh Hayes, "Red Rowland and the Ski Lifts," *Aspen Times,* December 16, 1976, C1; Kathleen Daily and Gaylord T. Guenin, *Aspen: The Quiet Years* (Aspen, Colo.: Red Ink, 1994), 415–16.

45. Mike Elliott, interview by the author, June 7, 1994, Purgatory, Colo.; Mahoney interview; Daily and Guenin, *Aspen,* 495, 499, 223.

46. "That probably enhanced [Pfeifer and Iselin's] ability to get lessons," he went on to say, "just the fact that they had the accent." Jim Snobble, interview by the author, July 11, 1994, Aspen, Colo., tape recording and transcript, 6, AHS.

47. Mary Eshbaugh Hayes, "Norwegian Invasion Brought New Blood to Skiing and Aspen," *Aspen Times,* December 6, 1984, C1; Paul Anderson, "He Never Ages, He Never Changes," *Aspen Times,* January 15, 1987, C9. See also Stein Eriksen, *Come Ski with Me* (New York: W. W. Norton, 1966); Morten Lund, "The One and Only Stein," *Skiing Heritage* 15 (March 2003), 9–16; Fred Iselin and A. C. Spectorsky, *The New Invitation to Skiing* (New York: Simon and Schuster, 1958); and Jean Claude Killy with Doug Pfeiffer, *Skiing . . . The Killy Way* (New York: Simon and Schuster, 1971).

48. Charles Paterson, interview by the author, June 28, 1994, Aspen, Colo., tape recording and transcript, 1, AHS; Whip Jones, interview by the author, July 12, 1994, Aspen, Colo., notes, AHS.

49. John Sabella, "The Mountain Moguls," *Aspen Times,* December 8, 1977, 2B.

50. "1960 Olympic Issue," *Ski,* as cited in John Rolfe Burroughs, *"I Never Look Back": The Story of Buddy Werner* (Boulder, Colo.: Johnson Publishing Company, 1967), 136.

51. Simonton, *Vail,* 72.

52. See MacCannell, *The Tourist,* 98–102.

53. See Sylvia Rodriguez, "Tourism, Whiteness, and the Vanishing Anglo," in Wrobel and Long, *Seeing and Being Seen,* 194–210; and Annie Gilbert Coleman, "The Unbearable Whiteness of Skiing," *Pacific Historical Review* (November 1996), 583–614.

54. Kingsbury Pitcher, in Rick Richards, *Ski Pioneers: Ernie Blake, His Friends, and the Making of Taos Ski Valley* (Helena, Mont.: Dry Gulch Publishing and Falcon Press, 1992), 145.

55. Paterson arrived in Aspen the weekend that the 1949 National Alpine Championships took place. He had a hard time finding a place to sleep and says that he was destined to become a hotel keeper there. Paterson interview, 3–4.

56. Natalie Gignoux, interview by Ruth Whyte, September 16, 1986, Aspen, Colo., tape recording and transcript, 1–2, AHS.

57. William A. Allen, "How to Ski for Free," *Ski* 12 (December 1947), 22.

58. Ibid., 35.

59. Janet Nelson, "Help Wanted in the Ski Industry," *Ski* 32 (December 1967), 61.

60. Janet Nelson, " . . . But They're Employed," *Ski* 34 (January 1970), 71.

61. Morten Lund, "They're Beautiful!" *Ski* 34 (January 1970), 66.

62. Ibid., 96.

63. For this to work, ski bums had to be white and live in town, and it helped if they were conversant in upper-class norms. When the ski industry came to depend on

a permanent working class of laborers in the late 1980s, a group largely defined by their color and immigrant status, resorts hid their labor from view in different ways.

64. Locals eager to promote the economic health of their home often invested in a ski resort that would change the shape of their town. Telluride residents invested in the ski resort in the late 1960s, even after losing money on a similar venture a decade earlier. They sold Frank Zoline their land and bought stock in his company. Durango residents, too, invested in the Purgatory ski area through the San Juan Development Corporation, a company formed by area developers Ray and Vincent Duncan. Mahoney interview; Elliott interview.

65. Ferenc Berko, Music Associates of Aspen "High Notes" talk, June 29, 1994, Aspen, Colo.

66. June Hodges, interview by the author, June 19, 1994, Denver, Colo., tape recording and transcript, 1, AHS; Litchfield interview, 4.

67. Friedl Pfeifer, interview by the author, July 21, 1994, Aspen, Colo., tape recording and transcript, 3, AHS; Gignoux interview.

68. Joe Alex Morris, "Aspen, Colorado," *Saturday Evening Post,* October 14, 1950, 27, Pamphlet file, CUA.

69. Pearl Anoe, "Aspen Was No Ghost Town," *Chrysler Event's Owner's Magazine* (August 1955), 15.

70. Peter J. Ognibene, "The Travail of Instant Tyrolia," *Denver Post Empire Magazine,* October 10, 1971, 11. Home owners hailed from places such as Texas and Mexico; businesspeople and resort managers came from as far away as the Northeast and Europe. See Simonton, *Vail,* 166–87. See also Hauk, "Vail Chronology," 6–7.

71. William Oscar Johnson, "A Vision Fulfilled," *Sports Illustrated,* January 30, 1989, 78.

72. Jane Nes, "Money Fever Is Running in Aspen Again," *Denver Post,* March 17, 1946, clipping, AHS; Morris, "Aspen, Colorado," 174; Al Nakkula, "Aspen, Where Everyone Skis," *Rocky Mountain News,* January 9, 1966, 52, clipping, AHS.

73. Morris, "Aspen, Colorado," 176; Peggy Clifford and John Macauly Smith, "The Distressing Rebirth of Aspen," *Denver Post Empire Magazine,* August 16, 1970, 9.

74. John Jerome, "Condominiums or Lodges: Which Should You Have?" *Skiing Area News* 4 (Spring 1969), 32–33.

75. Oral histories with area managers support this point. For a discussion of Vail's development, see Auran, "'Vail-Type Operation,'" 38–42. For a broader analysis of the ski industry as a whole, see Hal Clifford's *Downhill Slide: Why the Corporate Ski Industry Is Bad for Skiing, Ski Towns, and the Environment* (San Francisco: Sierra Club Books, 2002).

76. Clifford and Smith, "Distressing Rebirth of Aspen," 8.

77. Durrance interview (1993), 15.

78. Ognibene, "Travail of Instant Tyrolia," 11.

79. Mahoney interview, 5.

6. SHREDDING ASPEN

1. Grace Lichtenstein, "Singer Charged in Death of Skier," *New York Times,* April 8, 1976, 42.

2. Grace Lichtenstein, "Miss Longet Pleads Not Guilty in Killing," *New York Times,* June 11, 1976, 10.

3. Ibid., 10. For more on Aspen's lifestyle, see Ted Conover, *Whiteout: Lost in Aspen* (New York: Random House, 1991).

4. This skit aired on April 24, 1976. For the complete transcript, see http://snltranscripts.jt.org/75/75rski.phtml.

5. Timothy Egan, "Kellogg's Journal: Mining Town Given Lift in Effort to Be a Resort," *New York Times,* July 13, 1989.

6. Eugene F. Pilz, "Barbara Kidder — Queen of the Slopes," *Rocky Mountain Life* (December 1946), 47.

7. Smaller ski resorts geared toward day or weekend customers operated within a different kind of ski culture, one that emphasized skill on the slopes and local status over visible feats of consumption and leisure.

8. Continental Airlines, "Ski Colorado" (1976–77), pamphlet, 3, CHS; *Ski* 34 (January 1970), 5, 21.

9. "Aspen's New Silver Lode," *Business Week,* January 25, 1964, 30, clipping, Skiing 1963–64 file, AHS.

10. See Susan Douglas, *Where the Girls Are: Growing Up Female with the Mass Media* (New York: Times Books, 1995); John D'Emilio and Estelle B. Freedman, *Intimate Matters: A History of Sexuality in America,* 2nd ed. (Chicago: University of Chicago Press, 1997).

11. See Margaret Supplee Smith, "The Image of Skiing in American Popular Culture," in *Papers from the 2002 International Ski History Congress,* ed. E. John B. Allen (New Hartford, Conn.: International Skiing History Association, 2002), 141–45; Jonathan Runge, "A Brief History of Sex and Skiing," *Skiing* 49 (October 1996), 73–78.

12. *Skiing Trade News* 7 (Spring 1970), 54.

13. *Ski* 27 (November 1962), 72.

14. Nancy Greene, "The Woman Racer as a Woman," *Ski* 34 (January 1970), 57.

15. Al Nakkula, "Aspen, Where Everyone Skis," *Rocky Mountain News,* January 9, 1966, 52, clipping, Skiing 1966 file, AHS.

16. Pilz, "Barbara Kidder," 47.

17. Some who graduated from Yale include Walter Paepcke, William Hodges, George Berger, and Minot Dole. Quite a few 10th Mountain veterans graduated from similarly elite colleges.

18. John Fry, "The Sport of the Establishment," *Ski* (January 1963), 41–43.

19. John Jerome, "Condominiums or Lodges: Which Should You Have?" *Skiing Area News* 4 (Spring 1969), 33.

20. Three such films produced by Dick Durrance are "Snow Carnival," "Until We Meet in Aspen," and "The Aspen Album"; H. J. Heinz produced one called "Little Skier's Big Day," starring Fred Iselin, in 1956; videotapes, AHS.

21. Joy Caudill, interview by the author, July 26, 1994, Aspen, Colo., tape recording and transcript, 5, AHS.

22. June Hodges, interview by the author, June 19, 1994, Denver, Colo., tape recording and transcript, 3, AHS.

23. See Joshua Gamson, "The Assembly Line of Greatness: Celebrity in Twentieth-Century America," *Critical Studies in Mass Communication* 9 (1992), 1–24.

24. *Ski* 27 (October 1962), 22.

25. Earl S. Pomeroy, *In Search of the Golden West: The Tourist in Western America* (New York: Alfred A. Knopf, 1957; reprint, Lincoln: University of Nebraska Press, 1990), 209.

26. Pilz, "Barbara Kidder," 47.

27. *Ski* 60 (October 1995), 23; Charles Paterson, interview by the author, June 28, 1994, Aspen, Colo., tape recording and transcript, 8, AHS.

28. Jim Snobble, interview by the author, July 11, 1994, Aspen, Colo., tape recording and transcript, 6, AHS.

29. Alex Katz, "Sell the Look First," *Skiing Trade News* 3 (January 1966), 38; "How to Sell Expensive Fashions to the Nabob," *Skiing Trade News* 8 (Fall 1971), 55.

30. William Oscar Johnson, "A Vision Fulfilled," *Sports Illustrated,* January 30, 1989, 78.

31. Janet Nelson, "Help Wanted in the Ski Industry," *Ski* 32 (December 1967), 61.

32. Janet Nelson, " . . . But They're Employed," *Ski* 34 (January 1970), 71, 99.

32. Scott Bowie and Stacy Standley, "Ski Bum, R.I.P.," *Ski* 44 (November 1979), 143.

34. Martha Stine, "Ski Bum Shortage? Areas Say 'Yes,'" *Ski* 44 (November 1979), 204; Bill Mahoney, interview by the author, June 6, 1994, Telluride, Colo., tape recording and transcript, 7–8; Deborah Frazier, "Ski Resorts Offer Blizzard of Good Jobs," *Rocky Mountain News,* November 13, 1988, 28.

35. Colorado Ski Country USA, "Statistics," Denver, Colo., n.d., III-R-1, III-R-3, BRL; Charles R. Goeldner and Karen Duea, "Colorado Ski and Winter Recreation Statistics, 1981–82 Season," 70, BRL.

36. The next largest income bracket represented was the $50,000 to $75,000 group, with 17.4 percent. C. R. Goeldner and Jim Manire, "The Aspen Skier, 1983–84 Season" (Business Research Division, Graduate School of Business Administration, University of Colorado at Boulder, 1984), 11, BRL.

37. See Kirkpatrick Sale, *The Green Revolution: The American Environmental Movement, 1962–1992* (New York: Hill and Wang, 1993); Riley E. Dunlap and Angela G. Mertig, *American Environmentalism: The U.S. Environmental Movement, 1970–1990* (Washington, D.C.: Taylor and Francis, 1992); Roderick Nash, *Wilderness and the American Mind,* 3rd ed. (New Haven, Conn.: Yale University Press, 1982).

38. National Environmental Policy Act of 1969, Act of January 1, 1970 (PL 91–190, 83 Stat. 852; 42 USC 4321 [note], 4321, 4331–35, 4346a–b, 4347), sec. 101; *Planning Con-*

siderations for Winter Sports Resort Development (U.S. Department of Agriculture, Forest Service, in Cooperation with National Ski Areas Association, 1973), 1.

39. Paul Hauk, "Beaver Creek Ski Area Chronology," in *Ski Area Chronology: Chronologies of the Ski Areas on and Adjacent to the White River National Forest, Colorado* (Glenwood Springs, Colo.: U.S. Department of Agriculture, Forest Service, White River National Forest, 1979), 5.

40. See ibid., 3–10; Abbott Fay, *Ski Tracks in the Rockies: A Century of Colorado Skiing* (Evergreen, Colo.: Cordillera Press, 1984), 59–61.

41. Some tried anyway. The Little Annie Ski Corporation based in Aspen won the support of the Pitkin County commissioners but found itself mired in financial, environmental, and logistic concerns from which it could not extricate itself. An area near Rifle similarly failed. A proposed resort outside of Steamboat Springs called Lake Catamount Resort and one near Beaver Creek called Adams Rib were still fighting in 1995. Jack Cox, "Obstacles Still Strewn in Path of Little Annie," *Denver Post,* September 20, 1981, F1; U.S. Department of Agriculture, White River National Forest, "Little Annie, Proposed Ski Area Aspen, Colorado: Draft Environmental Impact Statement" (pamphlet, n.d.), Little Annie file, AHS; "1984 White River NF Forest Plan and Ski Area Statistics," U.S. Forest Service, Aspen Ranger District (1984).

42. Dirk Johnson, "On Ski Slopes of Colorado, a Battle of Snow vs. Water," *New York Times,* November 14, 1994, A1, A10; John Brinkley, "Snowmaking Imperils Snowmass Creek?" *Rocky Mountain News,* April 20, 1994, 8A; Hugh Dellios, "Ski Resorts, Environmentalists Battle over Snowmaking," *Denver Post,* January 22, 1995, 4C; Mark Obmascik, "Fish Can Only Squirm over Race to Make Snow," *Denver Post,* October 14, 1995.

43. Paul Anderson and Brighid Kelly, "Snowmass Power Struggle," *Aspen Times,* April 11, 1992, 1A; Cameron M. Burns, "Snowmass Unchained," *Aspen Times,* March 12, 1994, 1A; Paul Larmer, "Does Aspen Need Thousands More Skiers?" *High Country News,* October 4, 1993, 4; U.S. Department of Agriculture, White River National Forest, Aspen Ranger District, "Record of Decision Snowmass Ski Area: Final Environmental Impact Statement" (March 1994).

44. Katie Kerwin, "Settlement Nearing in Wetlands Destruction," *Rocky Mountain News,* September 26, 1993, 6A, 10A; Mark Obmascik, "Resort, Feds Reach Wetlands Deal," *Denver Post,* October 20, 1993, 1B, 5B; Katie Kerwin, "Judge Rejects Telluride Wetlands Plan," *Rocky Mountain News,* April 21, 1994, 8A; Joseph B. Verrengia, "EPA Broadens Telluride Wetlands Suit," *Rocky Mountain News,* November 7, 1994, 14A; Katie Kerwin, "Telluride Wins Round in Fight over Wetlands," *Rocky Mountain News,* May 5, 1995, 27A.

45. Kerwin, "Settlement Nearing," 10A.

46. James Brooke, "Group Claims Responsibility for Blazes at Vail Resort," *New York Times,* October 22, 1998, A14; David Johnson, "Vail Fires Were Probably Arson, U.S. Agents Say," *New York Times,* October 23, 1998, A16. See also Daniel Glick,

Powder Burn: Arson, Money, and Mystery on Vail Mountain (New York: PublicAffairs, 2001).

47. Mike Maginn, "The Problem with Doing Business in the Woods," *Skiing Area News* 5 (Summer 1970), 42; *Planning Considerations for Winter Sports Resort Development* (1973), 30; H. Peter Wingle, *Planning Considerations for Winter Sports Resort Development* (U.S. Department of Agriculture, Forest Service, Rocky Mountain Region, 1994), 28–31.

48. The median length of cross-country skiing experience was about 2.5 years. U.S. Department of Agriculture, Forest Service, "Growth Potential of the Skier Market in the National Forests," Research Paper WO-36 (1979), 6.

49. Almost 90 percent said they liked it because it is good exercise, and just over half said they liked it because it is less expensive than Alpine skiing. "Highlights from the 1987 Guide to Cross Country Skiing Survey," *Cross Country Skiing* (April 1978), 1–2.

50. Howard Pankratz and Chance Conner, "Liability Ruling Assessed," *Denver Post*, December 20, 1995, 4B.

51. "Ski Area Liabilities," *Ski Area News* 7 (Spring 1972), 39–41.

52. These fatalities resulted from collisions with people or objects; the figures do not include deaths from health-related problems such as heart attacks. This figure is, amazingly, the same as that of skiers killed by avalanches out of bounds. Pankratz and Conner, "Liability Ruling Assessed," 4B.

53. Howard Pankratz, "Ski-Area Lawsuits Upheld," *Denver Post*, December 19, 1995, 1A, 18A.

54. Douglas Pfeiffer, "Birth Pangs of an Olympic Winter Sport: A Personal Perspective," in Allen, *Papers from the 2002 International Ski History Congress*, 170.

55. Ibid., 170–73. The U.S. Skiing Association and Federation Internationale de Ski (FIS) soon sponsored competitions in ballet, mogul, aerial, and combined events, though only moguls and aerials became Olympic sports.

56. Guy Kelly, "Picking up a Spanish Accent," *Rocky Mountain News*, September 4, 1994, 12A; Bruce Finley, "'A Better Life': New Wave of Immigrants Lured by Resorts," *Denver Post*, October 30, 1995, 1A, 13A; Ray Ring, "The New West's Servant Economy," *High Country News*, April 17, 1995, 10, 12; Deborah Frazier, "Undocumented Workers Tax Ski Counties," *Rocky Mountain News*, November 9, 1993, 8A; "Aspen-Vail INS Sweep Nabs 30," *Denver Post*, December 7, 1995, 9B.

57. Ring, "New West's Servant Economy," 1. See also Hal Clifford, *Downhill Slide: Why the Corporate Ski Industry Is Bad for Skiing, Ski Towns, and the Environment* (San Francisco: Sierra Club Books, 2002).

58. Ring, "New West's Servant Economy," 1; Ray Ring, "Ski Bums Wrapped in Concrete," "Pedro Lopez, Entrepreneur," and "The Leadville-Indy 500," *High Country News*, April 17, 1995, 8–10; Gary Massaro, "Aspen Workers Commute from 'Edge of Hell,'" *Rocky Mountain News*, September 4, 1994, 13A; Deborah Frazier, "Privacy Exacts Price in Telluride," *Rocky Mountain News*, February 15, 1995, 10A;

Guy Kelly, "Resorts Face Urban Woes," *Rocky Mountain News,* September 4, 1994, 12A, 18A.

59. Ring, "New West's Servant Economy," 1; Ray Ring, "He Came to Ski and Stayed to Help," *High Country News,* April 17, 1995, 13; Kelly, "Resorts Face Urban Woes," 12A, 18A; Guy Kelly, "Church Housing Is a Godsend," *Rocky Mountain News,* September 5, 1994, 17A; Gary Massaro, "Nun Steers Hispanics to Shelter," *Rocky Mountain News,* September 5, 1994, 17A, 26A.

60. See the NBS website, www.nbs.org; Robert Jackson, "Make Pitch to Black Skiers, Industry Told," *Rocky Mountain News,* February 14, 1995, 12A; Robert Jackson, "Lack of Sponsors Puzzles Ski Group," *Rocky Mountain News,* February 15, 1994.

61. Rose Marie Cleese, "Building the Middle Week Throng," *Skiing Area News* 5 (Summer 1970), 23.

62. Sally Russell, "For Women Only," *Skiing* 41 (November 1988), 150, 153.

63. Deborah Frazier, "Gay Skiers Converge on Aspen," *Rocky Mountain News,* January 24, 1993, 10; Deborah Frazier, "Gays Stress Fund Clout at Aspen Ski Week," *Rocky Mountain News,* January 25, 1993, 10; Gil Rudawsky, "Gay Ski Week's Goal: A Gay Time," *Rocky Mountain News,* January 22, 1994, 6A. See also www.gayskiweek.com.

64. See Susanna Howe, *(Sick) a Cultural History of Snowboarding* (New York: St. Martin's Griffin, 1998).

65. Gavin Forbes Ehringer, "It's Tough to Ignore All These Dinosaurs on Snowboards, Dude," *Rocky Mountain News,* December 5, 1994, 20B.

66. See Douglas Booth, "From Bikinis to Boardshorts: *Wahines* and the Paradoxes of Surfing Culture," *Journal of Sport History* 28, no. 1 (Spring 2001), 3–22; Michael Brooke, *The Concrete Wave: The History of Snowboarding* (Los Angeles: Warwick Publishing, 1999); Judith Davidson, "Sport and Modern Technology: The Rise of Skateboarding, 1963–1978," *Journal of Popular Culture* 18, no. 4 (Spring 1985), 145–57.

67. Tom Sims, as quoted in Howe, *(Sick) a Cultural History of Snowboarding,* 29. See Howe (119–32) for a brief history of snowboarding women, and Annie Gilbert Coleman, "From Snow Bunnies to Shred Betties: Gender, Consumption, and the Skiing Landscape," in *Seeing Nature through Gender,* ed. Virginia Scharff (Lawrence: University Press of Kansas, 2003). See also Nelson George, *Hip Hop America* (New York: Penguin Books, 1998).

68. Scott Turner, "Stick Speak," *Boulder Quarterly* (Ski Guide 1996), 10; Deborah Frazier, "Ranks of Snowboarders Growing," *Rocky Mountain News,* February 13, 1994, 23A. For a more recent analysis of snowboarder stereotypes and self-images, see Robert Kenneth Karsted, "The Growing Sport of Snowboarding: An Analysis of Popular Images, Perceptions, and Stereotypes" (master's thesis, University of Colorado, 1996).

69. Howe, *(Sick) a Cultural History of Snowboarding,* 31–32, 47.

70. C. R. Goeldner and R. L. Wobbekind, "The Colorado Ski Industry: Highlights of the 1992–93 Ski Season" (Business Research Division, Graduate School of

Business Administration, University of Colorado at Boulder, 1993), 4–5, BRL.

71. Ibid., table 3, Rank by Lift Tickets Issued, 1982–83 to 1992–93, and table 4, Market Share 1981–82 to 1992–93; Brown, Bortz & Coddington, Inc., "Executive Summary: The Contribution of Skiing to the Colorado Economy 1987" (Ski Country USA, 1987), 3. It is, of course, difficult to generalize about a period of more than twenty years. Capital investments varied from year to year, with 1983 and 1985 ranking uncharacteristically high ($137 million and $130 million, respectively).

72. Alan Prendergast, "The Mid-Life Crisis of the Colorado Ski Industry," *Denver Post Empire Magazine,* April 8, 1984, 13.

73. Deborah Frazier, "State's Skier Numbers Drop 73,000 for Season," *Rocky Mountain News,* June 24, 1994, 14A; Charles Goeldner, personal e-mail correspondence with the author, September 1, 2003. A series of bad snow years and the events of September 11, 2001, are the clearest reasons for recent small declines.

74. James Brooke, "The Business of Skiing Gets Bigger," *New York Times,* September 9, 1996, B8. Clifford's *Downhill Slide* addresses this phenomenon in depth. Other giant corporations owned multiple ski resorts in other areas of the country. American Skiing Co., for instance, owned Killington, Mt. Snow, and Haystack and Sugarbush in Vermont; Sugarloaf and Sunday River in Maine; and Attitash in New Hampshire. This company controlled 3.0 million skier-days. Intrawest Corp. owned Blackcomb and Panorama in British Columbia, Mont Tremblant in Quebec, Mammoth in California, Stratton in Vermont, and Snowshoe/Silver Creek in West Virginia and accounted for 2.5 million visits. "The Urge to Merge," *Skiing* 49 (September 1996), 38; "Merger Madness, Part II," *Skiing* 49 (October 1996), 32. For another perspective on the industry's growth from 1976 to 1993, see Charles R. Goeldner, "We've Come a Long Way," *Ski Area Management* 33 (July 1994), 41.

75. David B. Rockland, "The Environment and Your Customer," *Ski Area Management* 33 (July 1994), 40, 58; John Fry, "Exactly What Are Their Environmental Attitudes?" *Ski Area Management* (November 1995), 45–47; Richard Needham, "Putting Spin on Environmental Good Deeds," *Ski Area Management* (January 1996), 68, 82–83; Janet Nelson, "Turning Trails into Classrooms," *Ski Area Management* (November 1995), 48.

76. "Highlights from the 1978 Guide to Cross Country Skiing Survey"; Jonathan B. Wiesel, "Cross Country Snowmaking: Where It's Been . . . Where It's Going," *Ski Area Management* (March 1982), 64, 67–68.

77. Michael Romano, "Going to Extremes," *Rocky Mountain News,* March 16, 1994, 1B; Charlie Meyers, "Taking the Risk Out of Extreme," *Denver Post,* February 16, 1996, 12D. Even backcountry skiing, though impossible to do in-bounds by definition, entered the ski industry through its high-tech fashion and equipment-oriented culture.

78. John Rebchook, "Telluride Hotel Going Western," *Rocky Mountain News,* May 10, 1994, 42A.

79. Chance Connor, "Vail Plans Mountain Social Club," *Denver Post,* September 14, 1995, 1C.

80. Sally Russell, "For Women Only," *Skiing* 41 (November 1988), 150, 153. See, for example, Bard Glenne, "What's a Woman's Ski?" *Skiing* 38 (October 1985), 93, and Sally Russell, "Deals for Skiing Families," *Skiing* 38 (January 1986), 32. These changes reflected the growing number of women working within the ski industry as instructors, equipment designers, marketers, and magazine writers. See also Janet Nelson, "The Trials of Jeannie Thoren," *Skiing* 44 (December 1991), and "Pioneer Spirit," *Skiing for Women* 2 (Winter 1995), 88–92, for some examples.

81. Dana White, "Shred Heads Go Mainstream," *Skiing* 41 (September 1988), 82, 84, 222; Bard Glenne, "How They Ride," *Skiing* 41 (January 1989), 62.

82. Turner, "Stick Speak," 10; Frazier, "Ranks of Snowboarders Growing," 23A.

83. Greta Gaines, from Wild Women Snowboard Camps website, coach biography (www.wildwomencamps.com/coach%20bios/gretabiobody.html).

84. C. R. Goeldner, "The Nature and Scope of Competition in the Colorado Ski Industry" (Business Research Division, Graduate School of Business Administration, University of Colorado at Boulder, 1974), 18, BRL.

SKIING AT THE BEACH

1. Janet Nelson, "How Disney Does It," *Ski Area Management* 34 (July 1995), 41; Walt Disney Travel Co., Inc., *1997 Walt Disney World Vacations,* 12.

BIBLIOGRAPHY

AHS   Aspen Historical Society, Aspen, Colo.

BRL   Business Research Division Library, Graduate School of Business Administration, University of Colorado, Boulder, Colo.

BWML   Buddy Werner Memorial Library, Steamboat Springs, Colo.

CHS   Colorado Historical Society, Denver, Colo.

CUA   Archives, University of Colorado at Boulder Libraries, Norlin Library, Boulder, Colo.

DPL   Denver Public Library, Denver, Colo.

GCHA   Grand County Historical Association, Hot Sulphur Springs, Colo.

GLHS   Grand Lake Historical Society, Grand Lake, Colo.

ARCHIVAL COLLECTIONS AND SOURCES

Allen, Gerald L. "Colorado Ski and Winter Recreation Statistics, 1968." Business Research Division, Graduate School of Business Administration, University of Colorado at Boulder, 1968. BRL.

———. "Colorado Ski and Winter Recreation Statistics, 1969." Business Research Division, Graduate School of Business Administration, University of Colorado at Boulder, 1969. BRL.

American Ski Annual, 1936–1949. CHS.

Andre Roch Biography file. AHS.

Aspen Ski Corporation file. AHS.

Aspen Skiing Corporation file. AHS.

Benson, Jack A. "Corn Snow in Colorado: The United States Forest Service and the Bankruptcy of a Ski Resort." Manuscript, n.d. Pamphlet file. CUA.

Berthoud Pass file. CHS.

"The Big Snow." *Colorado Magazine* 40 (April 1963), 113. CHS.

Blickensderfer, J. C. "Reminiscences of Skiing in Colorado, 1922–1968." Ski Collection. CHS.

Breckenridge file. CHS.

"Climax Ski Area Has Had a Lively, Exciting History." *Summit County Journal,* March 11, 1960, 4. Pamphlet file. CUA.

Colorado Department of Highways. *Paths of Progress.* Manuscript, n.d. CUA.

Colorado Ski Clubs and Associations Collection. CHS.

Colorado's Opportunities in the U.S. Ski Vacation Market. Toronto: Longwoods International, Inc., 1989. Prepared for the Colorado Tourism Board. BRL.

Continental Oil Co. Official Road Map of Colorado, 1928. CUA.

"The Cost of Recreation and Leisure Activities." Business Research Division, Graduate School of Business Administration, University of Colorado at Boulder, 1980. BRL.

Crampon, L. J., and Ronald D. Lemon. "Skiing in the Southern Rocky Mountain Region." Prepared for the Ski Area Operators Committee of the Southern Rocky Mountain Ski Association. Business Research Division, Graduate School of Business Administration, University of Colorado at Boulder, 1957. BRL.

Dabney, Page. *An Impact Study. The Colorado Ski Industry: A Study of the Influence of the Industry Upon the Economies of Selected Mountain Counties and Communities.* Denver: Colorado Ski Country USA, 1976. BRL.

Duke, H. Benjamin. "Skiing Soldiers to Skiing Entrepreneurs: Development of the Western Ski Industry." Paper presented at the Western Historical Association annual meeting, August 2, 1989. DPL.

Elizabeth Paepcke Biography file. AHS.

"Emerald Mountain Ski Lift" file. Routt County Collection. BWML.

Fellhauer, Cheryl. *The Economic Impact of the Colorado Ski Resort Industry: An Analysis of County Personal Income.* Prepared for Colorado Ski Country USA. Business Research Division, Graduate School of Business Administration, University of Colorado at Boulder, 1977. BRL.

Fred Iselin Biography file. AHS.

Frick, Ford, Dean Coddington, and Harvey Rubinstein. *The Contribution of Skiing to the Colorado Economy.* Prepared for Colorado Ski Country USA, 1982. BRL.

Fulton, Carl. "The Winter of the Deep Snow." *Colorado Magazine* 39 (January–October 1962), 38–41. CHS.

General Ski Collection. GCHA.

Goeldner, C. R. "The Aspen Skier: Lift Survey." Business Research Division, Graduate School of Business Administration, University of Colorado at Boulder, 1974. BRL.

———. "The Colorado Ski Industry: Highlights of the 1976–77 Season." Business Research Division, Graduate School of Business Administration, University of Colorado at Boulder, 1977. BRL.

———. "The Colorado Skier: 1977–78 Season: A Comparison of Five Skier Studies Conducted at Aspen, Vail, Steamboat, Winter Park and Copper Mountain." Business Research Division, Graduate School of Business Administration, University of Colorado at Boulder, 1978. BRL.

Goeldner, C. R., and Gerald Allen. "Colorado Ski and Winter Recreation Statistics, 1973." Business Research Division, Graduate School of Business Administration, University of Colorado at Boulder, 1973. BRL.

Goeldner, C. R., T. A. Buchman, C. E. Guernsey, and Gin Hayden. "Colorado Ski Industry Characteristics and Financial Analysis, 1987–88 Season." Business Research Division, Graduate School of Business Administration, University of Colorado at Boulder, 1989. BRL.

Goeldner, Charles R., and Karen Dicke. "Colorado Ski and Winter Recreation Statistics, 1978." Business Research Division, Graduate School of Business Administration, University of Colorado at Boulder, 1978. BRL.

———. "Colorado Ski Industry Characteristics and Financial Analysis, 1978–79 Season." Business Research Division, Graduate School of Business Administration, University of Colorado at Boulder, 1980. BRL.

Goeldner, Charles R., and Karen Duea. "Colorado Ski and Winter Recreation Statistics, 1981–82 Season." Business Research Division, Graduate School of Business Administration, University of Colorado at Boulder, 1982. BRL.

Goeldner, C. R., and Jim Manire. "The Aspen Skier, 1983–84 Season." Business Research Division, Graduate School of Business Administration, University of Colorado at Boulder, 1984. BRL.

Goeldner, C. R., and Yvonne Sletta. "Colorado Ski Industry Characteristics and Financial Analysis." Business Research Division, Graduate School of Business Administration, University of Colorado at Boulder, 1975. BRL.

Goeldner, C. R., and R. L. Wobbekind. "The Colorado Ski Industry: Highlights of the 1992–93 Season." Business Research Division, Graduate School of Business Administration, University of Colorado at Boulder, 1993. BRL.

Grand Lake Ski Club Account Book, 1938–1948. GLHS.

Groswold Ski Collection. GCHA.

Highland Bavarian Corporation file. AHS.

Kline, J. B. "Western Mountain Region Study: Recreation." Business Research Division, Graduate School of Business Administration, University of Colorado at Boulder, 1967. BRL.

McLaren Collection. GCHA.

National Ski Patrol Collection. CHS.

1987 Colorado Ski Areas. Denver: Mountain States Employers Council, Inc., 1987. BRL.

Norway: The Country with a Thousand Years of Ski History. Chicago: Norwegian America Line Agency, Inc., n.d. Pamphlet. Ski Collection. GCHA.

The Official American Ski Technique. 2d ed. Salt Lake City: Professional Ski Instructors of America, Inc., 1966. AHS.

Organizing Committee for the XII Olympic Winter Games, Denver, 1976. Denver 76 Official Bulletin. Spring 1972. CUA.

"Pioneering Near Steamboat Springs, 1885–1886, as Shown in Letters of Alice Denison." Colorado Magazine 28 (April 1951), 81–94. CHS.

Recreation — Skiing Collection. CHS.

Ridgeway, A. "A History of Transportation in Colorado." Manuscript, 1926. CUA.

Routt County Collection. BWML.

Ski Scrapbooks. GLHS.

Ski Town file. Routt County Collection. BWML.

Ski-Hi Stampede, 1939. Oversize Pamphlet file. CUA.

Skiing files. AHS.

Snowmass file. AHS.

State Highway Map of Colorado. Colorado Department of Highways, 1952. CUA.

Statistics: Colorado Ski Country USA: Ski Industry History/Growth/Economics. Denver: Colorado Ski Country USA, Inc., 1977. BRL.

"Steamboat Springs Colorado: Entering the International Tourism Marketplace." A Colorado Initiatives Project of Local Affairs, 1988. Manuscript. Tourism file. Routt County Collection, BWML.

Steamboat Springs Promotional Brochures file. Routt County Collection. BWML.

Texaco Touring Map of Colorado, 1939. CUA.

Thomas J. Flynn papers. DPL.

"Thrilling Winter Sport in Colorado, Top of the Nation." Pamphlet, 1941. CUA.

Tourism file. Routt County Collection. BWML.

Tournament Programs, 1920–1940. General Ski Collection and Groswold Collection. GCHA.

Tournament Programs, 1930s. GLHS.

U.S. Department of Agriculture, Forest Service. "Growth Potential of the Skier Market in the National Forests." USDA Research Paper WO-36, 1979. BRL.

Vail Associates Collection. DPL.

Vail file. CHS.

Will F. Ferrill Scrapbook, 3 vols. DPL.

Willoughby Biography file. AHS.

ORAL HISTORIES AND INTERVIEWS

Anderson, Chet. Interview by the author, June 7, 1994, Durango, Colo. Transcript.

Anderson, Hildur Hoaglund. Interview by Ramona Markalunas, January 18, 1979, Aspen, Colo. Tape recording. AHS.

Anderson, Tom. Interview by Jon Coleman, May 1995, Aspen, Colo. Tape recording and transcript. AHS.

Brennan, Tom. Interview by the author, August 24, 1995, Steamboat Springs, Colo. Transcript.

Brown, D. R. C. Interview by Jeanette Darnauer, April 10, 1979, Aspen. Tape recording #C10. AHS.

Caudill, Joy. Interview by the author, July 26, 1994, Aspen, Colo. Tape recording and transcript. AHS.

Durrance, Dick and Margaret (Miggs). Interview by Jeanette Darnauer, August 18, 1993, Aspen, Colo. Video recording and transcript. AHS.

Durrance, Dick and Margaret, and Ferenc Berko. "High Notes" talk, June 29, 1994, Aspen, Colo. Transcript. AHS.

Elliott, Mike. Interview by the author, June 7, 1994, Purgatory, Colo. Transcript.

Gerbaz, Michael. Interview by Jon Coleman, May 1995, Aspen, Colo. Tape recording and transcript. AHS.

Gignoux, Natalie. Interview by Ruth Whyte, September 16, 1986, Aspen, Colo. Tape recording and transcript. AHS.

Hodges, Ann V. Interview by Jon Coleman, May 1995, Aspen, Colo. Tape recording and transcript. AHS.

Hodges, June. Interview by the author, June 19, 1994, Denver, Colo. Tape recording and transcript. AHS.

Howard, Dorothy McLaren. Interview by the author, August 22, 1995, Grand Lake, Colo. Tape recording and transcript.

Hudson, Sally Niedlinger. Interview by Ruth Whyte, March 9, 1987, Aspen, Colo. Tape recording and transcript. AHS.

Jones, Whip. Interview by the author, July 12, 1994, Aspen, Colo. Transcript. AHS.

Kemp, Patience Cairns. Interview by the author, August 22, 1995, Grand Lake, Colo. Tape recording and transcript.

Knowlton, Steve. Interviews by the author, October 19, 1994, and November 14, 1995, Denver, Colo. Tape recording and transcript. AHS.

Kowinya, Ken. Interview by the author, August 24, 1995, Steamboat Springs, Colo. Transcript.

Kuen, Artur. Interview by the author, July 13, 1994, Aspen, Colo. Tape recording and transcript. AHS.

Langdon, Charles. Interview by the author, June 7, 1994, Durango, Colo. Tape recording and transcript.

Litchfield, John. Interview by the author, September 29, 1994, Denver, Colo. Tape recording and transcript. AHS.

Mahoney, Bill. Interview by the author, June 6, 1994, Telluride, Colo. Tape recording and transcript.

Marolt, Bill. Interview by the author, August 11, 1994, Boulder, Colo. Tape recording and transcript. AHS.

McCrudden, Dick. Interview by Jeanette Darnauer, August 10, 1993, Aspen, Colo. Video recording. AHS.

McLean, Barney. Interviews by Ruth Whyte, October 15, 1986, and March 1993, Aspen, Colo. Tape recordings #C89 and #C90. AHS.

Melville, Ralph and Marion. Interview by Judith Gertler, July 25, 1994, Aspen, Colo. Tape recording. AHS.

Nitze, Paul. Interview by the author, July 20, 1994, Aspen, Colo. Tape recording and transcript. AHS.

Oates, Cherie Gerbaz. Interview by the author, July 13, 1994, Aspen, Colo. Tape recording and transcript. AHS.

Obermeyer, Claus. Interview by Ruth Whyte, September 4, 1986, Aspen, Colo. Tape recording. AHS.

Paterson, Charles. Interview by the author, June 28, 1994, Aspen, Colo. Tape recording and transcript. AHS.

Pederson, Lorna. Interview by Jon Coleman, May 1995, Aspen, Colo. Tape recording and transcript. AHS.

Pederson, Tage. Interview by Judith Gertler, July 25, 1994, Aspen, Colo. Tape recording. AHS.

Pfeifer, Friedl. Interview by George Madsen, January 12, 1967, Aspen, Colo. Tape recording and transcript. AHS.

Pfeifer, Friedl. Interview by Judith Gertler, August 18, 1993, Aspen, Colo. Video recording. AHS.

Pfeifer, Friedl. Interview by the author, July 21, 1994, Aspen, Colo. Tape recording and transcript. AHS.

Rideout, Percy, Jack O'Brien, and Steve Knowlton. Interview by Ruth Whyte, March 24, 1991, Aspen, Colo. Tape recording and transcript. AHS.

Roch, Andre. Interview by George Madsen, February 16, 1967, Aspen, Colo. Tape recording #C55 and transcript. AHS.

Roush, Jim. Interview by the author, July 11, 1994, Aspen, Colo. Tape recording and transcript. AHS.

Rowland, Red. Interview by Elli Fox, February 12, 1987, Aspen, Colo. Tape recording #C57. AHS.

Ryan, Theodore S. Interview by George Madsen Jr., March 23, 26, and 30, 1965, Aspen, Colo. Transcript of three "Commentary" programs recorded and broadcast over WSNO. Highland Bavarian Corporation file. AHS.

Sabbatini, Thelma, and Dottie Danelli. Interview by Ruth Whyte, August 12, 1986, Aspen, Colo. Tape recording and transcript. AHS.

Sinclair, Elizabeth Oblock. Interview by the author, July 26, 1994, Aspen, Colo. Tape recording and transcript. AHS.

Snobble, Jim. Interview by the author, July 11, 1994, Aspen, Colo. Tape recording and transcript. AHS.

Stapleton, Sam and Elizabeth. Interview by the author, March 24, 1992, Aspen, Colo. Tape recording. AHS.

Stevens, Johnny. Interview by the author, June 6, 1994, Telluride, Colo. Transcript.

Toll, Giles. Interview by the author, February 2, 1996, Denver, Colo. Tape recording and transcript.

Trentaz, Art and Amelia. Interview by the author, March 26, 1992, Aspen, Colo. Tape recording. AHS.

Whyte, Ruth. Interview by the author, July 8, 1994, Aspen, Colo. Tape recording. AHS.

Wren, Gordon and Jean. Interview by the author, August 25, 1995, Steamboat Springs, Colo. Tape recording and transcript.

THESES, DISSERTATIONS, AND UNPUBLISHED PAPERS

Cornwell, Robert G., and Kristina J. Clebsch. "Ghost's Guide to Ashcroft." 1979. AHS.

Gilbert, Anne M. "The People of Aspen and the Roaring Fork Valley: A History of the Families and Daily Life of Miners and Ranchers, 1879–1960." 1991. AHS.

———. "Re-Creation through Recreation: Aspen Skiing from 1870 to 1970." 1995. AHS.

————. "Rural People with Connections: Farm and Ranch Families in the Roaring Fork Valley, Colorado." Master's thesis, University of Colorado, Boulder, 1992.

Hammond, Jennifer J. "Growth Management in Aspen, Colorado, 1960–1977." 1995. AHS.

Himes, Cindy L. "The Female Athlete in American Society: 1860–1940." Ph.D. diss., University of Pennsylvania, 1986.

Holland, Wendolyn S. "Parallel Tracks: A Study of Change in the Wood River Valley, Idaho." 1991.

Karsted, Robert Kenneth. "The Growing Sport of Snowboarding: An Analysis of Popular Images, Perceptions, and Stereotypes." Master's thesis, University of Colorado, Boulder, 1996.

Philpott, William Peter. "Consuming Colorado: Landscapes, Leisure, and the Tourist Way of Life." Ph.D. diss., University of Wisconsin, Madison, 2002.

————. "Visions of a Changing Vail: Fast-Growth Fallout in a Colorado Resort Town." Master's thesis, University of Wisconsin, Madison, 1994.

Rothman, Hal K. "East Goes West, West Goes East: The Structure of Tourism and Its Impact on Place in the Development of the Modern American West." 1994.

Sciullo, Henry Alfred. "An Analysis of Skiers to Colorado." Ph.D. diss., University of Missouri, 1971.

Thomas, Thomas Alexis. "Colorado and the Interstate Highways: A Study in the Continuity of Western Tradition." Ph.D. diss., University of Colorado, Boulder, 1991.

DOCUMENTARY FILMS

Fire on the Mountain. Produced and directed by Beth Gage and George Gage. Telluride, Colo., 1995. Videocassette.

Legends of American Skiing, 1840–1940. Produced and directed by Richard W. Moulton. *Skiing* magazine, 1986. Videocassette.

Soldiers on the Summit. Denver: Council for Public TV, Channel Six, Inc., 1987. Videocassette.

PRINTED PRIMARY SOURCES

Bird, Isabella L. *A Lady's Life in the Rocky Mountains.* New edition with an introduction by Daniel J. Boorstin. Norman: University of Oklahoma Press, 1960.

Bowles, Samuel. *The Switzerland of America: A Summer Vacation in the Parks and Mountains of Colorado.* Springfield, Mass.: Samuel Bowles and Co., 1869.

Dole, C. Minot. *Adventures in Skiing.* New York: Franklin Watts, 1965.

Durrance, Dick, and John Jerome. *The Man on the Medal: The Life and Times of America's First Great Ski Racer.* Aspen, Colo.: Durrance Enterprises, 1995.

Dusenbery, Harris. *Ski the High Trail: World War II Ski Troopers in the High Colorado Rockies.* Portland, Ore.: Binford and Mort Publishing, 1991.

Dyer, John L. *The Snow-Shoe Itinerant: An Autobiography of the Rev. John L. Dyer.* Cincinnati: Cranston and Stowe, 1890.

Eriksen, Stein. *Come Ski with Me.* New York: W. W. Norton, 1966.

Fuller, Z. "Rocky Mountain Snow-Shoeing." *Midland Monthly* 9 (1898), 204–8.

Gibson, E. C. "On Cooper Hill." *American Ski Annual* (1945), 60–61.

Hall, Alice Crossette. "Winter Sport in Switzerland." *Outing* 33 (March 1899), 391–95.

Harwood, W. S. "Ski Running." *Outing* 21 (February 1893), 339–46.

Hauk, Paul. *Ski Area Chronology: Chronologies of the Ski Areas on and Adjacent to the White River National Forest, Colorado.* Glenwood Springs, Colo.: U.S. Department of Agriculture, Forest Service, White River National Forest, 1979.

Ingersoll, Ernest. *The Crest of the Continent: A Record of a Summer's Ramble in the Rocky Mountains and Beyond.* Chicago: R. R. Donnelley and Sons, 1890.

———. *Knocking around the Rockies.* New York: Harper and Brothers, 1883.

Jackson, Rolf W. "A New Year's Day Ski Run." *Outing* 31 (January 1898), 395.

Johnsen, Theodore A. *The Winter Sport of Skeeing.* Portland, Me.: Theo. A. Johnsen Company, 1905. Reprint, New Hartford, Conn.: International Skiing History Association, 1994.

LaChapelle, Dolores. *Deep Powder Snow: 40 Years of Ecstatic Skiing, Avalanches, and Earth Wisdom.* Durango, Colo.: Kivaki Press, 1993.

Lang, Otto. *A Bird of Passage: The Story of My Life.* Helena, Mont.: Skyhouse Publishers, an imprint of Falcon Press, 1994.

Leopold, Aldo. "The Wilderness and Its Place in Forest Recreational Tourist Policy." *Journal of Forestry* 19 (1921), 719.

McNeil, Fred H. "Skiing and National Defense." *American Ski Annual* (1942), 5–22.

Miller, Warren. *On Film in Print: Forty-five Years on the Road with Camera, Skis, Boats, and Windsurfers.* Vail, Colo.: author, 1994.

———. *Wine, Women, Warren, and Skis.* Vail, Colo: author, 1958.

Mills, Enos. *The Rocky Mountain Wonderland.* Boston: Houghton Mifflin, 1915.

———. *The Spell of the Rockies.* Boston: Houghton Mifflin, 1911.

———. *The Story of Estes Park, Grand Lake and Rocky Mountain National Park.* Estes Park, Colo.: author, 1917.

Moomaw, Jack C. *Recollections of a Rocky Mountain Ranger.* With a foreword by Jack R. Melton and Lulabeth Melton. Denver: privately printed, 1963. Reprint, Denver: YMCA of the Rockies, 1994.

Pfeifer, Friedl, and Morten Lund. *Nice Goin': My Life on Skis.* Missoula, Mont.: Pictorial Histories Publishing Company, 1993.

Richards, Rick. *Ski Pioneers: Ernie Blake, His Friends, and the Making of Taos Ski Valley.* Helena, Mont.: Dry Gulch Publishing and Falcon Press, 1992.

Roch, Andre. "Un hiver aux Montagnes Rocheuses du Colorado." *Der Schnee-Hase* (1937). Reprint, translated by Ernest Blake. "A Once and Future Resort: A Winter in the Rocky Mountains of Colorado." *Colorado Heritage* 4 (1985), 17–23.

Schreiner, T. W. "Norway's National Sport." *Outing* 37 (March 1901), 711–15.

Schwartz, Gary H. *The Art of Skiing, 1856–1936.* Tiburon, Calif.: Wood River Publishing, 1989.

Templeton, Kenneth S., ed. *10th Mountain Division: America's Ski Troops*. Chicago: privately published, 1945.

U.S. Department of Agriculture, Forest Service, in cooperation with the National Ski Areas Association. *Planning Considerations for Winter Sports Resort Development*. 1973.

Warren, E. R. "Snow-shoeing in the Rocky Mountains." *Outing* 9 (January 1887), 350–53.

Wingle, H. Peter. *Planning Considerations for Winter Sports Resort Development*. U.S. Department of Agriculture, Forest Service, Rocky Mountain Region, 1994.

SELECTED SECONDARY SOURCES

Alba, Richard D. *Ethnic Identity: The Transformation of White America*. New Haven, Conn.: Yale University Press, 1990.

Allen, E. John B. *From Skisport to Skiing: One Hundred Years of an American Sport, 1840–1940*. Amherst: University of Massachusetts Press, 1993.

———. "The Modernization of Skisport: Ishpeming's Contribution to American Skiing." *Michigan Historical Review* 16 (1990), 1–20.

———. "Sierra Ladies on Skis in Gold Rush California." *Journal of Sport History* 17 (Winter 1990), 347–53.

———. "'Skeeing' in Maine: The Early Years, 1870s to 1920s." *Maine Historical Quarterly* 30 (1991), 146–65.

———. "Skiing Mailmen of Mountain America: U.S. Winter Postal Service in the Nineteenth Century." *Journal of the West* 29 (April 1990), 76–86.

———. "Winter Culture: The Origins of Skiing in the United States." *Journal of American Culture* 6 (Spring 1983), 65–68.

———, ed. *Papers from the 2002 International Ski History Congress*. New Hartford, Conn.: International Skiing History Association, 2002.

Allen, James Sloan. *The Romance of Commerce and Culture: Capitalism, Modernism, and the Chicago-Aspen Crusade for Cultural Reform*. Chicago: University of Chicago Press, 1983.

Allen, Theodore. *The Invention of the White Race*. New York: Verso, 1994.

Aron, Cindy S. *Working at Play: A History of Vacations in the United States*. New York: Oxford University Press, 1999.

Austin, Joe, and Michael Nevin Willard, eds. *Generations of Youth: Youth Cultures and History in Twentieth-Century America*. New York: New York University Press, 1998.

Baker, Alan R. H., and Gideon Biger, eds. *Ideology and Landscape in Historical Perspective: Essays on the Meaning of Some Places in the Past*. Cambridge: Cambridge University Press, 1992.

Barlow-Perez, Sally. *A History of Aspen*. Aspen, Colo.: Who Press, 1991.

Benson, Jack A. "Before Aspen and Vail: The Story of Recreational Skiing in Frontier Colorado." *Journal of the West* 22 (January 1983), 52–61.

————. "Before Skiing Was Fun." *Western Historical Quarterly* 8 (October 1977), 431–41.

————. "Skiing at Camp Hale: Mountain Troops during World War II." *Western Historical Quarterly* 15 (April 1984), 163–74.

Bernard, Paul P. *Rush to the Alps: The Evolution of Vacationing in Switzerland.* Boulder, Colo.: East European Quarterly, 1978. Distributed by Columbia University Press.

Besser, Gretchen. *The National Ski Patrol: Samaritans of the Snow.* Woodstock, Vt.: Countryman Press, 1983.

Betts, J. R. *America's Sporting Heritage: 1850–1950.* Reading, Mass.: Addison-Wesley, 1974.

Bjork, Kenneth. "'Snowshoe' Thompson: Fact and Legend." *Norwegian-American Studies and Record* 19 (1956), 62–88.

Bline, Elaine M., Diane E. Taub, and Lingling Han. "Sport Participation and Women's Personal Empowerment: Experiences of the College Athlete." *Journal of Sport and Social Issues* 17, no. 1 (April 1993), 47–60.

Booth, Douglas. "From Bikinis to Board Shorts: *Wahines* and the Paradoxes of Surfing Culture." *Journal of Sport History* 28, no. 1 (Spring 2001), 3–22.

Boutilier, Mary, and Lucinda San Giovanni. *The Sporting Woman.* Champaign, Ill.: Human Kinetics Publishers, 1983.

Brockman, Frank C. *Recreational Use of Wild Lands.* New York: McGraw-Hill, 1959.

Brooke, Michael. *The Concrete Wave: The History of Skateboarding.* Los Angeles: Warwick Publishing, 1999.

Browder, David. "First Winter at Camp Hale." *Sierra Club Bulletin* (June 1943), 67–68.

Burroughs, John Rolfe. *"I Never Look Back": The Story of Buddy Werner.* Boulder, Colo.: Johnson Publishing Co., 1967.

————. *Ski Town USA.* Steamboat Springs, Colo.: Pilot Press, 1962.

————. *Steamboat in the Rockies.* Fort Collins, Colo.: Old Army Press, 1974.

Burton, Hal. *The Ski Troops.* New York: Simon and Schuster, 1971.

Butler, Richard, C. Michael Hall, and John Jenkins, eds. *Tourism and Recreation in Rural Areas.* New York: John Wiley and Sons, 1998.

Butsch, Richard, ed. *For Fun and Profit: The Transformation of Leisure into Consumption.* Philadelphia: Temple University Press, 1990.

Cahn, Susan Kathleen. *Coming on Strong: Gender and Sexuality in Twentieth-Century Women's Sport.* New York: Free Press, 1994. Reprint, Cambridge: Harvard University Press, 1995.

Christensen, Bonnie. *Red Lodge and the Mythic West: From Coal Miners to Cowboys.* Lawrence: University Press of Kansas, 2002.

Clawson, Marion, and Jack L. Knetch. *The Economics of Outdoor Recreation.* Baltimore: Johns Hopkins Press, 1966. Published for Resources for the Future, Inc.

Clifford, Hal. *Downhill Slide: Why the Corporate Ski Industry Is Bad for Skiing, Ski Towns, and the Environment.* San Francisco: Sierra Club Books, 2002.

Cohen, Stan. *A Pictorial History of Downhill Skiing*. Missoula, Mont.: Pictorial Histories Publishing Company, 1985.

Conover, Ted. *Whiteout: Lost in Aspen*. New York: Random House, 1991.

Conzen, Michael P., ed. *The Making of the American Landscape*. Boston: Unwin Hyman, 1990.

Cornell, Virginia Miller. *Ski Lodge: Miller's Idlewild Inn Adventures in Snow Business*. Carpenteria, Calif.: Manifest Publications, 1993.

Cott, Nancy F. *The Grounding of Modern Feminism*. New Haven, Conn.: Yale University Press, 1987.

Cronon, William, ed. *Uncommon Ground: Towards Reinventing Nature*. New York: W. W. Norton, 1995.

Cutler, Phoebe. *The Public Landscape of the New Deal*. New Haven, Conn.: Yale University Press, 1985.

Daily, Kathleen, and Gaylord T. Guenin. *Aspen: The Quiet Years*. Aspen, Colo.: Red Ink, 1994.

Davidson, Judith A. "Sport and Modern Technology: The Rise of Skateboarding, 1963–1978." *Journal of Popular Culture* 18, no. 4 (Spring 1985), 145–57.

D'Emilio, John, and Estelle B. Freedman. *Intimate Matters: A History of Sexuality in Twentieth-Century America*. 2nd ed. Chicago: University of Chicago Press, 1997.

Douglas, Susan J. *Where the Girls Are: Growing Up Female with the Mass Media*. New York: Times Books, 1995.

Dudley, Charles M. *Sixty Centuries of Skiing*. Brattleboro, Vt.: Stephen Daye Press, 1935.

Dunleavy, J. E. "Skiing: The Worship of Ull in America." *Journal of American Culture* 4 (1981), 75–85.

Dyreson, Mark. "The Emergence of Consumer Culture and the Transformation of Physical Culture: American Sport in the 1920s." *Journal of Sport History* 16 (Winter 1989), 261–81.

Edington, John. *Ecology, Recreation, and Tourism*. Cambridge: Cambridge University Press, 1986.

Editors of *Ski* Magazine. *America's Ski Book*. With an introduction by Willy Schaeffler. New York: Scribner, 1973.

Eisen, George, and David K. Wiggins, eds. *Ethnicity and Sport in North American History and Culture*. Westport, Conn.: Greenwood Press, 1994.

Ewen, Stuart. *Captains of Consciousness: Advertising and the Social Roots of the Consumer Culture*. New York: McGraw-Hill, 1976.

Fay, Abbott. *Ski Tracks in the Rockies: A Century of Colorado Skiing*. Evergreen, Colo.: Cordillera Press, 1984.

Fetter, Richard L., and Suzanne Fetter. *Telluride: From Pick to Powder*. Caldwell, Idaho: Caxton Printers, 1990.

Fiester, Mark. *Blasted Beloved Breckenridge*. Boulder, Colo.: Pruett Publishing Co., 1973.

Findlay, John M. *Magic Lands: Western Cityscapes and American Culture after 1940.* Berkeley: University of California Press, 1992.

Flink, J. J. *The Car Culture.* Cambridge, Mass.: MIT Press, 1975.

Fox, Richard Wightman, and T. J. Jackson Lears, eds. *The Culture of Consumption: Critical Essays in American History 1880–1980.* New York: Pantheon Books, 1983.

———. *The Power of Culture: Critical Essays in American History.* Chicago: University of Chicago Press, 1993.

Frankenberg, Ruth. *White Women, Race Matters: The Social Construction of Whiteness.* Minneapolis: University of Minnesota Press, 1993.

Gamson, Joshua. "The Assembly Line of Greatness: Celebrity in Twentieth-Century America." *Critical Studies in Mass Communication* 9 (1992), 1–24.

George, Nelson. *Hip Hop America.* New York: Viking Press, 1998.

Glick, Daniel. *Powder Burn: Arson, Money, and Mystery on Vail Mountain.* New York: PublicAffairs, 2001.

Grand County Historical Association. *Winter Park: Colorado's Favorite for Fifty Years, 1940–1990.* Denver: Winter Park Recreation Association, 1989.

Grover, Kathryn, ed. *Fitness in American Culture: Images of Health, Sport, and the Body, 1830–1940.* Amherst: University of Massachusetts Press, 1989.

Guttmann, Allen. *Women's Sports: A History.* New York: Columbia University Press, 1991.

Hall, Colin Mitchell. *Tourism and Politics: Policy, Power and Place.* New York: John Wiley and Sons, 1994.

Hammitt, William E., and David N. Cole. *Wildland Recreation: Ecology and Management.* New York: John Wiley and Sons, 1987.

Hardy, Stephen. "Entrepreneurs, Organizations, and the Sport Marketplace: Subjects in Search of Historians." *Journal of Sport History* 13 (Spring 1986), 14–33.

Hart, John Fraser. *The Look of the Land.* Englewood Cliffs, N.J.: Prentice-Hall, 1975.

Hazard, Joseph T. "Winter Sports in the Western Mountains." *Pacific Northwest Quarterly* 44 (1953), 7–14.

Holland, Wendolyn Spence. *Sun Valley: An Extraordinary History.* San Francisco: Palace Press International, 1998.

Hovelsen, Leif. *The Flying Norseman.* Ishpeming, Mich.: National Ski Hall of Fame Press, 1983.

Howe, Susanna. *(Sick) a Cultural History of Snowboarding.* New York: St. Martin's Griffin, 1998.

Hyde, Anne F. *An American Vision: Far Western Landscape and National Culture, 1820–1920.* New York: New York University Press, 1990.

———. "Cultural Filters: The Significance of Perception in the History of the American West." *Western Historical Quarterly* 24 (August 1993), 351–74.

———. "Round Pegs in Square Holes: The Rocky Mountains and Extractive Industry." In *Many Wests: Place, Culture, and Regional Identity.* Edited by

David M. Wrobel and Michael C. Steiner. Lawrence: University Press of Kansas, 1997.

Ignatiev, Noel. *How the Irish Became White.* New York: Routledge, 1995.

Imbrie, John, and Hugh W. Evans, eds. *Good Times and Bad Times: A History of C Company 85th Mountain Infantry Regiment 10th Mountain Division.* Queechee, Vt.: Vermont Heritage Press, 1995.

Jackson, John Brinkerhoff. *Discovering the Vernacular Landscape.* New Haven, Conn.: Yale University Press, 1984.

———. *Landscapes: Selected Writings of J. B. Jackson.* Edited by Ervin H. Zube. Amherst: University of Massachusetts Press, 1970.

———. *A Sense of Place, a Sense of Time.* New Haven, Conn.: Yale University Press, 1994.

Jakle, John. *The Tourist: Travel in Twentieth-Century America.* Lincoln: University of Nebraska Press, 1985.

Jay, John. *Ski Down the Years.* New York: Universal Publishing, 1966.

Jenkins, McKay. *The Last Ridge: The Epic Story of the U.S. Army's 10th Mountain Division and the Assault on Hitler's Europe.* New York: Random House, 2003.

Jensen, Clayne R. *Outdoor Recreation in America: Trends, Problems, and Opportunities.* Minneapolis: Burgess Publishing Company, 1970, 1973, 1977.

Jubenville, Alan. *Outdoor Recreation Planning.* Philadelphia: W. B. Saunders, 1976.

Kingery, Hugh, and Elinor Eppich Kingery. *The Colorado Mountain Club: The First Seventy-five Years of a Highly Individual Corporation, 1912–1987.* Evergreen, Colo.: Cordillera Press, 1988.

Klein, Kerwin L. "Frontier Products: Tourism, Consumerism, and the Southwestern Public Lands, 1890–1990." *Pacific Historical Review* 62 (February 1993), 39–71.

Kraut, Alan M. *The Huddled Masses: The Immigrant in American Society, 1880–1920.* Arlington Heights, Ill.: Harlan Davidson, 1982.

Langdon, Charlie. *Durango Ski: People and Seasons at Purgatory.* Durango, Colo.: Purgatory Press, 1989.

Lavender, David. *The Telluride Story.* Ridgeway, Colo.: Wayfinder Press, 1987.

Lears, T. J. Jackson. "The Concept of Cultural Hegemony: Problems and Possibilities." *American Historical Review* 90, no. 3 (1985), 567–93.

———. *Fables of Abundance: A Cultural History of Advertising in America.* New York: Basic Books, 1994.

———. *No Place of Grace: Antimodernism and the Transformation of American Culture, 1880–1920.* New York: Pantheon Books, 1981.

Lee, Martyn J. *Consumer Culture Reborn: The Cultural Politics of Consumption.* New York: Routlege, 1993.

Lenskyj, Helen. *Out of Bounds: Women, Sport and Sexuality.* Toronto: Women's Press, 1986.

Lewis, Peirce F., David Lowenthal, and Yi-Fu Tuan. *Visual Blight in America.* Washington, D.C.: Association of American Geographers, 1973.

Lipsitz, George. *Time Passages: Collective Memory and American Popular Culture.* Minneapolis: University of Minnesota Press, 1990.

Mandell, Richard D. *Sport: A Cultural History.* New York: Columbia University Press, 1984.

Mangan, J. A., and Roberta J. Park. *From "Fair Sex" to Feminism: Sport and the Socialization of Women in the Industrial and Post-Industrial Eras.* London: Frank Cass and Company, 1987.

Marchand, Roland. *Advertising the American Dream: Making Way for Modernity, 1920–1940.* Berkeley: University of California Press, 1985.

Marx, Leo. *The Machine in the Garden: Technology and the Pastoral Ideal in America.* New York: Oxford University Press, 1964.

McCannell, Dean. *The Tourist: A New Theory of the Leisure Class.* New York: Schocken Books, 1976.

Meinig, Donald W., ed. *The Interpretation of Ordinary Landscapes: Geographical Essays.* New York: Oxford University Press, 1979.

Mergen, Bernard. *Snow in America.* Washington, D.C.: Smithsonian Institution, 1997.

Miller, Jean. "The Early Birds." *Grand County Historical Association Journal* 4 (January 1984; reprint, March 1988), 25–28.

———. "The Legacy." *Grand County Historical Association Journal* 4 (January 1984; reprint, March 1988), 52–54.

———. "The Skiing's Great at —." *Grand County Historical Association Journal* 4 (January 1984; reprint, March 1988), 38–51.

Mitchell, Don. *The Lie of the Land: Migrant Workers and the California Landscape.* Minneapolis: University of Minnesota Press, 1996.

Moss, Richard J. *Golf and the American Country Club.* Urbana: University of Illinois Press, 2001.

Mrozek, Donald J. "The Image of the West in American Sport." *Journal of the American West* 17 (July 1978), 3–15.

Nash, Roderick. *Wilderness and the American Mind.* 3rd ed. New Haven, Conn.: Yale University Press, 1982.

Needham, Richard. *Ski: Fifty Years in North America.* New York: Harry N. Abrams, 1987.

Nicholas, Liza, Elaine M. Bapis, and Thomas J. Harvey, eds. *Imagining the Big Open: Nature, Identity, and Play in the New West.* Salt Lake City: University of Utah Press, 2003.

Norris, Scott, ed. *Discovered Country: Tourism and Survival in the American West.* Albuquerque, N.M.: Stone Ladder Press, 1994.

Patterson, Steve, and Kenton Forrest. *Rio Grande Ski Train.* Denver: Tramway Press, 1984.

Peiss, Kathy. *Cheap Amusements: Working Women and Leisure in Turn-of-the-Century New York.* Philadelphia: Temple University Press, 1986.

Pfeifer, Luanne. *Gretchen's Gold: The Story of Gretchen Fraser*. Missoula, Mont.: Pictorial Histories Publishing Company, 1996.

Pomeroy, Earl S. *In Search of the Golden West: The Tourist in Western America*. New York: Alfred A. Knopf, 1957. Reprint, Lincoln: University of Nebraska Press, 1990.

Ponce de Leon, Charles L. *Self-Exposure: Human Interest Journalism and the Emergence of Celebrity in America, 1890–1940*. Chapel Hill: University of North Carolina Press, 2002.

Price, Jennifer. *Flight Maps: Adventures with Nature in Modern America*. New York: Basic Books, 1999.

Prown, Jules D. "Mind in Matter: An Introduction to Material Culture Theory and Method." *Winterthur Portfolio* 17 (Spring 1982), 1–19.

Raitz, Karl B. *The Theater of Sport*. Baltimore: Johns Hopkins University Press, 1995.

Rajtmajer, Dolfe. "The Slovenian Origins of European Skiing." *International Journal of the History of Sport* 11 (April 1994), 97–101.

Reiss, Steven A. "From Pitch to Putt: Sport and Class in Anglo-American Sport." *Journal of Sport History* 21 (Summer 1994), 138–84.

———. "Sport and the Redefinition of American Middle-Class Masculinity." *International Journal of the History of Sport* 8 (May 1991), 5–27.

Riebsame, William E., ed. *Atlas of the New West: Portrait of a Changing Region*. New York: W. W. Norton, 1997.

Robertson, Janet. *The Magnificent Mountain Women: Adventures in the Colorado Rockies*. Lincoln: University of Nebraska Press, 1990.

Rodriguez, Sylvia. "Applied Research on Land and Water in New Mexico: A Critique." *Journal of the Southwest* 32 (Fall 1990), 300–15.

———. "Art, Tourism, and Race Relations in Taos: Toward a Sociology of the Art Colony." *Journal of Anthropological Research* 45 (1989), 77–99.

———. "Ethnic Reconstruction in Contemporary Taos." *Journal of the Southwest* 32 (Winter 1990), 541–55.

———. "The Impact of the Ski Industry on the Rio Hondo Watershed." *Annals of Tourism Research* 14 (1987), 88–103.

Roediger, David R. *Towards the Abolition of Whiteness: Essays on Race, Politics, and Working Class History*. New York: Verso, 1994.

———. *The Wages of Whiteness: Race and the Making of the American Working Class*. New York: Verso, 1991.

Rothman, Hal K. *Devil's Bargains: Tourism in the 20th Century West*. Lawrence: University Press of Kansas, 1998.

Runte, Alfred. *National Parks: The American Experience*. 2nd rev. ed. Lincoln: University of Nebraska Press, 1987.

Sage, George E. *Power and Ideology in American Sport: A Critical Perspective*. Champaign, Ill.: Human Kinetics Books, 1990.

Sale, Kirkpatrick. *The Green Revolution: The American Environmental Movement, 1962–1992.* New York: Hill and Wang, 1993.

Savage, Kirk. *Standing Soldiers, Kneeling Slaves: Race, War, and Monument in Nineteenth-Century America.* Princeton, N.J.: Princeton University Press, 1997.

Saxton, Alexander. *The Rise and Fall of the White Republic: Class Politics and Mass Culture in Nineteenth-Century America.* New York: Verso, 1990.

Scharff, Virginia. *Taking the Wheel: Women and the Coming of the Motor Age.* New York: Free Press, 1991. Reprint, Albuquerque: University of New Mexico Press, 1992.

———, ed. *Seeing Nature through Gender.* Lawrence: University Press of Kansas, 2003.

Schein, Richard H. "Normative Dimensions of Landscape." In *Everyday America: Cultural Landscape Studies after J. B. Jackson.* Edited by Chris Wilson and Paul Groth. Berkeley: University of California Press, 2003.

———. "The Place of Landscape: A Conceptual Framework for Interpreting an American Scene." *Annals of the Association of American Geographers* 87, no. 4 (1997), 660–80.

Schmitt, Peter J. *Back to Nature: The Arcadian Myth in Urban America.* New York: Oxford University Press, 1969.

Schwantes, Carlos A. *In Mountain Shadows: A History of Idaho.* Lincoln: University of Nebraska Press, 1991.

Sears, John F. *Sacred Places: American Tourist Attractions in the Nineteenth Century.* New York: Oxford University Press, 1989.

Seibert, Peter W. *Vail: Triumph of a Dream.* Boulder, Colo.: Mountain Sport Press, 2000.

Shaffer, Marguerite S. *See America First: Tourism and National Identity, 1880–1940.* Washington, D.C.: Smithsonian Institution Press, 2001.

Shelton, Peter. *Climb to Conquer: The Untold Story of World War II's 10th Mountain Division Ski Troops.* New York: Scribner, 2003.

Simonton, June. *Vail: Story of a Colorado Mountain Valley.* Denver: Vail Chronicles, 1987.

Smith, Duane A. *Rocky Mountain Boom Town: A History of Durango, Colorado.* Niwot: University Press of Colorado, 1980, 1986, 1992.

———. *Rocky Mountain West: Colorado, Wyoming, and Montana, 1859–1915.* Albuquerque: University of New Mexico Press, 1992.

———. *When Coal Was King: A History of Crested Butte, Colorado, 1880–1952.* Golden, Colo.: Colorado School of Mines Press, 1984.

Smith-Rosenberg, Carroll. *Disorderly Conduct: Visions of Gender in Victorian America.* New York: Oxford University Press, 1985.

Sollors, Werner. *Beyond Ethnicity: Consent and Descent in American Culture.* New York: Oxford University Press, 1987.

Spears, Betty, and Richard A. Swanson. *History of Sport and Physical Activity in the United States.* Dubuque, Iowa: Wm. C. Brown Company Publishers, 1978.

Stilgoe, John. *Common Landscape of America, 1580–1845.* New Haven, Conn.: Yale University Press, 1982.

Takaki, Ronald T., ed. *From Different Shores: Perspectives on Race and Ethnicity in America.* New York: Oxford University Press, 1994.

"The 10th's Books." *Skiing Heritage: Journal of the International Skiing History Association* 7 (Fall 1995), 33.

Towler, Sureva. *The History of Skiing at Steamboat Springs.* Denver: Frederic Printing, 1987.

Tuan, Yi Fu. *Topophilia: A Study of Environmental Perception, Attitudes, and Values.* Morningside edition, with a new preface by the author. New York: Columbia University Press, 1990.

Urry, John. *Consuming Places.* New York: Routledge, 1995.

———. *The Tourist Gaze.* New York: Sage Books, 1990.

Veblen, Thorstein. *The Theory of the Leisure Class.* New York: Macmillan, 1899. Reprint, New Brunswick, N.J.: Transaction Publishers, 1992.

Vertinsky, Patricia. *The Eternally Wounded Woman: Women, Doctors, and Exercise in the Late Nineteenth Century.* Manchester: Manchester University Press, 1990.

———. "Feminist Charlotte Perkins Gilman's Pursuit of Health and Physical Fitness as a Strategy for Emancipation." *Journal of Sport History* 16 (Spring 1989), 5–26.

———. "Gender Relations, Women's History and Sport History: A Decade of Changing Enquiry, 1983–1993." *Journal of Sport History* 21 (Spring 1994), 1–24.

———. "Sport History and Gender Relations, 1983–1993: A Bibliography." *Journal of Sport History* 21 (Spring 1994), 25–58.

Waters, Mary C. *Ethnic Options: Choosing Identities in America.* Berkeley: University of California Press, 1990.

Wentworth, Frank L. *Aspen on the Roaring Fork.* Lakewood, Colo.: Francis B. Rizzari, 1950.

West, Elliott. "Selling the Myth: Western Images in Advertising." In *Wanted Dead or Alive: The American West in Popular Culture.* Edited by Richard Aquila. Urbana: University of Illinois Press, 1996.

———. *The Way to the West: Essays on the Central Plains.* Albuquerque: University of New Mexico Press, 1995.

White, Richard. *It's Your Misfortune and None of My Own: A New History of the American West.* Norman: University of Oklahoma Press, 1991.

Wier, Jim. "The Beginning of Skiing in Grand County." *Grand County Historical Association Journal* 4 (January 1984; reprint, March 1988), 9–12.

———. "Other Small Ski Areas and Skiing after 1950." *Grand County Historical Association Journal* 4 (January 1984; reprint, March 1988), 55–56.

———. "Skiing at Hot Sulphur Springs." *Grand County Historical Association Journal* 4 (January 1984; reprint, March 1988), 13–20.

———. "The Winter Park Ski Area." *Grand County Historical Association Journal* 4 (January 1984; reprint, March 1988), 29–37.

Wilkinson, Charles F. *The Eagle Bird: Mapping a New West.* New York: Vintage Books, 1992.

Wilkinson, Paul F. *Environmental Impact of Recreation and Tourism: A Bibliography.* Monticello, Ill.: Vance Bibliographies, 1978.

Williamson, Judith. *Decoding Advertisements: Ideology and Meaning in Advertising.* New York: Marion Boyars, 1984.

Wolf, Tom. *Ice Crusaders: A Memoir of Cold War and Cold Sport.* Boulder, Colo.: Roberts Rinehart Publishers, 1999.

Woods, Betty Jo. "Skiing at Grand Lake." *Grand County Historical Association Journal* 4 (January 1984), 21–24.

Woolsey, Elizabeth D. *Off the Beaten Track.* Wilson, Wyo.: Wilson Bench Press, 1984.

Worster, Donald. *Under Western Skies: Nature and History in the American West.* New York: Oxford University Press, 1992.

Wren, Jean. *Steamboat Springs and the "Treacherous and Speedy Skee": An Album.* Steamboat Springs, Colo.: Steamboat Pilot, 1972.

Wright, John B. *Rocky Mountain Divide: Selling and Saving the West.* Austin: University of Texas Press, 1993.

Wrobel, David M. *Promised Lands: Promotion, Memory, and the Creation of the American West.* Lawrence: University Press of Kansas, 2002.

Wrobel, David M., and Patrick T. Long, eds. *Seeing and Being Seen: Tourism in the American West.* Lawrence: University Press of Kansas, 2001.

Wyckoff, William. *Creating Colorado: The Making of a Western American Landscape, 1860–1940.* New Haven, Conn.: Yale University Press, 1999.

Zukin, Sharon. *Landscapes of Power: From Detroit to Disney World.* Berkeley: University of California Press, 1991.

INDEX